© **Copyright 2017 by Alex Zolini - All rights reserved**.

All rights Reserved. No part of this publication or the information in it may be quoted from form by means such as printing, sc otherwise without prior written perr holder.

Disclaimer and Terms of Use:

Effort has been made to ensure that the information in this book is accurate and complete, however, the author and the publisher do not warrant the accuracy of the information, text and graphics contained within the book due to the rapidly changing nature of science, research, known and unknown facts and internet. The Author and the publisher do not hold any responsibility for errors, omissions or contrary interpretation of the subject matter herein. This book is presented solely for motivational and informational purposes only.

Table of contents

Introduction..**22**

About Instant Pot..**23**

The benefits of Instant Pot.............................**24**

Measurement conversions **25**

    Abbreviations..25

Useful tips **26**

    Include in The Daily Diet and Stay Healthy 26

    12 Weight Loss Diet Tips 27

Instant Pot Porridge and Beans Dishes **28**

    Oatmeal (VEG, S&F)...29

    Pumpkin Steel Cut Oats (VEG) 29

    Honey Vanilla Steel Cut Oats 30

    Peach and Oats Crumble (VEG, S&F) 30

    Cranberry with Oatmeal (VEG, S&F) 31

    Blackberry Oatmeal (VEG, S&F) 31

    Carrot Cake Oatmeal...32

    Sweet Carrot Porridge.......................................32

    Minty Green Lentil (VEG) 33

    Three Lentil Chili (VEG) 33

    Lentil Risotto (VEG) 34

    Peaches & Cream Oatmeal (VEG, S&F) 35

    Quinoa (VEG, S&F) 35

    Creamy Pumpkin Porridge 36

    Cheese Grits 37

    Delicious Steel Cut Oats (VEG, S&F)..................37

Key Lime Coco Couscous (VEG, S&F)......................................38

Mango Dal...38

Herby Polenta Squares with Cheese.....................................39

Chickpeas Dish (VEG)...40

Jam-packed Curry Quinoa (VEG, S&F)....................................41

Banana and Chia Seed Porridge (VEG, S&F)............................42

Delicious chia porridge...42

Fruity Oatmeal (VEG, S&F)...43

Mushroom Thyme Oatmeal...44

Cinnamon Raisins Flat Oats (VEG, S&F)................................45

Multigrain mix...45

Baked Beans...46

Beans Stew...47

Pinto Beans Ala Tex-Mex...47

Spicy Black Bean and Brown Rice Salad................................48

Red Beans Over Rice..49

Bacon and Black Beans...50

Garlic Bacon Pinto Beans...51

Dried Beans Vegeratian Soup (VEG)....................................52

Black Bean Chili (VEG, S&F)...53

Mexican Chili Beans...54

Quick Ham & Beans...54

Instant Pot Rice Dishes.....................................55

White Rice (VEG, S&F)...56

Brown Rice (VEG, S&F)..56

Brazilian Black Beans (VEG)..57

Mango Pudding Rice (VEG, S&F)...58

Sweet Potato and Apple Risotto 58

Rice Pudding (VEG) 59

Nutty Brown Rice 60

Jasmine Rice (VEG, S&F) 61

Berry Banana Rice Porridge 61

Chinese Fried Rice (VEG) 62

Rice Pilaf with Peas, Parsley, and Carrots (VEG) 63

Rice and Black Beans..63

Rice Balls 64

Almond Saffron Risotto...65

Red Beans Over Rice 65

Lemon-Parmesan Risotto..66

Cherry Apple Breakfast Risotto..67

Apple Cherry Breakfast Rice Cream (VEG, S&F) 68

Savory Breakfast Porridge...69

Instant Pot Potatoes Dishes 70

Mashed Potatoes (VEG) 71

Potato Bacon Hash Browns..71

Baked Potatoes (VEG, S&F) 72

Baked Sweet Potatoes (VEG, S&F) 72

Cheesy Potatoes 73

Potato Salad..74

Red Potatoes (VEG)...74

Scalloped Potatoes...75

Simple Potato Frittata 76

Roasted Potatoes Garlic (VEG)...76

Crispy Potatoes (VEG) 77

Walnuts and Sweet Potato Crumble (VEG).............................78

Stir Fried Spiced Potatoes (VEG)..78

Potato Mash with Marjoram 79

Delicious Fingerling Potatoes...79

Hash Browns 80

Spanish Potatoes (VEG)..80

Sweet Potato Barley Porridge (VEG, S&F)..............................81

Egg Recipes 82

Breakfast Casserole..82

Spanish Casserole 82

Spread Of Eggplant And Olive 83

Hard-Boiled Eggs (S&F) 84

Soft-Boiled Egg (S&F) 84

Bell Pepper Poached Eggs 85

Egg Macaroni (S&F)..85

Egg and Tomato Omelet 86

Egg and Carrot Spread 86

Egg Scramble...87

Egg Balls 87

Egg and Onion Frittata 88

Egg and Spinach Cup Custards 88

Egg & Mushroom Breakfast 89

Egg Muffins 90

Eggs de Provence (S&F) 91

Cheesy Egg Cupcakes 91

Sweet egg toasts 92

Ham Frittata...93

Poached Tomato Eggs..93

Aromatic Bacon Eggs..94

Quick & Easy Salad 94

Easy, Quick Instant Pot Egg Bake 95

Chicken Omelette 96

Spinach Egg Omelet 96

Omelette-de-Corn..97

Korean Style Steamed Eggs...98

Scotch Eggs 98

Creamy Soufflé...99

Instant Pot Chicken Dishes 100

Aromatic whole chicken..100

Honey Sesame Chicken 100

The Greek Chicken 101

Instant Pot Chicken 102

Italian Chicken...102

Chicken Masala (S&F) 103

Chicken and Mushrooms Risotto 104

Potato Chicken Stew 104

Italian Chicken Parmesan..105

Apricot Chicken (S&F) 106

Hot Chicken Wings..106

Chicken Nuggets 107

Chicken with Cremini Mushrooms..107

Chicken with Herbs and Vegetables 108

Fantastic Chicken Fillets (S&F) 109

Hot Buffalo Wings..109

Sticky Sesame Chicken 110

Balsamic Chicken Thighs 111

Chipotle-Raspberry Pulled Chicken..111

Tuscan Garlic Chicken 112

Charred-Pepper Chicken Fajitas..113

Easy Spicy Chicken Wings 113

One-Pot Chicken Alfredo (S&F)..114

Spicy-Peanut Chicken Pasta 115

Baked Chicken Balls in Garlic Noodles 115

Creamy & Cheesy Chicken Risotto 116

Chicken with Potatoes 117

Chicken with Broccoli...117

Steamed chicken cutlets 118

Seasoned Chicken with Cheese..119

Chicken Risotto 120

Honey-Sriracha Chicken 120

Chicken Sandwiches..121

Chicken Cordon Blue Casserole 122

Chicken Cacciatore..122

Chipotle-Raspberry Pulled Chicken..123

Warm Chicken Salad 124

Feta Cheese Chicken Bowl 124

Green Pepper Chicken (S&F)..125

Family Baked Chicken (S&F)...125

Hot burrito 126

Instant Pot Turkey and Duck Dishes 127

Turkey Goulash 127

Zucchini Turkey 128

Ground Turkey Stew with Spinach 129

Balsamic Turkey Wings 129

Turkey-Stuffed Bell Peppers 130

Turkey Verde & Rice 131

Turkey Legs With Gravy 131

Turkey Wings Braised with Cranberry 133

Spiced Beans with Turkey 134

Turkey Chili 135

Thanksgiving Turkey Casserole 136

Turkey Drumsticks 136

Stuffed Bell Peppers 137

Ducks Legs in Orange Sauce 138

Duck Fat Risotto 139

Limy-Duck 140

Duck Chili 141

Spicy Shredded Duck 142

Instant Pot Beef Dishes 143

Beef & Broccoli 143

Russian Beef 143

Korean Beef 144

Italian Beef 145

Chili Con Carne 146

Marinated Steak 147

Beef Stifado 147

Beef Steak 148

Hot Chili Beef Stew 149

Beef Ragout 150

Texas Coffee Beef Ribs 150

Delicious Beef Casserole 151

Mongolian Beef 152

Moroccan Beef with Vegetables 152

Garlic Teriyaki Beef 153

Chinese Beef Stew 154

Beef and Tomato Gravy 154

Beef with Beans (S&F) 155

Beef Stroganoff 155

Spicy Barbacoa 156

Classic Corned Beef and Cabbage 157

Homemade Pastrami 157

Beef and Noodles 158

Autumn Vegetable Beef Stew 159

Country Beef Hash 160

Beef and Green Bean Soup 160

Beef Brisket with Tomatillo Sauce 161

Beef Bourguignon 162

Beefy Lasagna 162

Beef in Pepper Sauce 163

Teriyaki Short Ribs 164

Teriyaki-Garlic Flank Steak 165

Beef Taco Pie 166

Beef and Vegetable Chowder 166

Beef and Yogurt Curry (S&F) 167

Beef and Red Wine Sauce 168

Cuban-Style Braised Beef..169

Spaghetti with Bacon and Beef Sauce.........................169

Pulled BBQ Beef..170

Herbed Mustard Roast...170

Roast & Gravy 171

Instant Pot Pork and Lamb Dishes 172

Juicy Pork Belly..172

Barbeque Pork Roast 172

Pork Sausage Gravy..173

Pork Rice 173

Pork Teriyaki 174

Pulled Pork Flavorful 175

Pork Carnitas...176

Pork and Potatoes..177

Milk-Braised Pork...178

Pork Ragu 178

Pork and Egg Fried Rice..179

Northern Pork Roast with White Beans.......................180

Carrots with Pancetta, Butter, and Leeks 181

BBQ Baby Back Ribs 181

Juicy BBQ Pork 182

Cranberry BBQ Pulled Pork 183

Coconut Pork Curry (S&F) 184

Milk-Braised Pork...185

Chinese Pork Belly..185

Pork Stew 186

Citrus-Garlic Shredded Pork......................................187

Honey Pork Chops 188

Apple Cider Pork 188

Hawaiian Pork 189

Asian Pork Chops 190

Parmesan Honey Pork Roast 190

Collard Greens and Bacon 191

Mexican Pulled-Pork Lettuce Wraps 192

Four Ingredient Pulled Pork 193

Carnitas 193

Sausage and Peppers 195

Creamy savoy cabbage with bacon 196

Turnip Greens with Bacon 196

Barbecue Meatballs 197

Lamb and Feta Meatballs 198

Lamb Curry 199

Half-Hour Rosemary Lamb 200

Garlic Lamb Shanks 200

Lamb Shanks With Figs and Ginger 201

Mediterranean Lamb 202

Mexican Lamb 203

English Lamb Shanks 204

Lamb Stew 205

Seafood and Fish Recipes 206

Fish with Orange & Ginger Sauce 206

Mediterranean Tuna Pasta 206

Tuna and Pasta Casserole 207

Tuna and Capers Tomato Pasta 207

Steamed Fish Fillet...208

Teriyaki Salmon..209

Salmon Steaks with Yogurt Tartar Sauce 209

Salmon Al Cartoccio 210

Curried Fish Coconut Dish...211

Lemony Fish Fillets 212

Mediterranean Whitefish 212

Seafood Gumbo 213

Seafood Cranberries Plov..214

Scallop Chowder 215

White Fish with Beer and Potatoes (S&F)...........................215

White Fish with Orange Sauce 216

Spanish Style Fish (S&F) 216

Healthy Fish with Savory Sauce (S&F)..............................217

Salmon Fillets in Mayonnaise Sauce 218

Dijon Salmon...218

Mustard Crusted Salmon 219

Five-Spicer Tilapia 219

Cod with Mango Salsa...220

Green Chili Mahi-Mahi Fillets 221

Shrimp Bisque 221

Shrimp Jambalaya 222

Shrimp Creole 223

Shrimp Scampi (S&F)..223

Shrimp Paella 224

Shrimp Curry 224

Shrimp with Rice 225

Crispy Skin Salmom Fillet 226

Trout Hash 227

Sausage and Seafood Delight (S&F) 227

Clam Rolls..228

Quick Seafood Paella 228

Caramelized Haddock 229

Mustard Trout...230

Oysters in the Shell (S&F)..230

Cheesy Tuna...231

Crab Legs...231

Instant Pot Soups 232

Zucchini Soup (VEG)..232

Creamy Tomato Soup (VEG) 233

Minestrone Soup (S&F)...234

Tortilla Soup...234

Spanish Bean Soup..235

Red Pepper Soup...236

Wholesome Tomato Soup 237

Pork ribs soup with peas..238

Lentil Vegetable Soup (VEG) 239

Chicken Soup (S&F)..239

Chicken Curry Soup (S&F) 240

Chicken Cream Chesse Chili 241

Buffalo Chicken Soup 241

Tortilla Chicken Soup 242

Fish Soup...243

Rice Soup (S&F)...244

Leek Broccoli Cream Soup...244

Amazing Beef Soup 245

Smoked Turkey & Black Bean Soup 246

Pork and Hominy Soup 247

Beef, Tomato and Pasta Soup 248

Beef and Green Bean Soup 248

Italian-Style Beef Soup (S&F) 249

Barley and Beef Soup..250

Tasty Shrimp Soup (S&F)...251

Quick Matzo Ball Soup 252

Cheese soup..253

Simple Potato Frittata...254

Potato Soup With Leek and Cheddar (VEG) 255

Lentil, Potato, and Carrot Soup (VEG)..............................256

Easy and Quick Chicken Noodle Soup 257

Rainbow Soup (S&F) 258

Instant Pot Stocks and Sauces 259

Chicken Stock..259

Beef Bone Broth..259

Bone Broth 260

Fish Stock 261

Vegetable Stock (VEG) 262

Chicken and Beef Bone Broth 263

Tomato Sauce 264

Pasta and Spaghetti Sauce..265

Chipotle Honey BBQ Sauce 266

Cranberry Sauce (VEG, S&F)..267

Tabasco Sauce (VEG, S&F) 267

Mushroom Sauce (VEG) 268

Mango Chutney Sauce (VEG) 268

Orange Sauce (VEG) 269

Cheese Sauce 270

Vegetarian Recipes...........................271

Carrot and Pumpkin Stew 271

Steamed Broccoli (S&F) 271

Steamed Green Beans.............................272

Lentil and Veggie Soup............................272

Veggie Spaghetti 273

The Green Bowl 274

Hawaiian Black Beans 275

Spring Green Risotto 276

Basil Rice 276

Spiced Carrot Quinoa 277

Mexican Rice Mix (S&F) 278

Curry Tofu 278

Pumpkin Oats with Pecan Pie 279

Buttery Braised Cabbage 280

Instant Broccoli Mushroom Combo 280

Sesame & Napa Cabbage 281

Cajun Succotash 282

Creamy Mushrooms...............................283

Peanut Stew 283

Herbed Mashed Potatoes 284

Classic Ratatouille 285

Quick n Easy Zucchini...286

Couscous Burritos 286

Vegan Mousaka 287

Vegan Chili 288

Assorted Mushrooms Chili (S&F) 289

Vanilla Cake...290

Pineapple Crisps...290

Apricot and Cranberry Cake...291

Wintery Stew 292

White Vegetable Stew 293

Homemade Pumpkin Purée 293

Kidney Bean Salad..294

Farro and Cherry Salad 295

Hearty Mushroom-Bean Soup (S&F)..296

Sweet Potato Soup with Peanut Butter 297

Warm Russet Potato 297

Broccoli and Pineapple Salad 298

Broccoli and Garlic 299

Squash and Pineapple Treat 299

Maple Brussels Sprouts...300

Lemon-Garlic Corn on the Cob...301

Nutty Bulgur and Oat Porridge 301

Bean and Mint Salad...302

Yam Barley Congee (S&F)..302

Butter Bean Casserole...303

Butternut Squash Oatmeal 304

Spanish Paella 304

Mexican Chili Beans 305

Mexican Rice Mix (S&F) 306

Assorted Mushrooms Chili (S&F) 306

Asian Mushroom Dumpling 307

White Bean and Tofu Curry Bowl..308

Japanese Udon in Pumpkin Soup 309

Corn bread 310

Greek-Style Eggplant Stew...311

Eggplant Pasta...311

Vegan Pasta 312

Savoy Cabbage and Cream...313

Ratatouille...313

Couscous Burritos 314

Mexican "Baked" beans 315

Mung Beans Stew 316

Spaghetti Squash (S&F)..316

Vegan Feijoada...317

Corn with Cilantro Butter...318

Spanish Zucchini Tortilla 318

Vegan Rice and Veggies Dish 319

Tasty Millet and Veggies 320

Wheat Berry Salad 321

Easy Soy Yogurt...322

Gluten Free Quinoa Tabbouleh...322

Beet and Orange Salad...323

Beets with Blue Cheese..324

Babaganoush 324

Corn on the Cob 325

Corn With Lime Sauce 326

Vegetarian Burritos (S&F) 326

Zucchini and Mushrooms....................................327

Instant Pot Dessert Recipes 328

Fresh Berry Compote 328

Peach Compote 328

Fresh Currant Bread Pudding..............................329

Vegan Pumpkin Cake (VEG) 329

Frozen Lime..330

Festive Dessert with Prunes and Pecans.............331

Cheesecake with Cranberry Topping 332

Banana-Vanilla Rice Pudding (S&F).....................333

Orange Swirl Cheesecake....................................333

Black Chocolate Cake (S&F) 335

Star Anise Chocolate Cake 336

Tropical Tapioca Pudding (S&F)...........................336

Pumpkin Chocolate Bundt Cake.........................337

Vegan Key Lime Cheesecake (VEG).....................338

Sweet Coconut Rice with Walnuts 339

Rice Pudding 340

Vegan Vanilla Cake (VEG)...................................341

Butter Cake 341

Carrot Pecan Bread (VEG) 342

Carrot Cake 343

Mango Cake 344

Sweet Tapioca Pudding (VEG).............................344

Pineapple Crisps (VEG) 345

Greek Yogurt Cheesecake 346

Mini Pumpkin Puddings 347

Orange-Chocolate Bread Pudding 347

Red-Wine Baked Apples 348

Brownie Cakes 349

Cherry Jam 349

Raspberry Jam 350

Blueberry Jam 351

Pineapple whisked cake 352

Mocha Cheesecake 352

New York Cheescake 353

Chocolate Cheesecake 354

Strawberry Cheesecake 355

Strawberry and Mango Crunch 355

Applesauce 356

Apple Sweet Oatmeal 357

Apple Crisp 357

Apple Tacos 358

Baked Apples 359

Cream Cheese Coffee Cake 359

Vanilla Cake 360

Carrot Cake (VEG) 361

Mini Lava Cakes 362

Sweet Spaghetti Casserole 362

Strawberry Delight Bundt Cake 363

Banana Balls 364

Cream Mousse With the Strawberries................................364

Blueberry Muffins 365

Lemon Loaf 366

Cream Cheese Mousse................................366

Caramel Bites 367

Walnuts Bars 367

Cottage Cheese Prune Soufflé 368

Pears Stewed in Red Wine 369

Coconut Rice Pudding 370

Polenta with Honey and Pine Nuts 371

Pea And Pineapple Curry 372

Pina Collada Pudding 372

Lemon Marmalade................................373

Creme Brulee 374

Grated pie 375

Paleo Diet Recipes................................376

Baked Eggs 376

Beef + Broccoli Soup 376

Southern Glory Beef Chili................................377

Apple, Cabbage, and Beet Stew (S&F) 378

Chicken Veggie Lemon Soup 378

Chicken "Pho" 379

Chicken Pina Colada................................380

Caribbean Chicken 381

Sweet 'n Sour Mango Chicken 382

Butternut Squash Paleo Soup 383

Pork Egg Roll Soup 384

Pork Ribs 385

Pork Loin with a Cherry Apple Glaze................................386

Pork Carnitas...387

Southern Belle's Pulled Pork...387

Lime and Chili Salmon...388

Beef & Plantain Curry..389

French Beef with Red Wine Sauce 390

Olive and Lemon Chicken...390

Paleo Butter Chicken...391

Caribbean Chicken (S&F)..392

Quick Garlick Spanish Chicken (S&F)................................393

Enchilada Soup...394

Leftvofer Turkey Paleo Stew 396

Crab Legs..397

Paleo Chili 397

Paleo Sausage Stew 398

Chocolate Cake 399

Introduction

The book presented to you is a collection of recipes of various and incredibly delicious dishes. Here everyone will find something to their taste. The author of this book has selected for you the easiest and tastiest recipes for dishes made in a pressure cooker Instant Pot.

Using this book, you will get some advantages:

- You will be able to choose a remarkably delicious dish both for yourself and for the whole family.
- You will find many recipes for vegetarians in a special section or marked as VEG in other sections.
- Most recipes are SET&FORGET, marked with an S&F sign. It means that recipes are simple and easy.
- You will know the exact proportions of the ingredients and the cooking time of each dish.
- You will get a step-by-step instruction on making each dish in an Instant Pot.
- Useful tips and secrets of how to make dishes even tastier.
- And lots of other helpful information.

Eat with pleasure, creating a pleasant atmosphere for digesting, if possible.

About Instant Pot

Instant Pot it's essentially a multifunctional cooker, acting as a slow cooker, rice cooker, steamer, electric pressure cooker, sauté pan and even a yogurt maker - all in one. The combination of steam and pressure cooks your food quicker and safer than other devices, making everything from slow-and-low barbecue dishes and tender stews to perfectly prepared rice pilaf and steamed veggies much more Monday-night friendly.

The different buttons and features can seem confusing, but after some practice, you'll be a pro. One function you'll want to be super familiar with is the pressure cooking feature, which uses pressure to cook food faster. As the liquid and food heat up, steam increases the pressure inside, allowing dinner to make it to the table quicker. Essentially, a dish that takes five hours in a slow cooker could be done in one, thanks to the Instant Pot.

Most importantly, Instant Pot cooks meals faster with less energy while preserving more nutrients.

The benefits of Instant Pot

Convenient: 16 turn-key function keys for the most common cooking tasks. Planning the meal with delayed cooking up to 24 hours, reducing cooking time by up to 70%.

Cooking healthy, nutritious and tasty meals: smart programming for delicious healthy food, consistent every time.

Clean & Pleasant: absolutely quiet, no steam, no smell, no spills, no excessive heat in the kitchen. 6-in-1 capability reduces clutter in the kitchen.

Energy efficient: saves up to 70% of energy.

Safe and dependable: Instant Pot is UL/ULC certified UL Logo Instant Pot and has 10 fool-proof safety protections.

Measurement conversions

Use it for accurate measuring of the necessary ingredients.

Metric to standard	Fahrenheit to Celsius	Cups to tablespoons	Oz to grams
5 ml = 1 tsp	300 F = 150 C	3 tsp = 1 tbsp	1 oz = 29 g
15 ml = 1 tbsp	350 F = 180 C	1/8 cup = 2 tbsp	2 oz = 57 g
30 ml = 1 fluid oz	375 F = 190 C	1/4 cup = 4 tbsp	3 oz = 85 g
240 ml = 1 cup	400 F = 200 C	1/3 cup = 5 tbsp +	4 oz = 113 g
1 liter = 34 fluid oz	425 F = 220 C	1 tsp	5 oz = 142 g
1 liter = 4.2 cups	450 F = 230 C	1/2 cup = 8 tbsp	6 oz = 170 g
1 gram = .035 oz		3/4 cup = 12 tbsp	7 oz = 198 g
100 grams = 3.5 oz		1 cup = 16 tbsp	8 oz = 227 g
500 grams = 1.10 lb		8 fluid oz = 1 cup	10 oz = 283 g
		1 pint 2 cups = 16 fluid oz	20 oz = 567 g
			30 oz = 850 g
		1 quart 2 pints = 4 cups	40 oz = 1133 g
		1 gallon 4 quarts = 16 cups	

Abbreviations

oz = ounce

fl oz = fluid ounce

tsp = teaspoon

tbsp = tablespoon

ml = milliliter

c = cup

pt = pint

qt = quart

gal = gallon

L = liter

Include in The Daily Diet and Stay Healthy

15 FOODS THAT BOOST YOUR METABOLISM

GRAPEFRUIT	GREEN TEA	YOGURT	ALMONDS	COFFEE
TURKEY	APPLE	SPINACH	BEANS	JALAPENOS
BROCCOLI	CURRY	CINNAMON	SOY MILK	OATMEAL

Optimizing your metabolism is the key to weight loss (a high metabolism means you burn calories even at rest, making all lazy people's dreams come true).

Boosting your metabolism is also critical for many other bodily functions related to maintaining general health.

A strong metabolism is tied to more than a svelte body - it's beneficial for immune function, lower rates of infectious and degenerative diseases, fertility and a healthy sex drive, lean muscle mass, having more energy and vigor, brain functionality, longevity, and much more.

12 Weight Loss Diet Tips

12 WEIGHT LOSS DIET TIPS INFOGRAPHICS

HAVE **VEGETABLE** WITH EVERY MEAL ❶

LIMIT **PROCESSD FOODS** ❷

EAT **SLOWLY** ❸

DRINK MORE **WATER** ❹

❺ EAT **BREAKFAST**

❻ DO **YOGA**

❼ BUILD **MUSCLE**

❽ BAES EACH MEAL AROUND **PROTEIN**

❾ MEASURE YOURSELF **REGULARLY**

❿ GO FOR A **WALK**

⓫ EAT **FRUIT**

⓬ STOP DRINKING **SODA**

Instant Pot Porridge and Beans Dishes

In this book you will find fragrant and unforgettably tasty recipes for breakfast. Cook and enjoy!

Oatmeal (VEG, S&F)

(Prep + Cook Time: 4 minutes | Servings: 6)

Ingredients:
- 2 cups of steel cut oats
- 4 cups water
- Salt and butter to taste

Directions:

1. Add 2 cups of steel cut oats and 4 cups of water
2. Cook on HIGH pressure for 3 minutes
3. Then let it naturally release.
4. Add salt and butter to taste
5. Serve.

Pumpkin Steel Cut Oats (VEG)

(Prep + Cook Time: 30 minutes | Servings: 4)

Ingredients:
- 1 tbsp butter
- 1 cup steel cut oats
- 3 cups water
- 1 cup pumpkin puree
- ¼ cup maple syrup
- 2 tsp cinnamon
- 1 tsp pumpkin pie spice
- ¼ tsp salt

Directions:

1. Add butter to Instant Pot and select SAUTE. With the melted butter add the oats. Stirring constantly toast for 3 minutes.
2. Add water, pumpkin pie spice, pumpkin puree, cinnamon, maple syrup, and salt. Select HIGH pressure and 10 minutes cook time.
3. When Instant Pot beep sounds, turn off pressure cooker and allow a natural pressure release for 10 minutes, then perform a quick pressure release.
4. When the valve drops remove lid carefully. Stir oats.
5. Remove Inner pot from the pressure cooker and let oats cool in the cooking pot uncovered for up to 10 minutes or until oats thicken to a desired viscosity.
6. Serve warm with, milk, maple syrup and pecan pie granola if desired.

Honey Vanilla Steel Cut Oats

(Prep + Cook Time: 20 minutes | Servings: 4)

Ingredients:
- 1 cup steel cut oats
- 2 tbsp honey
- 1 tsp vanilla extract
- ½ vanilla bean (the caviar only)
- 1 tbsp coconut oil
- 1 tiny pinch of salt
- 1 ½ cups milk
- 1 ½ cups fresh water

Directions:
1. Select SAUTE. Add coconut oil to Instant Pot and when melted, add oats and toast for 3 minutes stirring constantly.
2. Add in the rest of the ingredients. Lock the lid in place and turn pressure value to seal. Cook on HIGH pressure for 10 minutes.
3. When Instant Pot beep sounds, turn off pressure cooker and allow a natural pressure release for 10 minutes, then perform a quick pressure release.
4. When the valve drops remove lid carefully.
5. Stir and enjoy.

Peach and Oats Crumble (VEG, S&F)

(Prep + Cook Time: 50 minutes | Servings: 4)

Ingredients:
- 2 cups oats
- ½ cup peach juice
- ¼ cup bilberries
- 1 peach, sliced
- 1 cup milk
- ¼ cup brown sugar
- 4 tbsp maple syrup
- 1 pinch salt
- 1 cup sour cream
- 2 tbsp butter, melted

Directions:
1. Combine oats, milk, peach juice, blueberries, maple syrup, sour cream, brown sugar, and salt in a bowl.
2. Brush the pot of pressure cooker with butter.
3. Transfer oats mixture to the Instant Pot and cover with lid.
4. Cook on SLOW cook mode for 35 minutes.
5. Transfer to serving dish and place peach slices.
6. Drizzle some maple syrup on top.
7. Serve and enjoy.

Cranberry with Oatmeal (VEG, S&F)

(Prep + Cook Time: 55 minutes | Servings: 4)

Ingredients:
- 2 cups oats
- 2 cups milk
- 1 egg, whisked
- 1 cup cranberry sauce
- ½ cup brown sugar
- 2 tbsp honey
- ½ tsp ginger powder
- 1 pinch salt
- 4 tbsp butter, melted
- 2 tbsp olive oil

Directions:
1. Grease Instant Pot with olive oil.
2. Combine oats, milk, egg, butter, cranberry sauce, honey, brown sugar, ginger powder, and salt in a bowl.
3. Transfer to greased Instant Pot and cover with lid.
4. Leave to cook on SLOW cook mode for 40 minutes.
5. Serve and enjoy.

Blackberry Oatmeal (VEG, S&F)

(Prep + Cook Time: 45 minutes | Servings: 2)

Ingredients:
- 1 cup oats
- 1 cup blackberries
- 1 cup cream milk
- ¼ cup caster sugar
- 4 tbsp honey
- 2 tbsp butter, melted

Directions:
1. Combine the oats, cream milk, sugar, and butter in a bowl. Transfer oats mixture to the Instant Pot and place the blackberries on top, cover with a lid.
2. Let it cook on PORRIDGE mode for 35 minutes. Drizzle honey on top while serving.
3. Serve and enjoy.

Carrot Cake Oatmeal

(Prep + Cook Time: 40 minutes | Servings: 6)

Ingredients:
- 1 tbsp butter
- 1 cup steel cut oats
- 4 cups water
- 1 cup grated carrots
- 3 tbsp maple syrup
- 2 tsp cinnamon
- 1 tsp pumpkin pie spice
- ¼ tsp salt
- ¾ cup raisins
- ¼ cup chia seeds

Directions:

1. Place butter into pressure cooking pot, select SAUTE. When butter is melted add the oats.
2. Toast, stirring constantly for 3 minutes. Continue to stir and add water, carrots pumpkin pie spice, maple syrup, cinnamon, and salt. Cook for 10 minutes on HIGH pressure.
3. When beep sounds, turn off pressure cooker and use a natural pressure release for 10 minutes.
4. When valve drops carefully remove lid. Stirring the oats stir in chia seeds and raisins.
5. Cover and let sit for 5 minutes until oats are at desired thickness.
6. Top with additional raisins, maple syrup, chopped nuts, and milk.

Sweet Carrot Porridge

(Prep + Cook Time: 30 minutes | Servings: 6)

Ingredients:
- 1 cup millet
- 3 cups coconut milk
- 2 carrots
- 4 tbsp honey
- 1 tbsp sugar
- 1 tsp ground ginger
- ¼ tsp salt

Directions:
1. Peel the carrot and chop it into the tiny pieces.
2. Combine the chopped carrot with the millet and transfer the mixture to the Instant Pot.
3. Add coconut milk, ground ginger, and salt. Stir the mixture gently and close the Instant Pot lid.
4. Cook the mixture at the RICE mode for 15 minutes.

5. Then open the Instant Pot lid and add honey. Stir it and cook the carrot porridge at the MANUAL mode for 5 minutes more.
6. When the time is over – chill the carrot porridge little.
7. Transfer it to the serving bowls.

Minty Green Lentil (VEG)

(Prep + Cook Time: 8 minutes | Servings: 2)

Ingredients:
- 1 tsp olive oil
- 1 medium onion, chopped
- ½ cup green lentils, rinsed
- ¾ cup veggie stock/water
- 1 medium carrot, grated
- 2 tbsp fresh mint, chopped
- 2 tbsp fresh cilantro
- ½ tsp grated lemon zest
- 1 tbsp lemon juice
- ½ tsp cumin powder
- Salt and pepper, to taste

Directions:
1. Select SAUTE and preheat your Instant Pot. Pour oil.
2. Add the chopped onion and sauté for a minute. Mix in the green lentils and water. Stir.
3. Secure the lid and cook for 5 minutes on HIGH Pressure. Allow the pressure to release naturally. Remove the lid and test for doneness.
4. If the lentils are not cooked well, cook for 1-2 minutes in the same procedure. Remove the lid and allow to cool.
5. Mix in all the remaining ingredients and stir well to mix.
6. Serve.

Three Lentil Chili (VEG)

(Prep + Cook Time: 35 minutes | Servings: 6)

Ingredients:
- 1 cup split red lentils, rinsed
- 2/3 cup brown lentils, rinsed
- 1 cup French green lentils, rinsed
- 1 medium-sized white onion, peeled and chopped
- 2 tsp minced garlic
- 2 medium-sized green bell peppers, seeded and chopped
- 28 ounce diced tomatoes
- 2 tbsp olive oil
- 1 tbsp salt
- ½ tsp ground black pepper
- 1 tsp red chili powder
- 1 tbsp ground cumin
- 7 cups vegetable stock

Directions:
1. Plug in and switch on a 6-quarts Instant Pot, select SAUTE option and add oil.
2. When the oil is heated, add onion and pepper and cook for 3-5 minutes or until onion is tender.
3. Then add garlic and sauté for 1 minute or until fragrant.
4. Add remaining ingredients into the pot, press CANCEL, select MULTIGRAIN option, secure pot with lid and then position pressure indicator.
5. When the timer beeps, switch off the Instant Pot and let pressure release naturally for 10 minutes and then do quick pressure release.
6. Then uncover the pot, stir and serve immediately.

Lentil Risotto (VEG)
(Prep + Cook Time: 30 minutes | Servings: 6)

Ingredients:
- 1 cup dry lentils, soaked overnight
- 1 celery stalk, chopped
- 1 medium-sized onion, peeled and chopped
- 1 tbsp minced garlic
- 1 tbsp olive oil
- 1 tbsp chopped parsley
- 1 cup Arborio rice, rinsed
- 3¼ cups vegetable broth

Directions:
1. Plug in and switch on a 6-quarts Instant Pot, select SAUTE option and add oil.
2. When the oil is heated, add onion and sauté for 2-3 minutes or until it begins to tenderize.
3. Add celery and parsley and cook for another minute. Then add garlic and rice, stir until mixed well and continue cooking for a minute.
4. Drain lentils and add to the pot along with vegetable broth. Mix well and press cancel and secure pot with lid.
5. Then select MANUAL option and adjust cooking time on timer pad to 5 minutes and let cook.

6. When the timer beeps, switch off the Instant Pot and let pressure release naturally for 10 minutes and then do quick pressure release.
7. Then uncover the pot, stir until mix well and serve immediately.

Peaches & Cream Oatmeal (VEG, S&F)
(Prep + Cook Time: 20 minutes | Servings: 4)

Ingredients:
- 2 cups rolled oats
- 4 cups water

Optional:
- ½ cup chopped almonds
- 2 tbsp flax meal

- 1 tsp vanilla
- 1 chopped peach

- Splash of cream, milk, or a non-diary milk
- Maple syrup

Directions:
1. Combine the water, peaches, oats, and vanilla in the Instant Pot.
2. Set to HIGH pressure using the PORRIDGE setting. Be sure the valve is sealed. Adjust the time to three minutes.
3. Allow the pressure to release naturally for ten minutes; then perform a quick release for the remainder of the pressure.
4. Garnish as desired and enjoy.

Quinoa (VEG, S&F)
(Prep + Cook Time: 20 minutes | Servings: 4)

Ingredients:
- 2 cup quinoa (any color)
- 3 cups water or chicken broth
- 2 pinches salt

- Juice of 1 lemon or apple cider vinegar

Optional:
Minced fresh herbs

Directions:
1. Thoroughly rinse the quinoa. It is best to soak it overnight using filtered water with one tablespoon of the lemon juice or vinegar, and strain.

2. Add the lemon juice, quinoa, broth, salt, and other herbs into the Instant Pot. Close and lock the lid. Use the manual (+) or (-) buttons to set the pot to one minute.
3. Allow the pot to do a natural release (up to 10 minutes).
4. Release the remainder of the pressure and serve.

Creamy Pumpkin Porridge

(Prep + Cook Time: 30 minutes | Servings: 5)

Ingredients:
- 1 cup milk
- 1 cup water
- 1-pound pumpkin
- 1 tsp cinnamon
- ½ tsp cardamom
- ½ tsp turmeric
- 1/3 cup millet
- 2 tsp brown sugar

Directions:
1. Peel the pumpkin and chop it roughly. Transfer the chopped pumpkin in the Instant Pot and add milk and water.
2. Sprinkle the mixture with the cinnamon, cardamom, turmeric, and brown sugar.
3. Add millet and mix up the mixture well. Close the Instant Pot lid and set the mode RICE. Cook the dish for 15 minutes.
4. When the time is over blend the mixture until smooth with the help of the hand blender.
5. Ladle the pumpkin porridge in the serving bowls. Enjoy!

Cheese Grits

(Prep + Cook Time: 20 minutes | Servings: 2)

Ingredients:
- 2 cups old fashion grits
- 2 cups milk
- 1 cup water
- 2 tbsp butter
- ½ cup cheddar cheese, shredded
- Pinch of sea salt and black pepper powder, to taste

Directions:
1. Mix the ingredients: cornmeal, water, butter, salt and pepper into your Instant Pot.
2. Hit the MANUAL and cook for 15 minutes on LOW pressure.
3. Once cooked, let depressurize naturally for about 10 minutes, then release manually.
4. Sprinkle the cheese and whisk continuously until smooth. Serve.

Delicious Steel Cut Oats (VEG, S&F)

(Prep + Cook Time: 15 minutes | Servings: 4)

Ingreduents:
- 1 cup steel cut oats
- 3 cups water

Directions:
1. Transfer the steel cut oats into the stainless steel bowl of your Instant Pot.
2. Add approximately 3 cups of water into the pot.
3. Close and secure the lid to its position, select the MANUAL option and then set the cooking time to 3 minutes.
4. Once the cooking cycle completes, wait for approximately 5 to 10 minutes and let the pressure to release naturally.
5. Feel free to add toppings of your choice, if desired.
6. Serve and enjoy.

Key Lime Coco Couscous (VEG, S&F)
(Prep + Cook Time: 15 minutes | Servings: 2)

Ingredients:
- 1 cup raw pearl couscous
- 1 can coconut milk
- ¼ cup water
- 1 zest of Key lime
- 1 juice of Key lime
- Pinch of iodized salt

Directions:
1. Place the pearl couscous, water, coconut milk, and salt in the Instant Pot.
2. Place the lid and seal it covering the pot.
3. Cook over HIGH pressure for 1 minute. After a minute let the steam naturally seep through. Uncover the pot.
4. Fluff the couscous using a pair of forks.
5. Add in the Key lime zest and juice. Stir well.
6. Serve on a plate. Enjoy.

Mango Dal

A classic Indian ingredient, mango and chana dal are the stars of this dish. Chana dal is a kind of chickpea with an earthy, sweet flavor.

(Prep + Cook Time: 50 minutes | Servings: 4)

Ingredients:
- 4 cups chicken broth
- 1 cup chana dal
- 2 peeled and diced mangoes
- 4 minced garlic cloves
- ½ cup chopped cilantro
- 1 minced onion
- 1 tbsp minced ginger
- 1 tbsp coconut oil Juice from
- ½ lime
- 1 tsp ground cumin
- 1 tsp sea salt
- 1 tsp ground coriander
- 1 tsp ground turmeric
- ⅛ tsp cayenne pepper

Directions:

1. Rinse the dal in a colander.
2. Turn the Instant Pot to SAUTE and heat coconut oil.
3. Add the cumin and cook for about 30 seconds. Toss in the onion and cook for 5 minutes, until soft.
4. Next, add the coriander, ginger, cayenne, garlic, and salt. Pour in the broth and add the dal and turmeric.
5. Keep the pot on sauté and bring the contents to a boil. It should boil for about 10 minutes. If it gets foamy, skim it off with a large spoon.
6. Add the mangoes. Secure the lid and hit BEANS/CHILI, and then 20 minutes.
7. When time is up, hit CANCEL and wait for the pressure to reduce naturally.
8. Add the lime juice and cilantro. Serve with rice.

Herby Polenta Squares with Cheese
(Prep + Cook Time: 10 minutes | Servings: 2)

Ingredients:

- 1 ¼ cups dry polenta
- ½ tsp cayenne pepper
- 1 tsp salt
- 2 ½ cups soy milk
- 1 ½ cups water
- 2 tbsp butter, room temperature
- ½ cup Ricotta cheese, for garnish
- 1 tbsp fresh marjoram, for garnish
- 1 tbsp fresh chopped Italian parsley, for garnish

Directions:

1. Simply fill your Instant Pot with the water, soy milk, butter, salt, and cayenne pepper. Press the SAUTE key.
2. Gradually stir the polenta into the boiling liquid, stirring continuously. Cover, push the MANUAL button and set the timer for 6 minutes.

3. Next, release the pressure naturally. Pour the polenta mixture into a baking sheet. Refrigerate it for 25 minutes.
4. Cut into squares and transfer to a plate. Sprinkle with fresh parsley and marjoram; serve topped with ricotta cheese.

Chickpeas Dish (VEG)

(Prep + Cook Time: 30 minutes | Servings: 8)

Ingredients:
- 16 oz chickpeas, soaked overnight and drained
- Salt and black pepper to the taste
- 3 cups coconut milk
- 1 tsp garlic, minced
- 1 cup cherry tomatoes, cut in halves
- ¾ pound sweet potatoes, cut in small chunks
- 1 tbsp curry paste
- 1 tbsp curry powder
- 1 tsp ginger, minced
- ½ cup basil leaves, finely chopped
- ¼ cup coriander, finely chopped
- 20 prunes, chopped
- 1 tbsp soy sauce

Directions:
1. Put the chickpeas in your Instant Pot, add garlic, coconut milk, sweet potatoes, curry powder and paste, tomatoes, coriander, salt, pepper and ginger.
2. Stir, cover and cook on HIGH pressure for 20 minutes.
3. Release pressure naturally, stir chickpeas mix and add prunes, basil and some soy sauce.
4. Stir again everything, divide amongst plates and serve.

Jam-packed Curry Quinoa (VEG, S&F)

(Prep + Cook Time: 50 minutes | Servings: 6)

Ingredients:
- 1 medium Russet potato, peeled and cubed
- 1 head cauliflower florets, coarsely chopped
- ½ white onion, diced
- 1 can chickpeas, rinsed and drained
- 1 can crushed tomatoes
- 2 can organic lite coconut milk
- ¼ cup raw quinoa
- 2 cloves garlic, minced
- 1 tsp ginger powder
- 1 tsp turmeric powder
- 1 tsp curry powder
- 1 tsp soy miso
- Salt and pepper to taste
- Red chili flakes for heat (optional)

Directions:
1. Place all the ingredients in the Instant Pot. Stir well using a spatula.
2. Cover and seal the lid. Select the MULTIGRAIN button and cook for 40 minutes.
3. Let the Instant Pot sit for 10 minutes after the set time. Uncover the lid.
4. Serve in a bowl. Enjoy.

Banana and Chia Seed Porridge (VEG, S&F)

(Prep + Cook Time: 10 minutes | Servings: 2)

Ingredients:
- 2 tbsp Chia seeds
- ½ cup green apple, grated
- ½ cup macadamia nuts, ground
- ½ cup fresh mixed berries
- 1 ¼ cups coconut milk
- ½ tsp cinnamon
- ½ tsp ground cloves
- 1 cup ripe bananas

Directions:
1. Add all of the above ingredients, except for the fresh berries, to your Instant Pot.
2. Set the machine to cook for 6 minutes at HIGH pressure.
3. Then, use the quick-release method.
4. Serve in individual dishes topped with fresh mixed berries.

Delicious chia porridge

(Prep + Cook Time: 10 minutes | Servings: 4)

Ingredients:
- 1 cup Greek yogurt
- 1 cup water
- 1 cup chia seeds
- 1 tbsp honey
- ½ tsp cinnamon
- 1 tsp lemon zest
- 2 apples
- ¼ tsp salt
- 1 tsp clove

Directions:
1. Combine the water and Greek yogurt together and mix up the mixture. After this, transfer the liquid mixture in the Instant Pot and add chia seeds.
2. Stir the mixture and sprinkle it with the honey, cinnamon, lemon zest, salt, and cloves.

3. Peel the apples and chop them into the convenient pieces. Add the chopped apple in the Instant Pot.
4. Then mix up the mixture to get the homogenous texture. Close the lid and set the Instant Pot mode STEAM. Cook the dish for 7minutes.
5. When the dish is cooked – remove it from the Instant Pot and mix it up gently.
6. Serve the chia porridge hot. Enjoy.

Fruity Oatmeal (VEG, S&F)

(Prep + Cook Time: 15 minutes | Servings: 4)

Ingredients:

- 1 cup steel cut oats
- ¼ tsp cinnamon powder
- 1 tbsp granulated sugar
- 3 cup water
- 1 cup sliced fruits in season

Directions:

1. Place the oats, water, cinnamon, and sugar in the Instant Pot.
2. Cover and seal the lid.
3. Cook over HIGH pressure for a minute. After a minute, let the pressure naturally release from the pot.
4. Uncover the pot and transfer the oats in a bowl. Let it cool for about 10 minutes.
5. Top each bowl with fresh fruits.
6. Serve and enjoy.

Mushroom Thyme Oatmeal

(Prep + Cook Time: 30 minutes | Servings: 4)

Ingredients:

- 1 14-ounce can of chicken broth
- ¼ tsp salt
- ½ medium onion, finely diced
- ½ cup water
- ½ cup smoked gouda (finely grated)
- 2 tbsp butter
- 2 cloves garlic, minced
- 1 cup steel cut oats
- 3 branches of fresh thyme (garnish)
- 2 tbsp olive oil
- 8 ounces Cremini mushrooms, sliced
- Salt and freshly ground pepper

Directions:

1. Place butter into pressure cooking pot, select SAUTE.
2. When butter is melted, Add in the onions and cook, stirring frequently, until soft for about 3 minutes.
3. Add the garlic and cook for 1 minute. Add oats and toast for 1 minute stirring frequently.
4. Add, water, thyme, broth and salt. Lock lid in place. Select HIGH pressure and a 10 minute cook time.
5. As the oats are cook, heat a large sauté pan over medium-high heat.
6. Add mushrooms and olive oil and cook until brown on both sides.
7. When Instant Pot beep sounds, turn off pressure cooker and allow a natural pressure release for 10 minutes, then perform a quick pressure release.
8. When the valve drops remove lid carefully. Stir oats. Stir in Gouda cheese until melted. Stir in mushrooms.
9. Season with salt and pepper to taste.
10. Garnish with thyme leaves. Serve.

Cinnamon Raisins Flat Oats (VEG, S&F)

(Prep + Cook Time: 15 minutes | Servings: 6)

Ingredients:
- 2 cup flat oats
- 2 cup almond milk
- 3 cup water
- 1 cup raisins
- 2 small barks cinnamon
- ½ tsp nutmeg
- 1 tsp vanilla extract
- ¼ cup maple syrup
- Pinch of salt

Directions:
1. Place all the ingredients except for the syrup, salt and vanilla extract in the Instant Pot.
2. Close and seal the lid. Press the PORRIGE button and set to 20 minutes.
3. Let the pressure naturally release from the Instant Pot before removing the lid.
4. Add in the rest of the ingredients.
5. Serve and enjoy.

Multigrain mix

(Prep + Cook Time: 40 minutes | Servings: 6)

Ingredients:
- ½ cup millet
- ½ cup white rice
- ½ cup brown rice
- 3 cups chicken stock
- 1 tsp salt
- 1 onion, diced
- 3 tbsp butter
- 3 oz. dates

Directions:
1. Combine the millet, white rice, and brown rice together in the mixing bowl. Add salt and diced onion.
2. Chop the dates and add them to the mixture too.
3. After this, transfer the grain mixture in the Instant Pot and add chicken stock. Mix up the mixture and close the lid.

4. Set the Instant Pot mode MULTIGRAIN and cook the dish for 30 minutes.
5. When the time is over – remove the mixture from the Instant Pot and transfer it to the mixing bowl.
6. Add butter and stir it carefully.
7. After this, transfer the dish in the serving plates.

Baked Beans

(Prep + Cook Time: 50 minutes | Servings: 8)

Ingredients:

- 1 pound dried northern beans
- 8 strips bacon, uncooked, chopped
- 2 tsp dry mustard
- 2 ½ cups chicken stock
- ¼ cup brown sugar, packed
- ½ tsp salt
- ½ tsp ground black pepper
- ½ cup molasses
- ½ cup ketchup
- 1 tbsp Worcestershire sauce
- 1 small-sized onion, diced

Directions:

1. In a large-sized container, soak the beans with just enough water to cover them for at least 6-8 hours or overnight.
2. Drain and rinse the beans. Discard the soaking water.
3. Press the SAUTE button. Put the bacon in the pot and sauté until crisp.
4. Transfer into a paper towel-lined plate and set aside. Put the onion in the pot. Sauté with the bacon grease in the pot until translucent.
5. Slowly add the broth in the pot. With a wooden spoon, scrape the bottom of the pot to loosen the browned bits.
6. Add the ketchup, molasses, dry mustard, brown sugar, Worcestershire sauce, salt, and pepper. Stir to mix. Stir in the beans.
7. Press CANCEL. Close and lock the lid. Turn the steam valve to SEALING. Press MANUAL and set the time to 45 minutes.
8. When the timer beeps, turn OFF the pot. Let the pressure release naturally for 10 minutes. Turn the steam valve to VENTING to release remaining pressure.
9. Check the tenderness of the beans. If needed, cook for another 3-5 minutes. Stir in the reserved bacon.
10. Serve.

Beans Stew

(Prep + Cook Time: 1 hour 30 minutes | Servings: 8)

Ingredients:
- 2 carrots, chopped
- 1 plantain, chopped
- 1 pound red beans, dry
- Salt and black pepper to the taste
- 1 tomato, chopped
- 2 green onions stalks, chopped
- 1 small yellow onion, diced
- ¼ cup cilantro leaves, chopped
- 2 tbsp vegetable oil

Directions:
1. Put the beans in your Instant Pot, add water to cover, cook on HIGH pressure for 35 minutes and release pressure for 10 minutes naturally.
2. Add plantain, carrots, salt and pepper tot the taste, cover Instant Pot again and cook on HIGH for 30 more minutes.
3. Meanwhile, heat up a pan with the vegetable oil over medium high heat, add yellow onion, stir and cook for 2 minutes.
4. Add tomatoes, green onions, some salt and pepper, stir again, cook for 3 minutes more and take off the heat. Release pressure naturally from your Instant Pot.
5. Divide cooked beans amongst plates, top with tomatoes and onions mix, sprinkle cilantro at the end and serve right away.

Pinto Beans Ala Tex-Mex

(Prep + Cook Time: 55 minutes | Servings: 6)

Ingredients:
- 20 ounces package pinto beans with ham (I used Hurst's HamBeens)
- ¼ cup cilantro, chopped
- ½ cup salsa verde
- 1 packet taco seasoning
- 1 onion
- 1 jalapeno, diced
- 1 clove garlic, diced
- 5 cups chicken broth
- Salt and pepper, to taste

Directions:

1. Rinse and sort out the dried beans. Put into the Instant Pot. Pour the broth in the pot.
2. Add garlic, onion, and jalapeno. Stir in the taco seasoning. Close and lock the lid.
3. Turn the steam valve to SEALING. Set the pressure to HIGH and set the timer for 42 minutes.
4. When the timer beeps, let the pressure release naturally for about 15 minutes.
5. Drain excess liquid from the pot. Stir in the salsa verde, ham seasoning, and cilantro.
6. Taste and season with salt to taste.
7. Serve in tacos, over rice, or as a side dish.

Spicy Black Bean and Brown Rice Salad
(Prep + Cook Time: 30 minutes | Servings: 8)

Ingredients:
- 1 can (14 ounces) black beans, drained and rinsed
- 1 cup brown rice
- 1 avocado, diced
- 1 ½ cups water
- ¼ cup cilantro, minced
- ¼ tsp salt
- 12 grape tomatoes, quartered

For the spicy dressing:
- 3 tbsp lime juice, fresh squeezed
- 3 tbsp extra-virgin olive oil
- 2 tsp Tabasco or Cholula
- 2 garlic cloves, pressed or minced
- 1/8 tsp salt
- 1 tsp agave nectar

Directions:

1. Combine the rice with the water and salt in the Instant Pot. Close and lock the lid.

2. Turn the steam valve to SEALING. Set the pressure to HIGH and set the timer for 24 minutes.
3. When the timer beeps, release the pressure naturally for 10 minutes. Turn the steam valve to VENTING to release any remaining pressure.
4. Carefully open the lid. Using a fork, fluff the rice and let cool to room temperature.
5. When cool, refrigerate until ready to use. In a large-sized bowl, stir the brown rice with the black beans, avocado, tomato, and cilantro.
6. In a small-sized bowl, except for the olive oil, whisk the dressing ingredients together.
7. While continuously whisking, slowly pour in the olive oil.
8. Pour the dressing over the brown rice mix and stir to combine.

Red Beans Over Rice

(Prep + Cook Time: 1 hour 25 minutes | Servings: 8)

Ingredients:

- 1 pound dry red kidney beans
- 1 ½ pounds ham, smoked sausage, tasso, cut into cubes
- 1 onion, diced
- 1 pepper, diced
- 1 teaspoon salt
- ½ tsp black pepper
- ½ tsp dried thyme
- ¼ tsp cayenne pepper (or more if you want it spicier)
- ¼ tsp white pepper
- 2 bay leaves
- 2 tbsp oil
- 2-3 stalks celery, chopped
- 3 garlic cloves, minced
- 5 ½ cups water

Directions:

1. Set the Instant Pot to normal SAUTE mode. Put the oil in the pot and heat.
2. When hot, add the celery, onion, and pepper. Sauté for about 5 minutes or until they start to soften. Add the garlic and chopped meat.
3. Cook for about 3-4 minutes, stirring often. Rinse the kidney beans and drain. Add all the ingredients into the Instant Pot.

4. Cover and lock the lid. Turn the steam valve to SEALING. Press PRESSURE, set to HIGH, and set the timer to 60 minutes.
5. When the timer beeps, let the pressure release naturally for about 10-15 minutes. Open the lid.
6. With a potato masher or a wooden spoon, mash about 1/ 3-1/2 of the beans and stir thoroughly – the mashed beans should thicken the broth into creamy gravy. Serve with rice.

Bacon and Black Beans
(Prep + Cook Time: 55 minutes | Servings: 6)

Ingredients:
- 1 pound dried black beans
- 3 strips bacon, cut into halves
- 1 small onion, cut in half
- 6 garlic cloves, crushed
- 1 orange, cut in half
- 2 bay leaves
- 2 quarts chicken stock, low-sodium
- 2 tsp kosher salt, more for seasoning

Directions:
1. Press the SAUTE key. Put the bacon in the pot and sauté for 2 minutes or until crisp and the fat is rendered.
2. Add the rest of the ingredients in the pot. Cover and close the lid. Turn the steam valve to SEALING. Set the pressure to HIGH and the timer to 40 minutes.
3. When the timer beeps, quick release the pressure – the beans will cooked, but still firm.
4. If you want a creamier and tender beans, let the pressure release naturally.
5. Open the lid. Discard the bay leaves, orange, and onion.
6. Season with salt to taste and serve.

Garlic Bacon Pinto Beans

(Prep + Cook Time: 1 hour 20 minutes | Servings: 8)

Ingredients:

- 1 pound bag of dried pinto beans
- 2 pounds thick cut bacon (cut into 2" pieces)
- cups of water
- 1 tsp garlic powder
- ½ tsp thyme
- 1 tsp sea salt
- ½ tsp black pepper
- 2 tbsp of Cholula hot sauce

Directions:

1. With your Instant Pot on SAUTE, cook your bacon until it's nice and crispy.
2. Drain half the grease out of your Instant Pot when done. Add in your dried beans, water, and all other seasonings.
3. Set to MANUAL high pressure for 38 minutes. When done, let it naturally release pressure. It should take about 22-26 minutes for this to happen (depending on elevation).
4. Take the lid off and allow to set for about 10 minutes before serving over some amazing jasmine rice.
5. Done and serve!

Dried Beans Vegeratian Soup (VEG)

(Prep + Cook Time: 45 minutes | Servings: 6)

Ingredients:

- 1 bag (20 ounces) 15 bean soup blend of Hurst Beans (save a seasoning packet for another use)
- 1 can (14.5 ounces) Red Gold petite diced tomatoes, undrained
- 1 dried bay leaf
- 1 lemon, fresh squeezed juice
- 1 red bell pepper, seeded and chopped
- 1 sweet onion, small-sized, chopped
- 1 tbsp olive oil
- ½ tsp ground red pepper
- 2 carrots, peeled and chopped
- 2 stalks celery, chopped with tops
- 2-3 sprigs fresh thyme
- 3 cloves garlic, chopped
- 8 cups vegetable stock, OR
- 4 cups water plus
- 4 cups stock Kosher salt and fresh black pepper to taste

Directions:

1. Sort the beans, rinse, and drain. Except for the lemon juice and tomatoes, put all of the ingredients into a 6-quart Instant Pot, ending with the olive oil.
2. Cover and lock the lid. Turn the steam valve to SEALING. Press the MANUAL key, set the pressure to HIGH, and set the timer for 45 minutes.
3. When the Instant Pot timer beeps, press the CANCEL key. Let the pressure release naturally for 10-15 minutes or until the valve drops.
4. Using an oven mitt or a long handled spoon, turn the steam valve to VENTING to release remaining pressure.
5. Unlock and carefully open the lid. Taste, and if needed, adjust seasoning.

6. Stir in the lemon juice and tomatoes. If desired, slightly mash a couple of beans. Serve.

Notes: If desired, you can cook the dish a bit longer on SAUTÉ mode after adding the lemon, tomato, and seasoning to meld the new added ingredients. Also, if you want softer beans, cover and lock the lid. Turn the steam valve to SEALING. Press the MANUAL key, set the pressure to HIGH, and set the timer for 5 minutes.

Black Bean Chili (VEG, S&F)

(Prep + Cook Time: 50 minutes | Servings: 8)

Ingredients:
- 1 lb dried black beans
- 4 medium finely chopped garlic cloves
- 3 tbsp vegetable oil
- 2 medium, cored, seeded and diced red bell peppers
- 2 medium diced red onions
- 2 tbsp chili powder
- 1 tbsp kosher salt
- 1 tbsp cumin
- 1 tbsp tomato paste
- 2 ½ c water
- 1 can crushed tomatoes
- 2 tbsp minced chipotles
- 2 cup corn kernels

Directions:
1. Soak your dried black beans overnight.
2. Cook up the red onions, garlic, and red bell peppers with the spices in the cooker until they are soft, about four minutes.
3. Add in the beans, tomatoes, and chipotles. Stir well.
4. Cook for 30 minutes on HIGH pressure with the lid locked down.
5. Add in corn about five minutes before the timer goes off.

Mexican Chili Beans

(Prep + Cook Time: 50 minutes | Servings: 6)

Ingredients:

- 2 cup dried red kidney beans
- 4 cup water
- 3 tbsp olive oil
- 1 white onion, diced
- 6 cloves garlic, minced
- 2 tbsp jalapeno chili, sliced
- Salt and pepper to taste
- 2 tbsp green onions, chopped (for topping)

Directions:

1. Place beans, one tablespoon of olive oil, and water in the Instant Pot. Cover and seal the lid. Select the MANUAL button and cook on HIGH pressure for 30 minutes.
2. Let the pressure naturally release after 30 minutes. Remove the lid.
3. Add the white onion, garlic, jalapeno, salt and pepper. Cover and seal the lid again. Select MANUAL and cook for another 10 minutes.
4. Mash the beans using a masher for better texture.
5. Serve in a bowl topped with green onions.

Quick Ham & Beans

(Prep + Cook Time: 40 minutes | Servings: 4)

Ingredients:

- 1.5-pounds of ham
- 36 oz of water
- 1 small, diced yellow onion
- 1 small, minced garlic clove
- 1 ½ pounds white beans (dry)
- 1 bay leaf Salt and pepper to taste

Directions:

1. Start by chopping up the onion and garlic.
2. Cut the ham into cubes. Rinse the beans and remove any beans that have become discolored.
3. Combine all of the ingredients in your Instant Pot. Season with salt and pepper. Close the lid and bring the pressure to HIGH and cook for 25 minutes.
4. Allow the pressure to drop naturally and then remove the bay leaf.
5. Serve after allowing the ham and beans to cool for a few minutes.
6. You could serve this over a bed of rice, with a salad, or with rolls or corn bread.

White Rice (VEG, S&F)

(Prep + Cook Time: 14 minutes | Servings: 4)

Ingredients:

- 1 cup long grain white rice
- 1 ½ cups water
- 1 tsp olive oil

Directions:

1. Add 1 cup long grain white rice, 1 ½ cups water, and 1 teaspoon olive oil to the Instant Pot.
2. Cook on HIGH pressure for 3 minutes.
3. Let it natural release for 10 minutes and quick release after.
4. Fluff and serve.

Brown Rice (VEG, S&F)

(Prep + Cook Time: 30 minutes | Servings: 4)

Ingredients:

- 1 cup brown rice
- 1 ¼ cups water
- 1 tsp olive oil

Directions:

1. Add 1 cup brown rice, 1 ¼ cups water, and 1 teaspoon olive oil to the Instant Pot.
2. Cook on HIGH pressure for 20 minutes.
3. Let it natural release for 10 minutes and quick release after. Fluff and serve.

Brazilian Black Beans (VEG)

(Total Time: 1 hour 45 minutes (plus soak time)

Servings: 8 servings

Ingredients:

- 1 smoked ham hock (or smoked pork chop) 6 oz.
- 2 bay leaves
- 1 lb package dried black beans
  For the sofrito:
- 1 large minced white onion
- 3 cloves garlic chopped
- 3/4 bunch of parsley finely chopped (no stems)
- Kosher salt and fresh cracked pepper to taste
- 2 tbsp extra virgin olive oil

Directions:

1. Soak bean over night. Discard water.
2. In the Instant Pot combine soaked beans, ham hock and bay leaves and add enough water to cover beans at least 3 inches, about 6 cups.
3. Bring to a boil, then cover and lock the lid. Cook 45 minutes in Instant Pot on MEDIUM heat.
4. After 45 minutes shut the heat off and wait for the pressure to come out of the pot before removing the lid.
5. Meanwhile, in a large sauté pan add oil; sauté onion, garlic, and parsley on a medium heat.
6. Add salt and pepper to taste and cook until onions are translucent, about 10-15 minutes.
7. Add onion mixture to the beans and cook uncovered 20-30 more minutes, or until beans have a thick consistency.Serve.

Mango Pudding Rice (VEG, S&F)

(Prep + Cook Time: 15 minutes | Servings: 4)

Ingredients:

- ¾ cup Arborio Rice
- 1 ½ cup water
- 1 cup coconut milk
- ½ tsp salt
- 1/3 cup brown sugar
- 1 tsp vanilla
- 1 mango, peeled and cubed
- ¼ cup shredded coconut
- ¼ cup almonds

Directions:

1. Add rice, water, coconut milk, sugar, and salt into the Instant Pot.
2. Use the manual setting and set the time to 7 minutes at HIGH pressure.
3. Let the cooker cool down naturally. Unlock the lid and uncover rice.
4. Add vanilla, and chopped mango. Stir together.
5. Serve in small bowls with toasted coconut and almonds over the top.

Sweet Potato and Apple Risotto

(Prep + Cook Time: 15 minutes | Servings: 4)

Ingredients:

- 1 tbsp butter
- 1 cup sweet yellow onion, chopped
- 2 cups Arborio rice
- ¼ cup dry white wine
- 1 cup sweet potato, peeled and cubed
- 1 cup apple, peeled and cubed
- 4 cups vegetable stock
- 1 tsp salt
- 1 tsp black pepper
- 1 tbsp fresh thyme
- 1 bay leaf
- ½ cup freshly grated
- Parmesan cheese, optional

Directions:

1. Set the Instant Pot to the SAUTE setting and add the butter. Once the butter has melted and is hot, add the onion and sauté for 2 minutes.

2. Next, add the Arborio rice and cook, stirring frequently, until lightly toasted, approximately 3-4 minutes.
3. Next, add the white wine and let it reduce by about half. Add the sweet potato, apple, and vegetable stock.
4. Season the mixture with salt, black pepper, thyme, and the bay leaf.
5. Switch the Instant Pot over to HIGH pressure cooker setting. Cover, seal, and cook for 7 minutes.
6. Release the steam from the device using the ten minute natural release option and carefully open the top and remove the bay leaf.
7. Stir in the freshly grated Parmesan, if using, and serve immediately.

Rice Pudding (VEG)
(Prep + Cook Time: 45 minutes | Servings: 4)

Ingredients:
- 1 cup Arborio rice
- 1 ½ cups water
- ¼ tsp salt
- 2 cups whole milk, divided*
- ½ cup sugar
- 2 eggs
- ½ tsp vanilla extract
- 3/4 cup raisins

*For a richer, creamier rice pudding you can also use half heavy cream.

Directions:
1. In the Instant Pot, combine rice, water, and salt. Lock the lid in place and select HIGH pressure and 3 minutes cook time.
2. When beep sounds turn off pressure cooker and use a natural pressure release for 10 minutes. After 10 minutes, release any remaining pressure with a quick pressure release.
3. Add 1 ½ cups milk and sugar to rice in pressure cooking pot; stir to combine.

4. In a small mixing bowl, whisk eggs with remaining ½ cup milk and vanilla. Pour through a fine mesh strainer into pressure cooking pot. Select SAUTE and cook, stirring constantly, until mixture starts to boil.
5. Turn off pressure cooker. Remove pot from the pressure cooker. Stir in raisins.
6. Pudding will thicken as it cools. Serve warm or pour into serving dishes and chill.
7. Served topped with whipped cream, and a sprinkle of cinnamon or nutmeg, if desired.

Nutty Brown Rice

(Prep + Cook Time: 20 minutes | Servings: 4)

Ingredients:
- 3 tbsp butter
- 2 cups long brown rice
- 4 chicken bouillon cubes
- 4 cups water
- Pepper to taste

Directions:
1. Add butter into the Instant Pot. Select the SAUTE setting on the Instant Pot.
2. When the butter stops foaming, add rice into the Instant Pot and stir to combine.
3. Add chicken bouillon cubes and water into the Instant Pot.
4. Close Instant Pot lid. Select MANUAL setting and select a 15 minute cook time.
5. Once the cook time is reached, select the CANCEL setting and allow pressure be released naturally for 15 minutes approximately, until the float valve drops down.
6. Open the Instant Pot lid.
7. Serve warm.

Jasmine Rice (VEG, S&F)
(Prep + Cook Time: 40 minutes | Servings: 4)

Ingredients:
1 package Jasmine rice
12 oz water

Directions:
1. Place the rice and water in the bottom of your pressure cooker.
2. Gently stir the rice to soak with water. Close the lid on your pressure cooker and bring to HIGH pressure and cook for 3 minutes.
3. Allow the pressure to naturally drop for the next 10 minutes. Release the remaining pressure and fluff the rice with a fork.
4. Close the lid and allow the rice to sit for 20 minutes before serving or using in another recipe.
5. Enjoy your perfect Jasmine rice!

Berry Banana Rice Porridge
(Prep + Cook Time: 20 minutes | Servings: 6)

Ingredients:
- 1 ½ cups pineapple juice
- 2 cups basmati rice
- 1 tbsp maple syrup
- 3 cups water
- 2 bananas, sliced
- ¼ tsp grated nutmeg
- ¼ tsp salt
- ½ tsp ground cloves
- 3 tsp butter
- 1/3 cup heavy cream
- 1 ¼ cups fresh mixed berries

Directions:
1. Melt the butter in your Instant Pot turned to the SAUTE function.
2. Stir in the mixed berries and the slices of banana; cook for two minutes, stirring often.
3. Stir in the rice, nutmeg, cloves, and a pinch of salt. Cook for an additional minute.

4. Pour in the water and pineapple juice; stir well to combine. Set the Instant Pot to cook at HIGH pressure for 12 minutes.
5. Then, use the quick-release method. Unlock and open the cooker.
6. Press the RICE button; stir in the cream and maple syrup.
7. Simmer for about 3 minutes. Unplug the machine, stir and serve warm.

Chinese Fried Rice (VEG)

(Prep + Cook Time: 40 minutes | Servings: 6)

Ingredients:
- 1 tbsp peanut oil
- 1 red onion, diced
- 2 cloves garlic, minced
- ½ tsp ginger powder
- 1 cup long grain brown rice
- ¼ cup light soy sauce
- 1 ½ cup vegan broth
- ½ cup frozen green peas
- 1 tbsp green onions, chopped (for topping)

Directions:
1. Select the SAUTE button and heat the oil. Sauté the onion and garlic. After a couple of minutes, add the ginger powder, rice, soy sauce, and vegan broth. Stir well.
2. Cover and seal the lid. Select the RICE button and cook for 12 minutes.
3. After 12 minutes, let the Instant Pot release its pressure naturally.
4. Remove the lid and stir in the green peas.
5. Serve on a plate topped with chopped green onions.

Rice Pilaf with Peas, Parsley, and Carrots (VEG)

(Prep + Cook Time: 15 minutes | Servings: 8)

Ingredients:

- 2 cups rinsed long-grain white rice
- 1 ¼ cups water
- 1 cup thawed frozen peas
- ½ cup toasted and sliced almonds
- 1 chopped onion
- 1 chopped carrot
- 1 chopped celery stalk
- 2 tbsp chopped parsley
- 1 tbsp butter
- Salt to taste

Directions:

1. Melt the butter in your Instant Pot on the SAUTE setting. When melted, add onions, carrots, and celery.
2. Stir and cook for 3-5 minutes, or until tender.
3. Add rice and stir for 1-2 minutes. Pour in broth and water, with a dash of salt.
4. Close and seal the lid. Select MANUAL and cook for 3 minutes on HIGH pressure.
5. When time is up, hit CANCEL and wait 5 minutes before quick-releasing.
6. Stir rice and add parsley, almonds, and peas.
7. Stir until the peas have warmed through. Serve.

Rice and Black Beans

(Prep + Cook Time: 35 minutes | Servings: 4)

Ingredients:

- 1 cup onion, diced
- 4 cloves garlic, crushed and then minced
- 2 cups brown rice
- 2 cups dry black beans
- 9 cups water
- 1 tsp salt
- 1-2 limes, optional
- Avocado, optional

Directions:

1. Put the garlic and the onion in the Instant Pot. Add the black beans and the brown rice.

2. Pour in the water and sprinkle the salt. Cover and lock the lid. Turn the steam valve to SEALING.
3. Press MANUAL and set the time to 28 minutes.
4. When the timer is up, press CANCEL or unplug the pot. Let the pressure release naturally.
5. You can let it sit for 20 minutes. Scoop into a serving bowl and squeeze a lime wedge over the bowl.
6. Serve with a couple of avocado slices for garnishing.

Rice Balls

(Prep + Cook Time: 35 minutes | Servings: 4)

Ingredients:

- 1 cup rice, cooked
- 2 eggs
- 1 carrot
- 1 white onion
- 1 tsp salt
- 3 tbsp flour
- 1 tbsp fresh dill
- 1 tbsp butter
- 1/3 cup ground chicken

Directions:

1. Peel the carrot and onion. Grate the vegetables and combine them together in the mixing bowl.
2. Add salt, flour, fresh fill, and ground chicken. Knead the smooth dough.
3. Then make the medium balls from the rice mixture.
4. Toss the butter in the Instant Pot and add the rice balls. Close the Instant Pot lid and set the Instant Pot mode STEAM.
5. Cook the dish for 25 minutes.
6. When the time is over – let the dish chill little.
7. Serve the rice balls warm.

Almond Saffron Risotto

(Prep + Cook Time: 20 minutes | Servings: 8)

Ingredients:

- 2 tbsp extra virgin olive oil
- ½ tsp saffron threads, crushed
- ½ cup onion, chopped
- 2 tbsp hot milk
- 1 ½ cups Arborio rice
- 3 ½ cups veggie stock
- A pinch of salt
- 1 tbsp honey
- 1 cinnamon stick
- 1/3 cup almonds, chopped
- 1/3 cup currants, dried

Directions:

1. In a bowl, mix hot milk with saffron, stir and leave aside.
2. Set your Instant Pot on SAUTE mode, add oil and heat it up.
3. Add onions, stir and cook for 5 minutes.
4. Add rice, veggie stock, saffron and milk, honey, salt, almonds, cinnamon stick and currants.
5. Stir, cover the pot and cook at HIGH for 5 minutes.
6. Release the pressure quick, fluff the rice a bit, sprinkle cinnamon. Serve.

Red Beans Over Rice

(Prep + Cook Time: 1 hour 15 minutes | Servings: 6)

Ingredients:

- 1 pound dry red kidney beans
- 1 ½ pounds ham, smoked sausage, tasso, cut into cubes
- 1 onion, diced
- 1 pepper, diced
- 1 tsp salt
- ½ tsp black pepper
- ½ tsp dried thyme
- ¼ tsp cayenne pepper (or more if you want it spicier)
- ¼ tsp white pepper
- 2 bay leaves
- 2 tbsp oil
- 2-3 stalks celery, chopped
- 3 garlic cloves, minced
- 5 ½ cups water

Directions:

1. Set the Instant Pot to normal SAUTE mode. Put the oil in the pot and heat. When hot, add the celery, onion, and pepper.

2. Sauté for about 5 minutes or until they start to soften.
3. Add the garlic and chopped meat. Cook for about 3-4 minutes, stirring often.
4. Rinse the kidney beans and drain. Add all the ingredients into the pot. Cover and lock the lid. Turn the steam valve to SEALING. Press PRESSURE, set to HIGH, and set the timer to 60 minutes.
5. When the timer beeps, let the pressure release naturally for about 10-15 minutes. Open the lid.
6. With a potato masher or a wooden spoon, mash about 1/3-1/2 of the beans and stir thoroughly – the mashed beans should thicken the broth into creamy gravy.
7. Serve with rice.

Notes: If the beans are still not tender after 60 minutes, cook on HIGH for 30 minutes more.

Lemon-Parmesan Risotto

(Prep + Cook Time: 15 minutes | Servings:)

Ingredients:

- 3½ cups veggie broth
- 1½ cups frozen baby peas
- 1½ cups Arborio rice
- 1 chopped onion
- 2 tbsp chopped parsley
- 2 tbsp butter
- 2 tbsp lemon juice
- 2 tbsp Parmesan cheese
- 1 tbsp olive oil
- 1 tsp lemon zest
- Salt and pepper to taste

Directions:

1. Turn on your Instant Pot to SAUTE and heat the oil and butter until shiny. Stir onion in for about 5 minutes, or until softened.
2. Stir in the rice to toast for 2-3 minutes. Pour in broth and lemon juice.
3. Close and seal lid. Press MANUAL and cook for 5 minutes. When time is up, turn off the cooker and quick-release.

4. Turn your Instant Pot back to the lowest setting of SAUTE and add rest of broth and the baby peas. Stir for 1-2 minutes until peas are warmed and tender.
5. Add parsley, cheese, 1 tablespoon of butter, and 1 teaspoon of lemon zest.
6. Season to taste before serving.

Cherry Apple Breakfast Risotto
(Prep + Cook Time: 15 minutes | Servings: 4)

Ingredients:
- 2 Large Apples (Cored & Diced)
- 2 tbsp of Butter
- 1½ tsp of Cinnamon
- 1½ cups of Arborio Rice
- 1/3 cup of Brown Sugar
- 3 cups of 1% Milk
- 1 cup of Apple Juice
- ½ cup of Dried Cherries
- ¼ tsp of Salt

Optional Toppings:
- Sliced Almonds
- Brown Sugar
- 1% Milk

Directions:
1. Heat your butter in your Instant Pot for approximately 2 to 3 minutes. Stir in your rice and cook, stirring frequently, until your rice becomes opaque. Should take approximately 3 to 4 minutes.
2. Add your apples, spices, and brown sugar. Stir in your juice and milk. Select HIGH pressure and cook for approximately 6 minutes.
3. After 6 minutes, turn off your Instant Pot and use a Quick pressure release. Carefully remove the lid and stir in your dried cherries.
4. Top with your sliced almonds, additional brown sugar, and a splash of milk. Serve and enjoy.

Apple Cherry Breakfast Rice Cream (VEG, S&F)

(Prep + Cook Time: 25 minutes | Servings: 6)

Ingredients:
- 1½ cups short-grain rice
- 2 apples, cored and diced
- ½ cup dried cherries
- 2 tbsp butter
- 1/3 cup brown sugar or sweetener
- 1 cup apple juice
- 3 cups milk
- 1¾ tbsp cinnamon
- ½ cup sliced almonds
- Sea salt
- Toppings on your choice (brown sugar, raisins, almonds)

Directions:
1. Put the butter in your Instant Pot and heat for a couple of minutes.
2. Add the rice and cook, stirring frequently until the rice becomes opaque. This should take 3 or 4 minutes.
3. Add the apples, spices, and brown sugar (or sweetener), then stir in the juice and the milk.
4. Secure the Lid on the Cooker and switch the Pressure Release Valve to Closed. Push the RICE button and set the time for 6 minutes.
5. Once the timer reaches 0, the cooker will automatically switch to KEEP WARM. Switch the pressure release valve to open. When the steam is completely released, remove the lid.
6. Carefully lift the lid and stir in the cherries before serving with toppings of your choice (brown sugar, raisins, almonds) and a dash of milk over the top.

Savory Breakfast Porridge

(Prep + Cook Time: 60 minutes | Servings: 4)

Ingredients:
- 2 cups chicken broth
- 2 cups water
- 4 eggs
- 4 chopped scallions
- ½ cup rinsed and drained white rice
- 1 tbsp sugar
- 1 tbsp olive oil
- 2 tsp soy sauce
- ½ tsp salt
- Black pepper

Directions:
1. Pour water, broth, sugar, salt, and rice into the Instant Pot.
2. Close the lid. Hit PORRIDGE and 30 minutes on HIGH pressure.
3. While that cooks, heat oil in a saucepan. Crack in the eggs one at a time, so they aren't touching each other.
4. Cook until the whites become crispy on the edges, but the yolks are still runny. Sprinkle on salt and pepper.
5. When the Instant Pot timer goes off, hit CANCEL and wait for the pressure to go down on its own.
6. If the porridge isn't thick enough, hit SAUTE and cook uncovered for 5-10 minutes.
7. Serve with scallions, soy sauce, and an egg per bowl.

Mashed Potatoes (VEG)

(Prep + Cook Time: 35 minutes | Servings: 2)

Ingredients:

- 4 potatoes
- 1 cup water
- ½ cup milk
- 2 tbsp unsalted butter
- 2 cloves garlic
- 1 tbsp parmesan cheese
- Kosher salt and pepper to taste

Directions:

1. Fill the pressure cooker with 1 cup of water. Place the steamer trivet in the cooker and add quartered potatoes in the steamer trivet.
2. Cook at HIGH pressure for 8 minutes then quick release. While the potatoes are cooking, heat a small saucepan over medium heat.
3. Melt the butter and add the garlic. Add a pinch of kosher salt.
4. SAUTE the garlic for 1 to 2 minutes until fragrant and golden in color.
5. Add the milk and deglaze the pan. Remove mixture from heat when it is hot. Remove the lid.
6. Mash the cooked potatoes in a medium mixing bowl with a potato masher.
7. Add half of the garlic butter mixture to the bowl. Continue to mash, stir, and add the mixture until desired consistency.
8. Add Parmesan cheese.
9. Taste and season with salt and pepper.
10. Serve warm.

Potato Bacon Hash Browns

(Prep + Cook Time: 30 minutes | Servings: 4)

Ingredients:

- 1 lb russet potatoes, peeled and grated
- 2 tbsp olive oil
- 2 tbsp parsley, finely chopped
- 8 oz crumbled bacon
- Salt and freshly ground pepper, to taste

Directions:
1. The grated potatoes need to be dry, so prepare them by grating, rinsing then pressing gently under paper towels.
2. Heat some olive in the Instant Pot. Put the potatoes in, season and sauté for 5 or 6 minutes, until brown, stirring occasionally.
3. Mix in the bacon and parsley and press the potatoes down firmly using a spatula or something that will give a nice even pressure.
4. Secure the lid on the cooker and switch the pressure release valve to close. Press the SOUP/ STEW button. Set for 10 minutes.
5. Once the timer reaches 0, the cooker will automatically switch to KEEP WARM. Switch the pressure release valve to open.
6. When the steam is completely released, remove the lid and serve.

Baked Potatoes (VEG, S&F)
(Prep + Cook Time: 12 minutes | Servings: 2)

Ingredients:
- 4 potatoes
- 1 cup water

Directions:
1. Wash potatoes and pierce them with a fork.
2. Place potatoes in the Instant Pot on the steam rack.
3. Add 1 cup of water to your pressure cooker.
4. Cook for 10 minutes at HIGH pressure.
5. Allow to natural release.
6. Serve.

Baked Sweet Potatoes (VEG, S&F)
(Prep + Cook Time: 18 minutes | Servings: 2)

Ingredients:
- 6 sweet potatoes
- 1 cup water

Directions:
1. Wash potatoes and pierce them with a fork.
2. Place potatoes in the Instant Pot on the steam rack.
3. Add 1 cup of water to your pressure cooker.
4. Cook for 16 minutes at HIGH pressure.
5. Allow to natural release.

Cheesy Potatoes
(Prep + Cook Time: 15 minutes | Servings: 4)

Ingredients:
- 6 peeled and ⅛-inch thick sliced potatoes
- 1 cup chicken broth
- 1 cup shredded cheese
- 1 cup panko bread crumbs
- ½ cup sour cream
- ½ cup chopped onion
- 2 tbsp butter + 3 tablespoons melted butter
- Pepper and Salt to taste

Directions:
1. Hit the SAUTE button on your Instant Pot and put in 2 tablespoons butter.
2. When melted, add the onion and cook for about 5 minutes.
3. Pour in 1 cup of chicken broth, salt, and pepper.
4. Lower in the steamer basket with the sliced potatoes inside. Lock the lid. Hit MANUAL and then select 5 minutes on HIGH pressure.
5. While the potatoes cook, melt 3 tablespoons of butter and mix with the panko.
6. Grease a 9x13 baking dish.
7. When the potatoes are ready, hit CANCEL and quick-release.
8. Remove the potatoes and layer them in the baking dish.
9. In the Instant Pot, mix cheese and sour cream into the cooking liquid.
10. Pour over potatoes and stir so they're thoroughly coated.
11. Pour over the panko/ butter topping.
12. Broil in the oven for 5-7 minutes. Serve.

Potato Salad

Just remember you need to chill the whole dish for at least an hour for the best taste.

(Prep + Cook Time: 15 minutes | Servings: 8)

Ingredients:
- 6 medium-sized peeled and cubed Russet potatoes
- 4 big eggs
- 1 ½ cups water
- 1 cup mayo
- ¼ cup chopped onion
- 2 tbsp chopped parsley
- 1 tbsp mustard
- 1 tbsp dill pickle juice
- Salt and pepper to taste

Directions:
1. Pour water in your Instant Pot. Add the potatoes and eggs in your steamer basket, and lower in the cooker.
2. Close and seal the lid. Press MANUAL and adjust time to 4 minutes on HIGH pressure. When time is up, hit CANCEL and quick-release.
3. Let the eggs cool in a bath of ice water while the potatoes cool in the steamer basket on the counter.
4. In a bowl, mix mayo, parsley, pickle juice, mustard, and onion.
5. Mix in the potatoes.
6. Dice three eggs and add to potato mixture.
7. Season with salt.
8. Chill for 1 hour before serving, topping with sliced eggs.

Red Potatoes (VEG)

(Prep + Cook Time: 25 minutes | Servings: 4)

Ingredients:
- 12 oz red potato
- 1 tsp ground pepper
- 1 tbsp kosher salt
- 1 tsp fresh basil
- 1 tsp oregano
- 1 tsp cilantro
- 1 tsp paprika
- ¼ cup chicken stock
- 1 tbsp butter
- 1/3 tsp nutmeg

Directions:
1. Combine the ground pepper, kosher salt, fresh basil, oregano, cilantro, paprika, and nutmeg. Mix up the mixture.
2. Wash the red potatoes carefully and cut them into 4 parts.
3. Then sprinkle the potato parts with the spice mixture and stir it carefully. Place the butter in the Instant Pot and melt it.
4. Add the spicy potato mixture and SAUTE the dish for 10 minutes. Stir it frequently. Then add chicken stock and close the lid. Cook the dish for 3 minutes in the HIGH pressure mode.
5. Then release the remaining pressure and open the Instant Pot lid.
6. Transfer the cooked dish in the serving plates.

Scalloped Potatoes
(Prep + Cook Time: 15 minutes | Servings: 6)

Ingredients:
- 6 peeled and thinly-sliced potatoes
- 1 cup chicken broth
- ⅓ cup milk
- ⅓ cup sour cream
- 2 tbsp potato starch
- 1 tbsp chopped chives
- 1 tsp salt
- Dash of pepper
- Dash of paprika

Directions:
1. Pour the broth into your Instant Pot. Add chives, potatoes, salt, and pepper. Close and seal the lid.
2. Select MANUAL and adjust time to 5 minutes on HIGH pressure. When time is up, turn off the cooker and quick-release.
3. Move the potatoes to a broiler-safe dish. Pour milk, sour cream, and potato starch into the liquid in your Instant Pot.
4. Turn back to SAUTE and whisk for 1 minute.
5. Pour everything over the potatoes and mix.
6. Add paprika and cook under the broiler for a few minutes, until the top is brown. Serve.

Simple Potato Frittata

(Prep + Cook Time: 35 minutes | Servings: 2)

Ingredients:

1 tbsp coconut oil

2 large potatoes, sliced

1 white onion, finely sliced

1 capsicum, sliced

2 cups water

2 free-range eggs

2 tbsp sour cream

4 tbsp cheddar cheese

Salt and pepper, to taste

Directions:

1. Select SAUTE and preheat your Instant Pot. Pour in the coconut oil. Once hot, add in the potato slices and saute for 3 minutes.
2. Remove from the pot. Throw in the chopped onion and capsicum and cook until fragrant.
3. Remove and turn off the pot. Add in the water and place a steam rack on top. Grease a 6 inch baking dish with cooking spray. Set aside.
4. Take a small mixing bowl and whisk in the egg with sour cream.
5. Sprinkle salt and pepper and mix everything up.
6. Distribute half of the potato-onion-capsicum mixture in the dish.
7. Pour half of the egg-cream mixture on top and spoon in 2 tablespoons of cheese.
8. Repeat this on remaining mixtures. Hit the MANUAL button and cook for 20 minutes on low pressure.
9. Once cooked, quick release the pressure and broil in the oven for 2 minutes (optional). Serve.

Roasted Potatoes Garlic (VEG)

(Prep + Cook Time: 15 minutes | Servings: 3)

Ingredients:

- 2 tbsp vegetable oil
- 1 lb. small potatoes
- 1 tsp black pepper

- 1 tsp minced garlic
- ¼ cup vegetable stock

Directions:

1. Wash and rinse the potatoes—don't need to peel them. Place the potatoes in the inner pot of an Instant Pot then add minced garlic into the pot.

2. Splash vegetable oil over the potatoes and pour vegetable into the pot. Cover the Instant Pot and seal properly then cook the potatoes on HIGH pressure for 7 minutes.
3. Once it is done, naturally release the Instant Pot, then open the lid.
4. Transfer the potatoes to a serving dish then sprinkle black pepper on top.
5. Serve and enjoy warm.

Crispy Potatoes (VEG)
(Prep + Cook Time: 15 minutes | Servings: 4)

Ingredients:
- 1.5 pounds fingerling or Yukon Gold potatoes
- (each one should be no more than 1 inch in diameter)
- 1 tbsp olive oil (or vegetable oil)
- Sea salt to taste
- ½ tsp turmeric powder
- ¼ tsp chili powder, or to taste
- 2 tsp Chinese black vinegar (or balsamic vinegar)
- ¼ cup chopped cilantro for garnish (Optional)

Directions:
1. Add ½ cup of water to the bottom of the Instant Pot fitted with a steamer insert. Place potatoes in the steamer
2. Cover the pot and cook at HIGH pressure for 5 minutes. Use natural release when the potatoes are done.
3. Carefully transfer the potatoes to a large plate to cool. When the potatoes are cooled enough to handle, peel the skin by hand.
4. Add olive oil to a large skillet and heat over medium-high heat until warm.
5. Add potatoes to the skillet. Evenly sprinkle salt, turmeric powder, and chili powder on top. Let cook for a minute.
6. Then gently shake the pan in a swirling motion, so that the potatoes are covered evenly with spices. Cook and stir until the surfaces are crisped.
7. Transfer potatoes to a serving plate. Drizzle a spoonful of vinegar over them and garnish with cilantro.

Walnuts and Sweet Potato Crumble (VEG)

(Prep + Cook Time: 55 minutes | Servings: 2)

Ingredients:

- 4 sweet potatoes, peeled, boiled
- 1 cup heavy milk
- ½ cup coconut milk
- ¼ cup coconut flakes
- 1 cup walnuts
- 2 eggs, whisked
- 1 tsp vanilla extracts
- ¼ tsp green cardamom powder
- ½ cup brown sugar
- ¼ cup all-purpose flour
- 1 pinch salt
- 4 tbsp butter, melted

Directions:

1. Mash sweet potatoes with folk and combine with walnuts and coconut flakes.
2. In a separate bowl combine flour, brown sugar, salt, cardamom powder, eggs, milk, coconut milk, and vanilla extract, mix well.
3. Mix this mixture with sweet potatoes and transfer to Instant Pot.
4. Leave to cook on SLOW cook mode for 40 minutes.
5. Serve and enjoy.

Stir Fried Spiced Potatoes (VEG)

(Prep + Cook Time: 25 minutes | Servings: 2)

Ingredients:

- 4 potatoes, peeled, boiled, diced
- ½ tsp chili flakes
- 1 tsp garlic paste
- ¼ tsp salt
- ¼ tsp cumin powder
- ¼ tsp cinnamon powder
- ¼ tsp black pepper
- ¼ tsp thyme
- 2 tbsp olive oil

Directions:

1. Heat oil in Instant Pot on sauté mod and fry garlic for 30 seconds.
2. Now add potatoes and fry for 10 minutes.
3. Add salt, chili flakes, thyme, cumin powder, and cumin powder.
4. Transfer to serving platter and serve.
5. Serve and enjoy.

Potato Mash with Marjoram

(Prep + Cook Time: 20 minutes | Servings: 4)

Ingredients:
- 4 cloves garlic, sliced
- 1 ¼ cups vegetable stock
- ½ tsp ground black pepper
- 1 tsp sea salt
- 1 tspn mustard powder
- ½ tsp onion powder
- 1 pound Yukon Gold potatoes, diced
- 1/3 cup non-dairy milk
- ¼ cup fresh marjoram, for garnish

Directions:
1. Place the potatoes, vegetable stock, and garlic in your Instant Pot. Close the lid and select MANUAL function; adjust the time to 10 minutes.
2. Carefully open the cooker. Mash the potatoes, adding the non-dairy milk, onion powder, mustard powder, salt, and black pepper.
3. Serve immediately garnished with fresh marjoram.

Delicious Fingerling Potatoes

(Prep + Cook Time: 20 minutes | Servings: 6)

Ingredients:
- 3/4 cup vegetable broth
- 2 ½ pounds fingerling potatoes
- 1 tsp dried dill weed
- 1 tsp sea salt
- ½ tsp cayenne pepper
- ½ tsp ground black pepper, or more to your liking
- 2 sprigs rosemary
- 3 garlic cloves, with outer skin
- 3 tbsp olive oil

Directions:
1. Use the SAUTE function to preheat your Instant Pot. Warm the olive oil; when the oil is hot, stir in the fingerling potatoes, rosemary, dill weed, and garlic; cook for 6 minutes.
2. Cook the fingerling potatoes, turning once or twice, for about 11 minutes.
3. Now, pierce in the middle of each potato with a sharp knife.

4. Stir in the vegetable broth, salt, ground black pepper, cayenne pepper to your liking.
5. Choose the MANUAL function and cook for 6 minutes.
6. Afterward, use a quick pressure release. Allow the garlic cloves to cool; peel and smash them.
7. Taste, adjust the seasonings and serve.

Hash Browns
(Prep + Cook Time: 20 minutes | Servings: 4)

Ingredients:
- 4 cups russet potatoes, peeled and grated
- 2 tbsp olive oil
- 2 tbsp butter, or vegan margarine, such as Earth Balance
- Salt and freshly ground pepper, to taste

Directions:
1. Prepare the potatoes and set aside.
2. Add the oil and butter to the Instant Pot and bring to temperature over medium heat.
3. Add the hash brown potatoes; sauté for 5 minutes, stirring occasionally, until they are just beginning to brown. Season with the salt and pepper.
4. Use a wide metal spatula to press the potatoes down firmly in the pan.
5. Lock the lid in place and bring to LOW pressure; maintain pressure for 6 minutes.
6. Remove from the heat and quick-release the pressure.
7. Serve.

Spanish Potatoes (VEG)
(Prep + Cook Time: 30 minutes | Servings: 4)

Ingredients:
- 1 tbsp water
- 1 ½ pounds red potatoes, cut in quarters
- 1 cup water
- Salt to the taste
- 1 tsp tomato paste
- 1 tsp smoked paprika
- 1 tsp hot paprika
- ½ tbsp brown rice flour
- ½ tsp garlic powder

Directions:

1. Put your potatoes in the Instant Pot, add 1 cup water and some salt, cover and cook on HIGH pressure for 4 minutes. Quick release the pressure, drain the potatoes and put them in a bowl.
2. In a small bowl, mix 1 tablespoon water with tomato paste and stir. In a third bowl, mix smoked paprika with hot paprika, flour, garlic powder and salt and stir well.
3. Pour the tomato paste over potatoes and toss to coat.
4. Sprinkle the spice mix over potatoes, stir gently, spread them on a lined baking sheet, introduce them in the oven at 400 degrees F and bake for 10 minutes.
5. Transfer the potatoes to a bowl and serve them.

Sweet Potato Barley Porridge (VEG, S&F)
(Prep + Cook Time: 50 minutes | Servings: 4)

Ingredients:
- 1 large sweet potato, peeled and cubed
- 3 cup water
- ¼ cup barley
- ¼ cup buckwheat
- 1 tbsp glutinous rice
- 1 tbsp chick peas
- 1 tbsp broken rice
- Pinch baking soda
- Maple syrup

Directions:

1. Place the sweet potato, rice, barley, buckwheat, chickpeas and baking soda in the Instant Pot.
2. Pour over the water. Cover and seal the lid. Press PORRIDGE and set to 45 minutes.
3. After 45 minutes, let the pot naturally release its pressure.
4. Serve in bowls and drizzle over some maple syrup.

Breakfast Casserole

(Prep + Cook Time: 30 minutes | Servings: 4)

Ingredients:
- 2 tbsp vegetable oil
- 1 onion, diced
- ½ green bell pepper, chopped
- 8 oz package Morningstar Farm Sausage Style Crumbles, or Gimme Lean Sausage
- 3 cups potatoes, peeled and shredded
- 6 eggs, beaten, or 16 ounces firm crumbled tofu
- 1 cup cottage cheese, or omit
- 2 cups Cheddar cheese, or 2 cups vegan Cheddar, such as Daiya Cheddar Style Shreds
- Salt and pepper, to taste

Directions:
1. Add the vegetable oil to the pressure cooker and sauté the onion and bell pepper until tender.
2. Add the crumbles and cook for 2–3 minutes more.
3. Add the rest of the ingredients to the Instant Pot.
4. Lock the lid into place; bring to high pressure and maintain for 5 minutes.
5. Remove from the heat and allow pressure to release naturally.
6. Serve.

Spanish Casserole

(Prep + Cook Time: 35 minutes | Servings: 4)

Ingredients:
- 1 cup spinach, chopped
- 8 oz cheddar cheese
- 8 oz mozzarella cheese
- 1 onion, chopped
- 4 eggs, whisked
- 1 yellow bell pepper, chopped
- ¼ tsp salt
- ¼ tsp
- Black pepper
- 2 tbsp olive oil

Directions:

1. In a bowl add eggs, spinach, mozzarella cheese, cheddar cheese, bell pepper, and onion, mix well.
2. Season with salt and pepper.
3. Grease Instant Pot with olive oil.
4. Transfer spinach mixture to Instant Pot and cover with lid.
5. Leave to cook for 25 minutes on SLOW cook mode.
6. Serve hot and enjoy.

Spread Of Eggplant And Olive

(Prep + Cook Time: 23 minutes | Servings: 2)

Ingredients:

- 4 tbsp of olive oil
- 2 pound of eggplant
- 3-4 garlic cloves with their skin on
- 1 tsp of salt
- ½ a cup of water
- ¼ a cup of lemon juice
- 1 tbsp of tahini
- ¼ cup of black pitted black olives
- Sprigs of fresh thyme
- Extra virgin olive oil

Directions:

1. Peel off the eggplants in alternative stripes of skin and no skin. Slice up the biggest possible chunk and cover up the bottom of the cooker.
2. Rest of the plant can be chopped up roughly In your preheated Instant Pot, add some olive oil and once heated, place the large chunks of eggplant face down trying to caramelize the side for about 5 minutes.
3. Once done, throw in your Garlic Cloves making sure that their skin is still on.
4. Flip over the eggplants and add the remaining chopped up pieces of eggplant alongside water and salt.
5. Close the lid and let it cook for about 3 minutes at HIGH pressure. Once done, release the pressure naturally.
6. Take the inner pot to a sink and discard the brown liquid.
7. Take out the garlic cloves and gently remove the skin.
8. Pour in the lemon juice, Tahini, all of the garlic cloves and black olives into an immersion blender and puree everything.
9. Pour the mixture and serve it with some fresh thyme sprinkled around with a dash of olive oil.

Hard-Boiled Eggs (S&F)
(Prep + Cook Time: 9 minutes | Servings: 6)

Ingredients:
- 12 large white eggs
- 1 cup of water

Directions:
1. In the Instant Pot Pour down about 1 cup of water into the bowl.
2. Place stainless steamer basket inside the pot.
3. Place the eggs in the steamer basket.
4. Boil 7 minutes on manual HIGH pressure
5. Then release the pressure through the quick release valve.
6. Open up the lid and take out the eggs using tongs and dunk them into a bowl of cold water.

Soft-Boiled Egg (S&F)
(Prep + Cook Time: 6 minutes | Servings: 2)

Ingredients:
- 4 eggs
- 1 cup of water
- Two toasted English muffins
- Salt and pepper to taste

Directions:
1. Pour 1 cup of water into the Instant Pot and insert the steamer basket. Put four canning lids into the basket before placing the eggs on top of them, so they stay separated.
2. Secure the lid.
3. Press the STEAM setting and choose 4 minutes.
4. When ready, quick-release the steam valve.
5. Take out the eggs using tongs and dunk them into a bowl of cold water.
6. Wait 1-2 minutes.
7. Peel and serve with one egg per half of a toasted English muffin.
8. Season with salt and pepper.

Bell Pepper Poached Eggs

(Prep + Cook Time: 7 minutes | Servings: 2)

Ingredients:

- 2 medium sized red bell peppers, tops sliced and seeds removed
- 2 free-range eggs
- Salt and pepper to taste
- Olive oil

Directions:

1. Crack one egg into each bell pepper cup. And drizzle the tops with a little bit of olive oil.
2. Cover with tin foil. Place on your pressure cooker's steamer rack and close the lid.
3. Set to MANUAL and cook for 4 minutes on high pressure.
4. Release the pressure and serve with your choice of sauce.

Egg Macaroni (S&F)

(Prep + Cook Time: 19 minutes | Servings: 2)

Ingredients:

- 2 eggs, whisked
- 1 tsp garlic powder
- ¼ tsp slat
- ½ tsp black pepper
- 1 onlon chopped
- 1 cup macaroni, boiled
- 1 tomato, chopped
- 3 tbsp oil

Directions:

1. Combine eggs with macaroni, onion, salt, pepper, and garlic powder, mix well.
2. Heat oil in Instant Pot on SAUTE mode.
3. Pour eggs mixture and spread all over evenly.
4. Cook for 1-2 minutes and then transfer to serving platter.
5. Serve hot and enjoy.

Egg and Tomato Omelet

(Prep + Cook Time: 20 minutes | Servings: 2)

Ingredients:
- 2 eggs, whisked
- 2 tomatoes, sliced
- 1 tsp garlic powder
- ¼ tsp slat
- ½ tsp chili powder
- 3 tbsp butter

Directions:
1. Melt butter in Instant Pot on SAUTE mode.
2. Add eggs and spread all over. Cook for 1-2 minutes then flip side.
3. Place tomato slices and cover pot with lid, let to cook on pressure cooker mode for 10 minutes.
4. Season with salt and chili powder.
5. Serve hot and enjoy.

Egg and Carrot Spread

(Prep + Cook Time: 40 minutes | Servings: 2)

Ingredients:
- 4 eggs, whisked
- 3 carrots, shredded and boiled
- ¼ tsp slat
- ½ tsp black pepper
- 3 tbsp butter

Directions:
1. In a blender, add carrots and blend till pureed.
2. Add to Instant Pot and let simmer for 2 minutes.
3. Add eggs, butter, salt, and pepper, stir continually for 10 - 15 minutes.
4. Cook for 10 minutes on STEW mode.
5. Serve hot and enjoy.

Egg Scramble

(Prep + Cook Time: 15 minutes | Servings: 2)

Ingredients:
- 4 eggs
- 1 pinch of salt
- ½ tsp black pepper
- 1 cup milk
- 3 tbsp butter

Directions:
1. Melt butter in Instant Pot on SAUTE mode.
2. Crack eggs in Instant Pot and add mllk, stirring continuously for 5 minutes.
3. Transfer to serving platter and scramble again with folk for 1 minute.
4. Serve and enjoy.

Egg Balls

(Prep + Cook Time: 45 minutes | Servings: 4)

Ingredients:
- 5 eggs, boiled
- 1 cup ground chicken
- 1 tsp salt
- 1 tsp ground black pepper
- ½ cup bread crumbs
- 1 tsp butter
- ½ tsp tomato paste
- 2 tbsp flour
- 1 tsp oregano

Directions:
1. Peel the eggs. Combine the ground chicken, salt, ground black pepper, tomato paste, and oregano together in the mixing bowl. Mix up the mixture.
2. Then make the balls from the ground chicken mixture and flatten them well.
3. Put the peeled eggs in the middle of the flatten ball and roll the eggs. Dip them in the flour.

4. Toss the butter in the Instant Pot and transfer the egg's balls. Close the lid and set the Instant Pot mode MEAT/STEW. Cook the dish for 30 minutes.
5. Open the Instant Pot during the cooking to turn the balls.
6. When the egg balls are cooked – remove them from the Instant Pot and chill little.
7. Serve and enjoy.

Egg and Onion Frittata

(Prep + Cook Time: 20 minutes | Servings: 2)

Ingredients:
- 4 eggs, whisked
- 1 onion, chopped
- 1 tbsp parsley, chopped
- 1 green chili, chopped
- ¼ tsp slat
- ½ tsp black pepper
- 3 tbsp butter

Directions:
1. In eggs, add onion, green chilies, parsley, salt, and pepper, mix well.
2. Melt butter in the Instant Pot on SAUTE mode.
3. Pour egg mixture and spread all over evenly.
4. Cook for 2-3 minutes on one side then flip it.
5. Cook for 1-2 minutes and then transfer to serving platter.
6. Serve hot and enjoy.

Egg and Spinach Cup Custards

(Prep + Cook Time: 8 minutes | Servings: 4)

Ingredients:
- 2 ½ cups milk
- 6 large-sized eggs
- 1 tsp dill weed
- 1/3 tsp salt
- 1 tsp cayenne pepper
- 1/3 tsp ground black pepper, or more to your liking
- 2 ½ cups baby spinach, chopped

Directions:
1. Set the pressure cooker rack in the Instant Pot; pour in 3 cups water.
2. Beat the eggs in a mixing bowl until frothy; now add the rest of the ingredients. Divide the mixture among four heat-safe ramekins.
3. Cover the ramekins with foil tightly. Lock the lid onto the pot. Set the machine to cook at HIGH pressure. Cook for about 8 minutes.
4. Use the quick-release method and open the cooker.
5. Transfer the ramekins to a wire rack to cool before serving.
6. Serve at once.

Egg & Mushroom Breakfast
(Prep + Cook Time: 5 minutes | Servings: 2)

Ingredients:
- 4 large Portobello mushrooms
- 2 cups cooked spinach
- 4 large eggs
- ½ cup shredded gouda cheese
- ½ cup crumbled bacon

Directions:
1. Remove the stems of the mushrooms and then place them upside down on a plate.
2. Season the cooked spinach with salt and pepper and then divide them equally among the mushroom caps.
3. Crack the eggs and pour one egg into each mushroom cap. Now, sprinkle the crisped bacon and shredded cheese.
4. Coat the Instant Pot cooker with some cooking spray and carefully place the arranged mushroom caps inside the cooker.
5. Close the lid and cook on MANUAL setting for 4 minutes.
6. Use the quick release button to release the pressure.
7. Serve the mushrooms with the sauce of your choice.

Egg Muffins
(Prep + Cook Time: 30 minutes | Servings: 4)

Ingredients:
- 1 green onion
- 4 eggs
- ½ tsp lemon pepper seasoning
- 4 tbsp grated cheddar cheese
- 4 slices bacon, cooked
- 12 oz water

Directions:
1. Take a standard 4 cups dark muffin pan, line each cup with a paper liner and lightly drench with non-stick cooking spray until just evenly coated, or dip a paper towel in oil and grease each cup generously, set aside until require.
2. In a large mixing bowl crack eggs and using electric mixer beat in lemon pepper until blend.
3. Peel and dice onion, and crumble beef. Evenly divide green onion, bacon and cheese among muffin cups, then evenly pour egg mixture and using fork stir until mix.
4. Into the pot of electric pressure cooker, pour water, insert steamer basket and place muffin tray. Close and lock with lid, switch on cooker, position valve, select HIGH pressure and enter 8 minutes cooking time on timer pad.
5. When time is up and timer buzz, switch off cooker and quickly release pressure.
6. Uncover cooker when pressure indicator has gone down and carefully remove the muffin tray.
7. Insert wooden toothpick into dough, if toothpick comes out clean then muffins are cook.
8. Let muffins cool on cooling rack for 10 minutes and then turning out.
9. Serve immediately.

Eggs de Provence (S&F)

(Prep + Cook Time: 25 minutes | Servings: 4)

Ingredients:

- 6 eggs
- 1 cup of chopped kale leaves
- 1 cup of cooked ham
- 1 chopped onion
- 1 tbsp of Herbs de Provence
- 1 cup of cheddar cheese
- ½ cup of heavy cream
- ½ tbsp of salt
- ½ tbsp of pepper

Directions:

1. Whisk your eggs with your heavy cream.
2. Put in the rest of your ingredients and mix together well.
3. Put your mixture in your heatproof dish and cover it.
4. Put 1 cup of water inside your Instant Pot, then your trivet, and then your eggs.
5. Set your Instant Pot on MANUAL with HIGH pressure for approximately 20 minutes with a Natural pressure release.
6. Remove from your Instant Pot once finished. 7. Serve and Enjoy.

Cheesy Egg Cupcakes

(Prep + Cook Time: 20 minutes | Servings: 4)

Ingredients:

- ¼ cup cooked bacon (crispy and diced)
- ½ tsp salt
- ½ cup shredded cheese
- ½ cup potatoes peeled and finely diced
- Four ½ pint mason jars
- 7 large eggs
- 1 tbsp heavy whipping cream
- 1 scallion diced (reserve half)
- 1 cup water

Directions:

1. Grease inside of mason jars with non-stick cooking spray.
2. Beat eggs, salt and cream together pour into four mason jars.
3. In a bowl mix potatoes, 1/4 cup cheese, 1/2 the scallions and bacon. Dish into the mason jars.

4. Pour a cup of water into the pressure pot. Place a trivet into the pot. Close and lock lid in place.
5. Cook at HIGH Pressure for 5 minutes. When cooking cycle completes allow for 10 minutes natural pressure release. Open the lid once pressure is fully released.
6. Leaving the egg muffins inside the pot, sprinkle the remaining cheese over the egg muffins.
7. Reclose the lid and leave for 1 minute.
8. Garnish with chopped scallions, serve warm.

Sweet egg toasts
(Prep + Cook Time: 20 minutes | Servings: 6)

Ingredients:
- 4 eggs
- 1 cup milk
- 3 tbsp brown sugar
- 1 tsp vanilla sugar
- 1 tbsp butter
- 1 pound white bread

Directions:
1. Slice the bread. Beat the eggs in the mixing bowl and add milk. Whisk the mixture carefully and add brown sugar.
2. Then sprinkle the egg mixture with the vanilla sugar and stir it carefully until sugar is dissolved.
3. Then dip the bread slices into the egg mixture. Toss the butter in the Instant Pot. Add the dipped bread slices and close the lid.
4. Set the Instant Pot mode SAUTE and cook the dish for 4 minutes on the each side.
5. When the toasts are cooked – remove them from the Instant Pot and chill little.
6. Serve the dish warm.

Ham Frittata

(Prep + Cook Time: 25 minutes | Servings: 6)

Ingredients:
- 7 eggs
- ½ cup milk
- 1 tsp salt
- ½ tsp paprika
- ½ cup parsley
- 8 oz ham
- 1 tsp white pepper
- 1 tbsp lemon zest
- 1 tsp olive oil
- 1 tomato

Directions:
1. Beat the eggs in the mixing bowl. Add milk, salt, paprika, white pepper, and lemon zest. Mix up the mixture carefully with the help of the hand mixer.
2. Then chop the tomato and add it to the egg mixture. Chop the ham and sprinkle the egg mixture with the ham too. Stir it carefully until you get homogenous mass. Chop the parsley.
3. Spray the Instant Pot with the olive oil inside. Then transfer the egg mixture in the Instant Pot. Sprinkle it with the chopped parsley and close the lid.
4. Cook the frittata for 10 minutes at the mode STEAM.
5. When the time is cooked – let the dish cool little.
6. Serve.

Poached Tomato Eggs

(Prep + Cook Time: 10 minutes | Servings: 4)

Ingredients:
- 4 eggs
- 3 medium tomatoes
- 1 red onion
- 1 tsp salt
- 1 tbsp olive oil
- ½ tsp white pepper
- ½ tsp paprika
- 1 tbsp fresh dill

Directions:
1. Spray the ramekins with the olive oil inside. Beat the eggs in every ramekin. Combine the paprika, white pepper, fresh dill, and salt together in the mixing bowl. Stir the mixture.
2. After this, chop the red onion. Chop the tomatoes into the tiny pieces and combine them with the onion. Stir the mixture.

3. Then sprinkle the eggs with the tomato mixture. Add spice mixture and transfer the eggs to the Instant Pot. Close the lid and set the Instant Pot mode STAEM.
4. Cook the dish for 5 minutes. Then remove the dish from the Instant Pot and chill it little.
5. Serve the dish immediately. Enjoy!

Aromatic Bacon Eggs
(Prep + Cook Time: 15 minutes | Servings: 4)

Ingredients:
- 7 oz. bacon
- 4 eggs, boiled
- 1 tsp cilantro
- ½ cup spinach
- 2 tsp butter
- ½ tsp ground white pepper
- 3 tbsp cream

Directions:
1. Slice the bacon and sprinkle it with the ground white pepper, and cilantro. Stir the mixture.
2. Peel eggs and wrap them in the spinach leaves. Then wrap the eggs in the sliced bacon.
3. Set the Instant Pot mode MEAT/STEW and transfer the wrapped eggs. Add butter and cook the dish for 10 minutes.
4. When the time is over – remove the eggs from the Instant Pot and sprinkle them with the cream.
5. Serve the dish hot.

Quick & Easy Salad
(Prep + Cook Time: 14 minutes | Servings: 2)

Ingredients:
- 1 cup tap water
- 1 stalk celery, finely chopped
- 4 medium free-range eggs
- 4 tbsp mayonnaise
- 1 tsp dijon mustard
- 1 tsp lemon juice, freshly squeezed
- 2 tsp parsley, freshly minced
- Salt and pepper, to taste

Directions:

1. Pour the water into your Instant Pot. Place a steam rack on top. Distribute the eggs on the rack and secure the lid. Select MANUAL and cook for 7 minutes on LOW pressure.
2. In the meantime, take a medium mixing bowl and add in the celery, mayonnaise, parsley, dijon, lemon juice, salt and pepper.
3. Stir and combine. Once cooked, release the pressure manually.
4. Rinse the eggs under cool water, peel and add to a medium bowl.
5. Mash using a fork and stir in the dijon mixture.
6. Serve.

Easy, Quick Instant Pot Egg Bake

(Prep + Cook Time: 20 minutes | Servings: 6)

Ingredients:

- 9 eggs
- ½ cup milk (can use unsweetened almond or soy as well –or cream)
- 6 pieces of raw bacon, diced
- 1 cup shredded sharp cheddar cheese
- 2 cups frozen hash brown potatoes, thawed
- ¼ tsp salt or to taste
- Chives for garnish

Directions:

1. Add the bacon to the Instant Pot and lightly brown for about 1-2 minutes.
2. Once browned, leave the bacon in the Instant Pot, you will be layering with the other ingredients. Layer the hash brown potatoes over the top of the bacon.
3. Sprinkle 1/2 cup of the cheese atop of the potatoes. In a medium bowl, beat the eggs together with the milk and salt, and then pour right over the top of the potatoes and bacon layers.

4. Sprinkle with the remaining 1/2 cup cheese. Place the lid on the Instant Pot to lock. Close the valve. Set the timer for manual (high) for 7 minutes, and walk away.
5. After the 7 minutes is up and the pot has beeped, there should be NO pressure to release.
6. Open the pot and serve in bowls - add any additional salt/pepper to taste.

Chicken Omelette
(Prep + Cook Time: 25 minutes | Servings: 4)

Ingredients:
- 8 eggs
- 1 cup milk
- 1 cup sharp cheddar cheese
- 1½ tsp hot sauce
- 1 cup cooked and shredded chicken

Directions:
1. Beat the eggs in a bowl and add all the other ingredients with the egg.
2. Remember to season eggs with salt and pepper.
3. Coat a glass bowl with cooking spray and pour the egg mixture into it.
4. Cover the bowl with a foil and place it inside the steamer basket of the Instant Pot.
5. Pour required amount of water inside the pot. Close the pot and cook on MANUAL setting for 22 minutes. Let the pressure release naturally.
6. Remove the foil and slice the omelette into four slices.
7. Serve by garnishing with some more cheese.

Spinach Egg Omelet
(Prep + Cook Time: 15 minutes | Servings: 4)

Ingredients:
- 2 cups spinach
- 8 eggs
- ½ cup milk
- 1 tsp salt
- 1 tbsp olive oil
- 1 tsp ground black pepper
- 4 oz. Parmesan

Directions:
1. Beat the eggs in the mixing bowl and whisk them. Chop the spinach and add it to the whisked egg mixture.
2. After this, add milk, salt, olive oil, and ground black pepper. Mix up the mixture. Grate Parmesan cheese.
3. Transfer the egg mixture to the Instant Pot and close the lid. Set the Instant Pot mode STEAM and cook the dish for 6 minutes.
4. When the time is over – remove the omelet from the Instant Pot and transfer it to the serving plate.
5. Sprinkle the dish with the grated cheese.
6. Serve it.

Omelette-de-Corn
(Prep + Cook Time: 25 minutes | Servings: 4)

Ingredients:
- 8 eggs
- 1 cup milk
- 1 cup shredded cheddar cheese
- 2 tbsp salsa
- 1 cup fresh corn

Directions:
1. Beat the eggs in a bowl and add all the other ingredients with the egg.
2. Remember to season eggs with salt and pepper.
3. Coat a glass bowl with cooking spray and pour the egg mixture into it.
4. Cover the bowl with a foil and place it inside the steamer basket of the Instant Pot.
5. Pour required amount of water inside the pot.
6. Close the pot and cook on MANUAL setting for 22 minutes. Let the pressure release naturally.
7. Remove the foil and slice the omelette into four slices.
8. Serve by garnishing with some more cheese.

Korean Style Steamed Eggs
(Prep + Cook Time: 10 minutes | Servings: 2)

Ingredients:
- Scallions, fresh & chopped
- 2 egg, large
- Pinch of each pepper, salt & garlic powder
- ⅓ cup water
- Pinch of sesame seeds

Directions:
1. Mix egg together with the cold water in a bowl, preferably small size.
2. Using a fine mesh strainer; strain the egg mixture into a bowl, preferably heat proof.
3. Add in the remaining ingredients; mix well and set aside.
4. Add a cup of water to your Instant Pot.
5. Place the steamer basket or trivet inside the pot. Place the egg mixture bowl in the steamer basket or trivet. Tightly close the lid, closing the vent valve.
6. Choose the MANUAL setting & set the cooking time to 5 minutes, preferably on HIGH.
7. When you are done with the cooking, quick release the pressure.
8. Serve immediately with some hot rice.

Scotch Eggs
(Prep + Cook Time: 25 minutes | Servings: 4)

Ingredients:
- 4 Large Eggs
- 1 pound of Country Style Ground Sausage
- 1 tbsp of Vegetable Oil

Directions:
1. Put your steamer basket in your Instant Pot. Add 1 cup water and your eggs. Lock the lid in place and cook on HIGH pressure for approximately 6 minutes.

2. When the timer beeps, let the pressure release naturally for about 6 minutes. Then turn off your Instant Pot and do a Quick pressure release.
3. When the pressure is released, carefully remove your lid. Remove your steamer basket from the Instant Pot. Put your eggs into ice cold water to cool.
4. When your eggs are cool remove their shells. Divide your sausage into four equal-sized pieces. Flatten each piece into a flat round. Place your hard boiled egg in the center and gently wrap your sausage around the egg.
5. Heat your Instant Pot on SAUTE. When your pot is hot, add your oil and brown your Scotch eggs on four sides. Remove your Scotch eggs from the Instant Pot and add 1 cup of water. Put a rack in your Instant Pot and place your Scotch eggs on the rack.
6. Lock the lid in place and pressure cook on HIGH pressure for approximately 6 minutes. When the timer beeps, do a Quick pressure release.
7. When all of the pressure is released, carefully remove your lid.
8. Serve and Enjoy!

Creamy Soufflé
(Prep + Cook Time: 30 minutes | Servings: 6)

Ingredients:
- 3 eggs
- 1 cup cream
- 6 oz cottage cheese
- 4 tbsp butter
- 1/3 cup dry apricots
- 1 tbsp sour cream
- 2 tbsp sugar
- 1 tsp vanilla extract

Directions:
1. Whisk the eggs and combine them with cream.
2. Transfer the cottage cheese to the mixing bowl and mix it well with the help of the hand mixer.
3. Then add whisked eggs, butter, sour cream, sugar, and vanilla extract. Mix up the mixture carefully until you get smooth mass.
4. Then add dry apricots and stir the mixture well. Transfer the soufflé in the Instant Pot and close the lid. Set the Instant Pot mode STEW and cook the dish for 20 minutes.
5. When the time is over – let the soufflé cool little.
6. Serve it.

Aromatic whole chicken
(Prep + Cook Time: 45 minutes | Servings: 8)

Ingredients:

- 2-pound whole chicken
- 3 red apples
- 1 tbsp salt
- 1 tsp ground black pepper
- 1 tbsp olive oil
- 1 tsp butter
- 1 tsp fresh rosemary
- 1 lemon
- 1 tbsp sugar
- 1 cup water
- 1 tsp coriander
- ½ tsp cayenne pepper
- ¼ tsp turmeric

Directions:

1. Wash the whole chicken carefully.
2. Combine the salt, ground black pepper, fresh rosemary, sugar, coriander, cayenne pepper, and turmeric together. Stir the mixture.
3. After this, rub the whole chicken with the spice mixture carefully. Wash the red apples and chop them.
4. Combine the chopped apples with the butter and fill the whole chicken with the fruit mixture.
5. Then sprinkle the chicken with the olive oil. Pour the water in the Instant Pot and place the stuffed whole chicken.
6. Close the lid and cook the dish at the MANUAL pressure mode for 30 minutes.
7. When the time is over – release the remaining pressure (approximately 10 minutes) and open the Instant Pot lid.
8. Remove the whole chicken from the Instant Pot.
9. Chill it little. Serve the dish!

Honey Sesame Chicken
(Prep + Cook Time: 25 minutes | Servings: 6)

Ingredients:

- 4 large boneless skinless chicken breasts, diced (about 2 lbs.)
- 1 tbsp vegetable oil
- ½ cup diced onion
- 2 cloves garlic, minced
- ½ cup soy sauce
- ¼ cup ketchup
- 2 tsp sesame oil
- ½ cup honey
- ¼ tsp red pepper flakes
- 2 tbsp cornstarch
- 3 tbsp water
- 2 green onions, chopped
- Sesame seeds, toasted
- Salt and pepper to taste

Directions:

1. Salt and pepper chicken. Preheat pressure cooking pot using the SAUTE setting.
2. Add oil, onion, garlic, and chicken to the pot and sauté occasionally stirring until onion is softened, about 3 minutes.
3. Add soy sauce, ketchup, and red pepper flakes to the pressure cooking pot and stir to combine.
4. Pressure cook on HIGH for 3 minutes. When timer beeps, turn pressure cooker off and do a quick pressure release.
5. Add sesame oil and honey to the pot and stir to combine. In a small bowl, dissolve cornstarch in water and add to the pot. Select SAUTE and simmer until sauce thickens. Stir in green onions.
6. Serve over rice sprinkled with sesame seeds.

The Greek Chicken

(Prep + Cook Time: 25 minutes | Servings: 2)

Ingredients:

- 4 small chicken breasts with skin and bone in
- ¼ cup extra virgin olive oil, divided and more for garnish
- 4 large garlic cloves cut small
- 2 rosemary sprig torn into bits
- ½ tbsp oregano dried
- ½ tsp red pepper flakes
- 1 large potato peeled, washed and pricked
- 2 cups chicken broth
- ½ cup frozen peas
- 1 medium lemon
- ¼ cup olives
- Kosher salt
- Fresh black pepper powder

Directions:

1. Rub pepper and salt on chicken and smear 2 tablespoon oil on top.
2. Sprinkle red pepper flakes, rosemary, oregano and marinate for 40 minutes.
3. Select SAUTE and preheat the pot.
4. Pour 1 tablespoon oil, add chicken, and cook without stirring.
5. The skin side should touch the pan. Cook until crispy.
6. Once done, remove the chicken and transfer to a plate.
7. Pour broth in Pot and add potatoes, place fried chicken on top and rest of marinade Cook on HIGH on Manual option for about 10 minutes.

8. Release pressure naturally, removes the chicken, add peas and stir until cooked in the heat.
9. Serve chicken topped with peas and potatoes and drizzle oil if you like.

Instant Pot Chicken
(Prep + Cook Time: 35 minutes | Servings: 4)

Ingredients:
- ¼ cup honey
- 3 tbsp tamari
- ½ tsp finely ground black pepper
- ¼ cup ghee
- 2 tsp garlic powder
- 1½ tsp sea salt
- 3 tbsp ketchup
- 2 pounds boneless chicken thighs

Directions:
1. Place the ingredients in the Instant Pot and stir to mix and then close the lid ensuring the valve is in the seal position.
2. Press MANUAL and set 18 minutes for fresh chicken or 40 minutes for frozen chicken.
3. After the set cooking time elapses, do a quick release.
4. Remove and shred the chicken.
5. Press CANCEL and then press the SAUTE function and let the sauce cook for 5 minutes.
6. Serve with vegetables and rice.

Italian Chicken
(Prep + Cook Time: 30 minutes | Servings: 4)

Ingredients:
- ¾ cup mushrooms, thinly sliced
- 2 lbs. chicken breasts
- 2 tbsp pesto
- ¾ cup marinara
- ¼ tsp salt
- ½ cup red bell pepper
- ½ cup green bell pepper
- ¾ cup onion
- 1 tbsp olive oil

Directions:
1. Press the SAUTE option and once it says hot, add the oil.
2. Add onion and bell peppers and season with salt and then cook for 3-4 minutes before adding the chicken, pesto and marinara.

3. Set the time for 12 minutes on high for thawed chicken and 20 minutes for frozen chicken.
4. Once the set time elapses, remove the chicken breasts and shred and then remove 2/3 cup of liquid.
5. Do not remove the vegetables. You can use the liquid you removed to make rice or soup if you wish.
6. Add the mushrooms to the Instant Pot and cook for another 2-3 minutes on the SAUTE setting.
7. Place the shredded chicken in the Instant Pot and stir to combine.
8. Serve over rice and enjoy.

Chicken Masala (S&F)
(Prep + Cook Time: 35 minutes | Servings: 4)

Ingredients:
- 4 chicken thighs
- 1 sweet potato
- 1 can of drained chickpeas
- 1 jar of Indian Simmer Sauce
- Salt and pepper to taste

Directions:
1. Combine 4 chicken thighs, in chunks, one diced sweet potato, one can of drained chickpeas, and any jar of Indian Simmer Sauce (any Patak's Simmer Sauce or masala will work).
2. Pressure cook for 20 minutes on HIGH pressure and quick release when done.
3. Serve with rice.

Chicken and Mushrooms Risotto

(Prep + Cook Time: 50 minutes | Servings: 8)

Ingredients:

- 1 cup rice
- 3 cups chicken stock
- 1 tbsp salt
- 2 tbsp butter
- 2 big carrots
- 1 white onion
- 8 oz. mushrooms
- 1 tbsp dry dill
- 1 tbsp cream
- 1 tsp rosemary
- 1 tsp ground cumin
- 1 tsp paprika
- 1 tsp oregano
- 1 tbsp cilantro
- 1 tsp chives
- 1-pound chicken breast

Directions:

1. Peel the carrots and onions and slice the vegetables. Then slice the mushrooms.
2. Combine the cream, rosemary, ground black pepper, paprika, oregano, cilantro, and chives together. Stir the mixture.
3. Chop the chicken breast roughly. Place the chopped chicken breast in the cream mixture and leave it. Put the butter in the Instant Pot and melt it.
4. Then add the sliced vegetables and sauté them at the MANUAL mode for 10 minutes.
5. Stir the mixture frequently. Then add the cream chicken mixture and chicken stock. Add the rice. Close the lid and cook the dish at the MEAT/STEW mode for 25 minutes.
6. When the dish is cooked – remove the dish from the Instant Pot and stir it carefully.
7. Place the cooked dish in the serving bowls.

Potato Chicken Stew

(Prep + Cook Time: 30 minutes | Servings: 6)

Ingredients:

- 1 cup sliced mushrooms
- 5 cups skinless, boneless chicken breast, cut into bite-sized pieces
- 1 tbsp olive oil
- 1 cup diced onion
- 2 cups diced carrots
- 1 tsp sage, dried
- 6 cups chicken stock
- 1 tsp basil leaves, dried
- 1 tsp parsley, dried
- 10 oz mixed vegetables, frozen or thawed
- ½ cup diced celery
- 4 cups diced red potatoes
- Salt and pepper to taste

Directions:

1. Chop the chicken breast into bite-sized pieces.
2. Pour the oil into the bottom of the Instant Pot, and add the chicken, browning each side for about three minutes on the SAUTE setting.
3. Afterward, add the mushrooms, onion, and carrots, and cook for an additional three minutes, allowing the onion to become fragrant.
4. Add the chicken stock, sage, basil, parsley, mixed vegetables, celery, and the potatoes, and stir well.
5. Place the lid on the pressure cooker, sealing the valve
6. Cook the stew on HIGH pressure for 18 minutes.
7. After 18 minutes, quick release the soup, allowing the steam to exit away from your face.
8. Serve the stew warm, and enjoy.

Italian Chicken Parmesan

(Prep + Cook Time: 30 minutes | Servings: 10)

Ingredients:

- 3 pounds chicken breasts
- 1 cup olive oil
- 1 cup grated Parmesan cheese
- ½ tsp. garlic powder
- ½ stick butter
- 50 ounces tomato sauce
- Mozzarella cheese for serving
- Salt and pepper to taste

Directions:

1. Add the olive oil to the Instant Pot, heating on the SAUTE setting.
2. Add the chicken, and brown it for approximately 5 minutes, stirring it to ensure you brown all sides.
3. Next, add the Parmesan cheese, garlic powder, tomato sauce, and butter, and stir well.
4. Place the lid on the pressure cooker, and close the valve.
5. Cook the chicken on HIGH pressure for 15 minutes.
6. After 15 minutes, quick release the pressure, and then add mozzarella cheese to the top of the dish.
7. Allow it to melt in the pressure cooker for five minutes.
8. Serve and enjoy.

Apricot Chicken (S&F)

(Prep + Cook Time: 35 minutes | Servings: 6)

Ingredients:
- 1 cup apricot Jam
- 1 small bottle Russian Salad Dressing
- 1 package onion soup mix
- 5-6 chicken breasts

Directions:
1. Place chicken breasts in the Instant Pot.
2. Pour sauce over chicken.
3. Select POULTRY setting and a cook time of 30 minutes.
4. Serve.

Hot Chicken Wings

(Prep + Cook Time: 40 minutes | Servings: 2)

Ingredients:
- 4 chicken wings
- 1 tsp garlic powder
- 1 cup all-purpose flour
- 2 tbsp soya sauce
- ½ tsp salt
- ½ tsp chili powder
- ½ tsp cinnamon powder
- 1 cup oil, for frying
- ¼ cup water

Directions:
1. In a bowl, combine flour, soya sauce, salt, chili powder, and cinnamon powder.
2. Add water to make a thick paste.
3. Heat oil in the Instant Pot on SAUTE mode.
4. Dip each chicken piece into the flour mixture and transfer to oil.
5. Fry each chicken wing till golden and place on paper towel to drain out excess oil.
6. Transfer to serving dish and serve with mint sauce.
7. Serve and enjoy.

Chicken Nuggets

(Prep + Cook Time: 40 minutes | Servings: 2)

Ingredients:

- 2 chicken breast, cut into small pieces
- 1 tsp garlic powder
- 1 tsp onion powder
- ½ cup bread crumbs
- 1 tsp salt
- ½ tsp black pepper
- ½ tsp cinnamon powder
- ½ tsp cumin powder
- 1 egg, whisked
- 1 cup oil, for frying

Directions:

1. In a bowl, mix garlic powder, bread crumbs, onion powder, cinnamon powder, salt, pepper, and cumin powder.
2. Dip chicken pieces into egg and roll out into bread crumb mixture.
3. Set Instant Pot on SAUTE mode and heat oil well.
4. Deep fry each chicken nugget till nicely golden.
5. Transfer to paper towel.
6. Serve with boiled rice or any sauce.

Chicken with Cremini Mushrooms

(Prep + Cook Time: 30 minutes | Servings: 6)

Ingredients:

- 4 chicken thighs
- 4 tbsp corn starch
- 1 onion, chopped
- 1 cup Cremini mushrooms, quartered
- 4 cloves garlic
- 2 tbsp chopped parsley
- 1 cup dry sweet wine
- 1 cup chicken broth
- Salt and pepper to taste

Directions:

1. Season chicken with salt and pepper and roll in cornstarch.
2. Put the internal pot into the Instant Pot. Press the MEAT/STEW button. Press the TIMER button and set to 15 minutes.
3. Add the oil and sauté onion and garlic. Add the mushrooms and cook for 2-3 minutes.
4. Return chicken to internal pot, and add the wine, stock, parsley and corn starch; blend.

5. Put the lid on the Instant Pot and Lock. Switch the Pressure release valve to close.
6. Once the clock achieves 0, the cooker will naturally change to KEEP WARM. Press the CANCEL.
7. Switch the Pressure release valve to open.
8. Serve hot.

Chicken with Herbs and Vegetables
(Prep + Cook Time: 50 minutes | Servings: 4)

Ingredients:
- 3 stalks celery, cut into thirds
- 1 medium sweet onion, peeled and quartered
- ¾ tsp dried thyme
- 1 whole chicken, about 3 pounds
- Sea salt to taste
- 8 small carrots, peeled
- ½ cup chicken broth or water
- ¼ cup dry white wine
- 3 tbsp butter
- 2 cups coarse dried bread crumbs
- Fresh parsley for garnish, optional

Directions:
1. Arrange the celery pieces in the bottom of the pot of your Instant Pot and put the onion wedges on top.
2. Sprinkle with thyme. Rinse the chicken and season it with salt. Put it on top of the celery and onions.
3. Toss the carrots over the chicken and around it. Add the broth or water and white wine.
4. Lock the lid into position. Set the pot to low pressure for 25 minutes.
5. Let the pressure release in a natural way for 5 minutes, then use the quick release.
6. Serve and enjoy.

Fantastic Chicken Fillets (S&F)

(Prep + Cook Time: 15 minutes | Servings: 4)

Ingredients:
- 1¼ lb chicken fillets, cut into four equal portions
- ¼ cup reduced fat sour cream
- 2 tbsp stone-ground mustard
- 2 tsp lemon juice
- Salt and pepper

Directions:
1. Heat the Instant Pot and place the chicken fillets in the pot.
2. Make a paste with all the other ingredients and spread the mixture with a spoon over the chicken fillets.
3. Close the pot and cook on HIGH pressure for 15 minutes. Let the pressure release naturally before removing the lid.
4. Serve the chicken by garnishing with lime wedges.

Hot Buffalo Wings

(Prep + Cook Time: 20 minutes | Servings: 6)

Ingredients:
- 4 pounds chicken wing, sectioned, frozen or fresh
- 1-2 tbsp sugar, light brown
- ½ tsp kosher salt
- ½ cup cayenne pepper hot sauce (I used frank's red hot)
- ½ cup butter
- 1 tbsp Worcestershire sauce 6 ounces water

Directions:

For the sauce:

In a microwavable container, mix the hot sauce with the Worcestershire sauce, butter, salt, and brown sugar; microwave for 15 seconds or until the butter is melted.

For the wings:

1. Pour the water into the Instant Pot. Set a trivet in the bottom of the pot. Put the chicken wings on the trivet. Cover and lock the lid.
2. Turn the steam valve to SEALING. Press the MANUAL key, set the pressure to HIGH, and set the timer for 5 minutes.
3. When the Instant Pot timer beeps, release the pressure naturally for 5 minutes, then turn the steam valve to VENTING to quick release the pressure.
4. Unlock and carefully open the lid. Put the oven rack in the center of the oven. Turn the oven to the broil.
5. Carefully transfer the chicken wings from the pot into a cookie sheet. Brush the tops of the chicken wings with the sauce.
6. Place the cookie sheet in the oven and broil for 5 minutes.
7. Turn the chicken wings and brush the other side with the remaining sauce.
8. Serve with celery sticks and blue cheese dressing.

Sticky Sesame Chicken
(Prep + Cook Time: 30 minutes | Servings: 4)

Ingredients:
- 6 boneless chicken thigh fillets
- 4 peeled and crushed garlic cloves
- 5 tbsp hoisin sauce
- 5 tbsp sweet chili sauce
- ½ cup chicken stock
- 1 chunk of peeled, grated fresh ginger
- 1 ½ tbsp sesame seeds
- 1 tbsp rice vinegar
- 1 tbsp soy sauce

Directions:
1. Spread chicken thighs flat and place them into the Instant Pot.
2. Whisk garlic, ginger, chili sauce, hoisin, vinegar, sesame seeds, broth, and soy sauce into a sauce.
3. Pour over chicken and stir.
4. Select MANUAL and cook 15 minutes on HIGH pressure.
5. When time is up, hit CANCEL and wait for a natural pressure release.
6. When all the pressure is gone, open up the cooker and serve the chicken with rice.

Balsamic Chicken Thighs

(Prep + Cook Time: 25 minutes | Servings: 2)

Ingredients:
- 1 pound boneless, skinless chicken thighs
- ½ cup balsamic vinegar
- ⅓ cup cream sherry wine
- 2 tbsp chopped cilantro
- 2 tbsp olive oil
- 2 tbsp minced green onion
- 1 ½ tsp minced garlic
- 1 tsp dried basil
- 1 tsp garlic powder
- 1 tsp Worcestershire sauce
- ½ tsp black pepper

Directions:
1. Mix basil, salt, garlic, pepper, sherry, Worcestershire, onion, and vinegar in a plastic bag.
2. Add chicken and squish around, so the chicken becomes completely coated.
3. Turn your Instant Pot on and select SAUTE.
4. Pour in the olive oil and cook the minced garlic, stirring, until fragrant.
5. Turn the pot to POULTRY and pour in the chicken and sauce. Secure the lid. The POULTRY setting defaults to 15 minutes, which is the correct length of time for this recipe.
6. When it beeps, quick-release the pressure.
7. Serve with chopped cilantro and a side dish like rice or veggies.

Chipotle-Raspberry Pulled Chicken

(Prep + Cook Time: 30 minutes | Servings: 6)

Ingredients:
- 3 pounds boneless, skinless chicken thighs
- 1 (28-ounce) can of drained, whole tomatoes
- 1 cup raspberry jam
- 1 seeded, minced chipotle pepper
- ¼ cup packed, dark brown sugar
- 2 tbsp red wine vinegar
- 1 ½ tbsp smoked paprika
- 1 tbsp Worcestershire sauce
- 1 tsp ground cumin
- ½ tsp ground cinnamon
- ¼ tsp ground cloves

Directions:

1. In a food processor, mix jam, tomatoes, brown sugar, chipotle, paprika, cumin, cloves, cinnamon, Worcestershire, and vinegar. Pour this mixture into your Instant Pot.
2. Add chicken thighs and turn, so they become covered in sauce. Close and seal the lid. Select MANUAL and cook on HIGH pressure for 22 minutes.
3. When the timer beeps, hit CANCEL and quick-release the pressure. Remove the chicken thighs with tongs and shred.
4. To thicken the cooking liquid into a sauce, turn the cooker to SAUTE and reduce.
5. Serve.

Tuscan Garlic Chicken

(Prep + Cook Time: 15 minutes | Servings: 4)

Ingredients:

- 2 pounds halved and pounded boneless, skinless chicken breasts
- 1 cup chopped spinach
- ¾ cup heavy cream
- ½ cup sun-dried tomatoes
- ½ cup Parmesan cheese
- ½ cup chicken broth
- 2 minced garlic cloves
- 2 tbsp olive oil
- 2 tsp Italian seasoning
- ½ tsp salt

Directions:

1. Prep your chicken. Add the pounded chicken to a bowl and add olive, salt, garlic, and Italian seasoning. Rub into the chicken.
2. Add salt to your cream. Turn your Instant Pot to SAUTE and when hot, put the chicken along with its marinade inside.
3. Brown on all sides for a few minutes. Pour in broth and deglaze.
4. Close and seal the lid. Select MANUAL and cook on high pressure for 3 minutes.
5. When time is up, turn off the Pot and quick-release.
6. Turn the pot back to SAUTE and pour in salted cream. Let the dish simmer for 5 minutes before mixing in cheese.
7. Lastly, add sun-dried tomatoes and spinach. Simmer until the spinach leaves wilt.
8. Serve.

Charred-Pepper Chicken Fajitas

(Prep + Cook Time: 15 minutes | Servings: 4)

Ingredients:

- 4 frozen chicken breasts
- 4 tortillas
- 1 ½ cups chicken broth
- 2 bell peppers
- 1 quartered yellow onion
- 1 quartered red onion
- 2 garlic cloves
- 1 tsp paprika
- 1 tsp cumin
- 1 tsp dried rosemary
- Salt and pepper to taste

Directions:

1. Put chicken breasts in your Instant Pot and add seasonings. Add the yellow onion and garlic cloves before pouring in the broth. Close and seal lid. Select MANUAL and cook on HIGH pressure for 5 minutes.
2. When time is up, wait 10 minutes after turning off the cooker, and then quick-release any remaining pressure.
3. While waiting for the natural pressure release, prepare the bell peppers and red onion by cooking on a grill or skillet until soft and charred slightly.
4. Shred the chicken and serve with onion and peppers in a tortilla.
5. Optional toppings include cheese, sour cream, and so on.
6. Serve and enjoy.

Easy Spicy Chicken Wings

(Prep + Cook Time: 15 minutes | Servings: 4)

Ingredients:

- 3 pounds chicken wings
- ½ cup chicken broth
- ¼ cup light brown sugar
- 2 tbsp olive oil
- ½ tsp garlic powder
- ½ tsp paprika
- ½ tsp cayenne pepper
- ½ tsp salt
- ½ tsp black pepper

Directions:

1. Rinse and dry the chicken wings with a paper towel. Tumble into a mixing bowl.

2. In a separate bowl, mix the seasonings. You want about 3 tablespoons total of the mixed spice rub, so feel free to add more of whatever spice you like.
3. More sugar will make it sweeter, more pepper will make it spicier.
4. Add olive oil and your spice rub to the chicken wings, and rub.
5. Pour chicken broth in your cooker and add wings. Close and seal the lid. Select MANUAL and cook on HIGH pressure for 9 minutes.
6. When time is up, hit CANCEL and quick-release.
7. For really crispy skin, broil for 5-6 minutes, flipping halfway through.
8. Serve with hot sauce on the side!

One-Pot Chicken Alfredo (S&F)
(Prep + Cook Time: 5 minutes | Servings: 4)

Ingredients:
- 8 oz fettuccine
- 2 cups water
- One 15-ounce jar of Alfredo sauce
- 1 cup diced chicken
- 2 tsp chicken seasoning
- 1 tbsp roasted garlic
- ½ tsp black pepper

Directions:
1. Break pasta in half before adding to the Instant Pot along with water and chicken seasoning.
2. Add diced raw chicken. Close and seal the lid. Select MANUAL and cook for just 3 minutes on HIGH pressure. When time is up, hit CANCEL and quick-release the pressure.
3. Mix garlic and Alfredo sauce. Drain the pasta and add to bowl. Mix in sauce and black pepper.
4. If you are using pre-cooked chicken, add now.
5. Season with black pepper and serve.

Spicy-Peanut Chicken Pasta

(Prep + Cook Time: 20 minutes | Servings: 4)

Ingredients:

- 1 pound boneless, skinless chicken breasts (cut into bite-sized pieces)
- One 14-ounce can of diced tomatoes
- 2 ¼ cups chicken broth
- 8 oz whole-wheat ziti pasta
- 6 tbsp creamy, natural peanut butter
- 1 chopped yellow onion
- 2 tbsp peanut oil
- 1 tbsp dark brown sugar
- 1 tbsp fresh, minced ginger
- 2 tsp minced garlic
- ½ tsp ground allspice
- ½ tsp salt
- ½ tsp ground cloves
- ½ tsp ground cinnamon
- ¼ tsp cayenne

Directions:

1. Heat your oil in the Instant Pot on the SAUTE setting. When hot, stir the ginger, garlic, and onion until the onion is clear.
2. Next, add the chicken and cook until it becomes opaque. You're not browning it, but you do want it to not look raw.
3. Add peanut butter, tomatoes, seasonings, and brown sugar, and mix well until the peanut butter has melted.
4. Pour in the broth and pasta and stir one last time.
5. Close and seal the lid. Select MANUAL and adjust the time to 8 minutes on HIGH pressure.
6. When time is up, hit CANCEL and turn the valve to VENTING for a quick-release.
7. Stir before serving.

Baked Chicken Balls in Garlic Noodles

(Prep + Cook Time: 10 minutes | Servings: 4)

Ingredients:

- 7 oz fettuccine noodles
- 10 garlic cloves
- 2 tsp red chilli flakes
- Baked chicken balls
- ½ cup salsa sauce

Directions:

1. Put the pasta in the Instant Pot and pour just enough water to cover the pasta.

2. Add one tablespoon olive oil to prevent the pasta from foaming while cooking.
3. Cook on MANUAL setting for 6 minutes and then let the pressure release naturally.
4. Place the pasta under running water to avoid overcooking.
5. Add the remaining olive oil in the Instant Pot and cook the chilli flakes for half minute.
6. Add the salsa sauce and cook for another 10 seconds. Add the cooked pasta and toss the entire ingredients for some time.
7. Now, add the baked chicken balls and salsa sauce and then toss the entire content to coat the chicken balls and noodles with the salsa sauce.
8. Serve the dish warm.

Creamy & Cheesy Chicken Risotto
(Prep + Cook Time: 15 minutes | Servings: 4)

Ingredients:
- 2 cups risotto rice
- 1 cup cooked chicken chilli
- 4 oz heavy cream
- 2 tbsp parmesan cheese
- 1 onion
- 2 garlic cloves, minced
- 4 oz sherry
- 4 cups of chicken stock

Directions:
1. Turn your Instant Pot to SAUTE and heat oil.
2. Sweat the onion and garlic for a minute. Add the other ingredients (except cheese and heavy cream) and stir the contents in the pot thoroughly.
3. Close the lid and cook on MANUAL setting for 12 minutes. Let the pressure release and then open the lid.
4. Add the heavy cream and parmesan cheese and then stir once again thoroughly to blend the cheese and cream well.
5. Serve the risotto warm.

Chicken with Potatoes

(Prep + Cook Time: 50 minutes | Servings: 4)

Ingredients:

- 1 cup chicken, minced
- 2-3 potatoes, peeled, diced
- 1 onion, chopped
- 2-3 garlic cloves, minced
- 2 tomatoes, chopped
- 1 tsp salt
- ¼ tsp turmeric powder
- ½ tsp chili powder
- 2 tbsp olive oil
- 1 bunch coriander, chopped
- ½ cup chicken broth

Directions:

1. Heat oil in the Instant Pot on SAUTE mode and fry garlic with onion for 1 minute.
2. Add ground chicken and stir fry for 5-10 minutes.
3. Add tomatoes, salt, turmeric powder, and chili powder and fry till tomatoes are softened.
4. Add potatoes and fry for 5-10 minutes.
5. Add chicken broth and cook on manual mode for 25 minutes.
6. Transfer to serving dish
7. Serve and enjoy.

Chicken with Broccoli

(Prep + Cook Time: 30 minutes | Servings: 4)

Ingredients:

- 2 oz chicken, cut into small pieces
- 1 cup broccoli florets
- 2-3 garlic cloves garlic, minced
- 1 tsp salt
- ½ tsp cayenne pepper
- 3 tbsp butter
- 1 cup chicken broth

Directions:

1. Melt butter in the Instant Pot on SAUTE mode and fry garlic for 1 minute.
2. Add chicken and fry till lightly golden.
3. Season with salt and pepper.
4. Add broccoli and pour in chicken broth. Cook on manual mode for 10 minutes.
5. Transfer to serving the dish and serve hot.

Steamed chicken cutlets

(Prep + Cook Time: 35 minutes | Servings: 8)

Ingredients:

- 14 oz ground chicken
- 1 tsp ground black pepper
- 1 tsp paprika
- 1 tsp cilantro
- 1 tsp oregano
- ½ tsp minced garlic
- 2 tbsp starch
- 1 tsp chili flakes
- 1 tbsp oatmeal flour
- 1 egg

Directions:

1. Place the ground chicken in the mixing bowl. Sprinkle it with the ground black pepper, cilantro, and oregano.
2. Add paprika and minced garlic.
3. Mix up the mixture with the help of the hands.
4. Then beat the egg in the separate bowl and whisk it.
5. Add the starch and oatmeal flour and stir the mixture until you get the homogenous texture.
6. Add the egg mixture in the ground meat.
7. Then add chili flakes and mix up it carefully with the help of the spoon.
8. After this, make the medium cutlets from the ground chicken mixture.
9. Transfer the chicken cutlets in the Instant Pot trivet and place the trivet in the Instant Pot.
10. Close the lid and cook the dish at the STEAM mode for 25 minutes.
11. When the dish is cooked – remove it from the Instant Pot.
12. Chill it little. Serve the dish immediately.

Seasoned Chicken with Cheese

(Prep + Cook Time: 25 minutes | Servings: 6)

Ingredients:

- ¼ tsp ground black pepper, or more to taste
- 3/4 tsp kosher salt
- 2 ½ cups whole skinless and boneless chicken, cut into bite-sized chunks
- 3 tbsp oil
- 3 cloves garlic, minced
- 1 cup onions, finely chopped
- 1 ½ tsp bouillon granules
- 1 tbsp molasses
- 1 ½ tsp dried basil
- 1 ½ tsp dried oregano
- 2 (10-ounce) cans tomato sauce
- 2 tbsp butter, at room temperature
- 1 ½ tbsp flour
- 1 ½ cups Cheddar cheese, grated
- 1 ¼ cups olives, pitted and halved

Directions:

1. Generously season your chicken with salt and black pepper.
2. Heat oil and sauté chicken chunks until they start to brown.
3. Add onion and garlic and sauté for 5 minutes or until they are tender.
4. Now add tomato sauce, molasses, oregano, basil, and bouillon granules and cook an additional 5 minutes. Stir to combine.
5. Secure the lid and select the MANUAL mode. Cook for 15 minutes.
6. Carefully remove the lid (according to the manufacturer's instructions) and add the cheese; stir to blend. Combine flour and butter in a mixing bowl.
7. Add this mixture to the Instant Pot to thicken the sauce.
8. Serve warm garnished with olives.

Chicken Risotto

(Prep + Cook Time: 20 minutes | Servings: 4)

Ingredients:
- 1/3 cup butter, at room temperature
- 2 garlic cloves, chopped
- 1 ¼ pounds chicken, diced
- 1 cup onion, chopped
- 4 ½ cups chicken stock
- 1/2 cup white wine
- 1 ½ cups rice
- 1 tsp sea salt
- 1 sprig rosemary
- ¼ tsp freshly ground black pepper
- ¼ cup chopped fresh parsley, for garnish

Directions:
1. Use the SAUTE function to preheat your cooker.
2. Now warm the butter, and cook the onion, garlic, and chicken for about 5 minutes.
3. Stir in the rice and wine. Add the chicken stock, rosemary, salt, and black pepper.
4. Use MANUAL mode, and adjust the time to 13 minutes.
5. Give it another good stir. Now seal the lid.
6. Serve topped with fresh parsley.

Honey-Sriracha Chicken

(Prep + Cook Time: 15 minutes | Servings: 4)

Ingredients:
- 4 diced chicken breasts
- ¼ cup sugar
- 5 tbsp soy sauce
- 2-3 tbsp sriracha
- 2-3 tbsp honey
- 2 tbsp cornstarch
- 2 tbsp water + 2 tablespoons cold water
- 1 tbsp minced garlic

Directions:
1. Mix soy sauce, honey, sriracha, sugar, 2 tablespoons of water, and garlic in your Instant Pot.
2. Add chicken and mix to coat in the sauce. Close and seal the lid. Select MANUAL and cook for 9 minutes on HIGH pressure.

120

3. When time is up, quick-release the pressure after turning the cooker off.
4. In a cup, mix 2 tablespoons of cold water with cornstarch.
5. Turn the pot to SAUTE and pour in the cornstarch mixture. Stir constantly until the pot boils and the sauce begins to thicken.
6. Serve over rice.

Chicken Sandwiches
(Prep + Cook Time: 25 minutes | Servings: 6)

Ingredients:
- 1 pound boneless, skinless chicken breasts
- 1 and ½ cups canned orange juice
- 2 tbsp lemon juice
- 15 oz canned peaches and their juice
- 1 tsp soy sauce
- 20 ounces canned pineapple and its juice
- 1 tbsp cornstarch chopped
- ¼ cup brown sugar
- 8 hamburger buns

Directions:
1. In a bowl, mix orange juice with soy sauce, lemon juice, canned pineapples pieces, peaches and sugar and stir well.
2. Pour half of this mix in your Instant Pot, add chicken and pour the rest of the sauce over meat.
3. Cover the pot and cook at HUGH for 12 minutes.
4. Release the pressure quick, take the chicken and put on a cutting board.
5. Shred meat and leave aside for now. In a bowl, mix cornstarch with 1 tablespoon cooking juice and stir well.
6. Transfer the sauce to a pot, add cornstarch mix and chicken, stir and cook for a few more minutes.
7. Divide this chicken mix on hamburger buns, top with grilled pineapple pieces and serve.

Chicken Cordon Blue Casserole

(Prep + Cook Time: 40 minutes | Servings: 2)

Ingredients:

- 16 oz Rotini pasta
- 1 pound boneless skinless chicken breast
- 1 pound Cubed Ham
- 16 oz Swiss cheese
- 1 oz Gouda cheese
- 1 oz heavy cream
- 2 cups chicken broth
- 1 tbs spicy mustard
- 2 tbs butter
- 1 cup panko bread crumbs

Directions:

1. Pour uncooked pasta into your Instant Pot cover with 2 cups chicken broth. Place thin chicken strips and ham on top.
2. Place on MANUAL setting on HIGH Pressure for 25 minutes.
3. Do a quick release Stir and pour heavy cream, mustard and both of the cheeses into the pan.
4. Stir until creamy and smooth.
5. In a small pan melt butter and add panko bread crumbs stir until all are toasty and golden brown about 2-3 minutes.
6. Sprinkle on top of cordon blue.

Chicken Cacciatore

(Prep + Cook Time: 20 minutes | Servings: 6)

Ingredients:

- 8 chicken drumsticks, or approximately two pounds of chicken
- 1 cup chicken stock
- 1 bay leaf
- 1 diced onion
- 1 tsp garlic power
- 1 tsp oregano
- 28 oz stewed tomatoes, canned
- ½ cup pitted black olives

Directions:

1. First, preheat the pressure cooker by pressing the SAUTE button. Next, add the chicken stock to the Instant Pot, along with salt, and the bay leaf. Stir well.
2. Next, add the chicken, garlic powder, onion, tomatoes, and the oregano. Give the mixture a good stir to coat the chicken well.
3. Next, place the lid on the pressure cooker, and cook for 15 minutes at HIGH pressure.

4. After 15 minutes, allow the pressure to release naturally.
5. After the pressure releases completely, remove the lid, tilting it away from your face.
6. Stir the mixture well, remove the bay leaf, and throw it away.
7. Use a slotted spoon to remove the chicken and the tomatoes from the electric cooker and place them on a serving dish.
8. Next, increase the heat in the electric pressure cooker to reduce the cooking liquid.
9. Serve the chicken coated with the cooking liquid, along with the black olives over rice.

Chipotle-Raspberry Pulled Chicken
(Prep + Cook Time: 30 minutes | Servings: 6)

Ingredients:
- 3 pounds boneless, skinless chicken thighs
- 1 (28-ounce) can of drained, whole tomatoes
- 1 cup raspberry jam
- 1 seeded, minced chipotle pepper
- ¼ cup packed, dark brown sugar
- 2 tbsp red wine vinegar
- 1 ½ tbsp smoked paprika
- 1 tbsp Worcestershire sauce
- 1 tsp ground cumin
- ½ tsp ground cinnamon
- ¼ tsp ground cloves

Directions:
1. In a food processor, mix jam, tomatoes, brown sugar, chipotle, paprika, cumin, cloves, cinnamon,
2. Worcestershire, and vinegar. Pour this mixture into your Instant Pot.
3. Add chicken thighs and turn, so they become covered in sauce.
4. Close and seal the lid. Select MANUAL and cook on HIGH pressure for 22 minutes.
5. When the timer beeps, hit CANCEL and quick-release the pressure. Remove the chicken thighs with tongs and shred.
6. To thicken the cooking liquid into a sauce, turn the cooker to SAYTE and reduce.
7. Serve.

Warm Chicken Salad

(Prep + Cook Time: 35 minutes | Servings: 6)

Ingredients:

- 1 whole chicken or one pound chicken breasts
- 1 cup water
- 1 cup mayonnaise or sour cream
- 1 tsp garlic powder
- 1 tsp black pepper
- 3 cups baby spinach
- 3 tomatoes, diced
- 1 avocado, sliced

Directions:

1. Place the chicken and water in the Instant Pot. Use the HIGH pressure setting to cook. Press in the MANUAL button to add minutes for a total of 30 minute cooking time or press the POULTRY button.
2. In the meantime, prepare the salad by combining the spinach, tomatoes and avocado in a salad bowl.
3. Mix the mayo or sour cream with the garlic powder and black pepper.
4. When the chicken is ready, open the Instant Pot.
5. Cut the chicken into pieces (removing the bone if not boneless) and mix in the mayo or sour cream dressing.
6. Serve warm over the salad.

Feta Cheese Chicken Bowl

(Prep + Cook Time: 45 minutes | Servings: 6)

Ingredients:

- 7 oz Feta cheese
- 10 oz chicken fillet
- 1 tsp basil
- 1 tbsp onion powder
- 1 tsp olive oil
- 1 tbsp sesame oil
- 4 oz green olives
- 2 cucumbers
- 1 cup water
- 1 tsp salt

Directions:

1. Place the chicken fillet in the Instant Pot. Add water, basil, and onion powder. Stir the mixture gently and close the lid.
2. Cook the dish at the MANUAL mode for 30 minutes.
3. Meanwhile, chop Feta cheese roughly and sprinkle it with the olive oil. Slice the green olives.

4. Chop the cucumbers into the medium cubes.
5. Combine the chopped cheese, sliced green olives, and cucumbers together in the mixing bowl.
6. Sprinkle the mixture with the salt and sesame oil.
7. When the chicken is cooked – open the Instant Pot and remove it from the machine.
8. Chill it well and chop the chicken roughly.
9. Add the cooked chopped chicken in the cheese mixture.
10. Mix it gently with the help of the help of the 2 forks.
11. Serve the dish immediately.

Green Pepper Chicken (S&F)

(Prep + Cook Time: 15 minutes | Servings: 4)

Ingredients:

- 2 chicken breasts, cut into pieces
- 2 cups chicken broth
- ½ cup sour cream
- 1 green pepper, sliced lengthwise
- 1 red pepper, sliced lengthwise
- 1 red onion, sliced into rings
- 2 tbsp garlic powder

Directions:

1. Place all of the ingredients in the Instant Pot.
2. Cook on HIGH pressure setting for 8 minutes.
3. Allow pressure to naturally release.
4. Serve with salad and bread.

Family Baked Chicken (S&F)

(Prep + Cook Time: 30 minutes | Servings: 6)

Ingredients:

- 1 (2 ½ pounds) whole chicken
- 1 (1-inch) piece of ginger, minced
- 1 ½ tbsp sugar
- ¼ tsp ground black pepper
- ½ cup shallot, minced
- 1 tsp salt
- 2 tbsp wine
- 1 ½ tbsp soy sauce

Directions:

1. Sprinkle the chicken with sugar and ½ teaspoon of salt.

2. Cover the bottom of the inner pot with the remaining ½ teaspoon of salt.
3. Lay the chicken in the inner pot. Now, add black pepper, ginger, soy sauce, and wine.
4. Choose the POULTRY mode and cook for 30 minutes.
5. Serve with minced shallot and enjoy!

Hot burrito

(Prep + Cook Time: 60 minutes | Servings: 6)

Ingredients:
- 8 oz. tortilla
- 1-pound chicken
- ½ cup chicken stock
- 1 tbsp tomato paste
- 1 tsp sour cream
- 1 tsp ground black pepper
- ½ tsp paprika
- 1 tsp cilantro
- ½ tsp turmeric
- 1 white onion
- 2 sweet peppers
- ½ cup sweet corn
- 1 cup water

Directions:
1. Chop the chicken roughly and transfer it to the Instant Pot. Add chicken stock, tomato paste, sour cream, and water.
2. Sprinkle the mixture with the ground black pepper, paprika, cilantro, and turmeric. Peel the onion and remove the seeds from the sweet peppers.
3. Sprinkle the Instant Pot mixture with the sweet corn and close the lid. Set the Instant Pot mode STEAM and cook the dish for 30 minutes.
4. Then add chopped onion and peppers and cook the dish for 15 minutes.
5. When the time is over – shred the chicken and transfer all the mixture in the tortillas.
6. Wrap the tortillas and serve the dish immediately.

Turkey Goulash

(Prep + Cook Time: 35 minutes | Servings: 4)

Ingredients:
- 1 ½ diced turkey
- 3 tbsp plain flour
- Salt and freshly ground black pepper
- 2 tbsp sunflower oil
- 2 onions, chopped
- 1 garlic clove, crushed
- 1 green pepper, diced
- 2 carrots, peeled and cut into thick slices
- ¾ cup chicken stock
- ¾ cup passata
- 1 tbsp sweet paprika
- ½ tsp caster sugar
- 4 large potatoes, peeled and cut into chunks

Directions:
1. Toss the turkey in the flour, seasoned with a little salt and pepper. Heat the oil in the pressure cooker and fry the onions, stirring, for 2 minutes until softened but not browned.
2. Add the turkey and brown on all sides, stirring. Add the remaining ingredients except for the potatoes.
3. Cover with the lid and bring up to High pressure, then reduce the heat and cook for 6 minutes.
4. Remove from the heat and reduce the pressure quickly under cold water.
5. Stir the goulash, taste and re-season. Add a little extra stock or water if necessary. Add the potatoes.
6. Cover with the lid, bring back to HIGH pressure and cook for a further 4 minutes.
7. Reduce the pressure quickly under cold water again.
8. Stir gently. Spoon into bowls and serve garnished with soured cream or crème fraîche and a sprinkling of chopped parsley.

Zucchini Turkey
(Prep + Cook Time: 25 minutes | Servings: 4)

Ingredients:

- ¾ pound boneless, skinless turkey breast
- 2 tbsp olive or vegetable oil
- 2 medium zucchini, sliced thick
- 1 medium eggplant, peeled and diced
- 1 medium sweet onion, peeled and diced
- 1 medium green bell pepper, seeded and diced
- 1 can sliced mushrooms, drained
- 1 (28-ounce) can diced tomatoes
- 3 tbsp tomato paste
- 2 cloves garlic, peeled and minced
- 2 tsp fresh basil, chopped
- ¼ tsp dried red pepper flakes
- Sea salt and freshly ground black pepper, to taste
- Parmigiano-Reggiano cheese, grated (optional)

Directions:

1. Cut the turkey into bite-sized chunks. Heat the oil in the cooker over medium. Add the turkey and fry for 5 minutes, until it begins to brown.
2. Add the zucchini, eggplant, onion, peppers, mushrooms, diced tomatoes, tomato paste, garlic, basil, and red pepper flakes.
3. Lock the lid into position. Set the pot to low pressure and cook for 5 minutes. Use the quick release method for releasing the pressure.
4. Add salt and pepper if needed. Top with Parmigiano-Reggiano cheese.
5. Serve and enjoy.

Ground Turkey Stew with Spinach

(Prep + Cook Time: 20 minutes | Servings: 8)

Ingredients:

- 7 cups chicken broth
- 1 pound ground turkey
- 1 cup tomatoes, seeded and chopped
- 1 tsp salt
- 1 tsp dried thyme
- ½ tsp black pepper, to taste
- 1 tsp marjoram
- 1 tsp cayenne pepper
- 1 tsp dried rosemary
- 3 tbsp butter
- ½ cup celery, chopped
- 1 cup onions, diced
- 1 cup carrots, diced
- 1 ½ cups spinach, chopped
- 1/3 cup white wine
- 10 ounces noodles, cooked

Directions:

1. Choose the SAUTE function. Warm the butter and brown the meat, adding the seasonings.
2. Cook till the meat has browned, about 5 minutes. Stir in the onion, carrots, and celery; cook for about 5 minutes.
3. Add the wine to deglaze the pot. Add the remaining ingredients, except the noodles; give it a good stir and cook for 10 minutes.
4. Serve warm with cooked noodles.

Balsamic Turkey Wings

(Prep + Cook Time: 70 minutes | Servings: 4)

Ingredients:

- 1/3 cup water
- 1 ¼ cups chicken stock
- ½ tsp ground black pepper
- 1 tsp dried rosemary
- 1 tsp sea salt
- 4 tbsp flour
- 1 tsp dried sage
- 3 cloves garlic, minced
- ¼ cup balsamic vinegar
- 1 ½ pounds turkey thighs

Directions:

1. Set the cooker to SAUTE; brown the turkey thighs.
2. Add the chicken stock and balsamic vinegar. Choose the POULTRY setting and cook turkey for 55 minutes.
3. Reserve prepared turkey thighs. To make the sauce, whisk the garlic, rosemary, sage, salt, black pepper, flour and water.

4. Whisk the flour mixture into the cooking liquid. Turn your Instant Pot to KEEP/WARM setting and simmer the sauce for 13 minutes.
5. Serve the thighs with the sauce on the side.

Turkey-Stuffed Bell Peppers
(Prep + Cook Time: 35 minutes | Servings: 4)

Ingredients:
- 1 pound ground turkey
- 4 big bell peppers (red or green)
- One 4 ½-ounce can of mild green chiles
- 1 cup shredded sharp cheddar cheese
- 1 chopped yellow onion
- ½ cup corn kernels
- 2 tbsp butter
- 2 tsp minced garlic
- 1 tsp ground cumin
- 1 tsp dried oregano
- ¼ tsp salt
- ¼ tsp (or less) cayenne

Directions:
1. Melt the butter in your Instant Pot on the SAUTE setting. Cook the onion until it becomes soft in about 3 minutes.
2. Add the ground turkey, breaking it up with a spatula, and cook for 3 minutes.
3. Add cayenne, garlic, oregano, cumin, and salt. After half a minute of stirring, move everything to a large bowl to cool for 20 minutes.
4. Stir in the corn, cheese, and chiles into the turkey.
5. Prep your peppers by cutting off the tops and scraping out the seeds. Stuff the peppers with the turkey filling.
6. Wipe the inside of the cooker with a paper towel and lower in the steamer rack.
7. Pour in 1 cup of water and arrange the peppers on top of the rack. Lock and seal the lid. Hit MANUAL and cook for 7 minutes on HIGH pressure.
8. When the timer beeps, turn off the cooker and quick-release.
9. Serve.

Turkey Verde & Rice

(Prep + Cook Time: 30 minutes | Servings: 2)

Ingredients:

- ⅔ cup chicken broth
- 1¼ cups long grain brown rice
- 1 small yellow onion, sliced
- 1½ lb. Jennie-O turkey tenderloins
- ½ cup salsa Verde
- ½ tsp salt

Directions:

1. Add the chicken broth and rice into the Instant Pot. Top with the sliced onions, turkey and salsa verde. Sprinkle with salt and close the lid.
2. Close the vent to pressure cooker mode and set on HIGH for 18 minutes.
3. When the timer beeps, and the cooking is complete, do NOT open the lid. Let the pot sit for 8 additional minutes.
4. After 8 minutes turn off the Instant Pot, open the lid and the turkey and rice are ready to serve.
5. Optional: garnish with fresh cilantro.

Turkey Legs With Gravy

(Prep + Cook Time: 40 minutes | Servings: 4)

Ingredients:

- 2 pieces turkey legs
- 1 cup chicken stock, homemade, unsalted
- 1 dash sherry wine
- 1 onion, small-sized, sliced
- 1 pinch rosemary
- 1 pinch thyme
- 1 stalk celery, chopped
- 1 tbsp light soy sauce
- 1 tbsp olive oil
- 2 bay leaves
- 3 cloves garlic, roughly minced
- Kosher salt and ground black pepper, to taste

Directions:

1. Generously season the turkey legs with salt and pepper.

2. Press the SAUTE key of the Instant Pot and select the MORE option. Wait for the indicator to show HOT.
3. When the pot is hot, put in the 1 tablespoon olive oil, making sure the bottom of the pot is coated. Add the turkey legs into the pot.
4. Cook or about 2 to 3 minutes each side or until browned. Transfer onto a plate. Set aside until ready to use.
5. Press the CANCEL key to the SAUTE function and then press the SAUTE function again to set the heat MEDIUM.
6. Stir in the onion in the pot. Season with a pinch of salt and pepper and cook for 1 minute or until the onion is soft.
7. Add the garlic and sauté for about 30 seconds or until fragrant.
8. Add the celery and sauté for 1 minute. If desired, season with another pinch of salt and pepper. Add the bay leaves. Slightly scrunch the thyme and the rosemary and then add them in the pot. Stir to combine.
9. Pour in 1 dash wine to deglaze the pot, scraping any browned bit off the bottom using a wooden spoon. Let cook until the alcohol is evaporated.
10. Add the stock. Stir in the soy sauce. Taste and, if needed, season to taste with salt and pepper.
11. Press CANCEL to stop the sauté function. Cover and lock the lid. Press the MANUAL key, set the pressure to HIGH, and set the timer for 18 or 20 minutes.
12. When the Instant Pot timer beeps, let the pressure release naturally for 10 minutes. Turn the steam valve to VENTING to quick release the pressure.
13. Unlock and carefully open the lid. Remove the turkey legs. If desired, filter the turkey gravy. If you want a thicker sauce, mix 3 tablespoons cornstarch with 1 tablespoon water.
14. Pour about 1/3 of the mixture at a time into the pot until the sauce reaches your desired thickness.

Turkey Wings Braised with Cranberry

(Prep + Cook Time: 35 minutes | Servings: 4)

Ingredients:
- 4 turkey wings (2-3 pounds total)
- 2 tbsp oil
- 2 tbsp butter
- 1 onion, medium-sized, roughly sliced
- 1 cup walnuts, shelled
- 1 cup orange juice, fresh squeezed, OR prepared juice, without added sugar
- 1 cup dry cranberries ("crasins"), soaked in boiling water for
- 5 minutes), OR 1 ½ cup fresh cranberries, OR 1 cup canned cranberries, rinsed
- 1 bunch fresh thyme
- Salt and pepper, to taste

Directions:
1. Press the SAUTE key of the Instant Pot and wait until the display shows HOT.
2. Put the butter in the pot and melt. Swirl in the olive oil. Add the turkey wings, season with pepper and salt, and cook until both sides are browned and the skin sides are nicely colored.
3. When the wings are cooked and browned, transfer them to a plate.
4. Put the onion on the pot and immediately put the browned wings on top, with the browned skin faced up.
5. Add the walnuts, cranberries, and thyme. Pour the orange juice over the turkey. Press the CANCEL key to stop the sauté function.
6. Cover and lock the lid. Turn the steam valve to SEALING. Press the MANUAL key, set the pressure to HIGH, and set the timer for 15-20 minutes.
7. When the Instant Pot timer beeps, press the CANCEL key. Let the pressure release naturally for 10-15 minutes or until the valve drops.
8. Using an oven mitt or a long handled spoon, turn the steam valve to VENTING to release remaining pressure. Unlock and carefully open the lid. Remove the thyme.

9. Carefully transfer the wings into an oven-safe serving dish – they might be fall-apart-tender.
10. Slide the serving dish under the broiler and broil for about 5 minutes or until the wings are caramelized.
11. Meanwhile, press the SAUTÉ key of the Instant Pot. Cook the sauce until the sauce is reduced in half.
12. Pour the sauce over the broiled wings.

Spiced Beans with Turkey
(Prep + Cook Time: 30 minutes | Servings: 6)

Ingredients:
- ¼ cup white wine
- ½ tsp freshly ground pepper
- 3 ½ cups chicken stock
- 1 tsp sea salt
- 1 ¼ pounds dried beans
- 2 medium-sized onions, diced
- 1 cup tomatoes, diced
- 3 cloves garlic, peeled and minced
- 2 ½ tbsp vegetable oil
- 1 ½ pounds turkey breast, cut into pieces
- 2 Serrano peppers, seeded and diced
- 1 tsp paprika
- 1 cup bell pepper, seeded and thinly sliced
- 1 ½ tbsp parsley

Directions:
1. Press the SAUTE button and warm the vegetable oil. Then, sear the turkey on all sides, stirring occasionally.
2. At the pan sauté the onions, garlic, and peppers and add to the cooker
3. Add the remaining ingredients.
4. Place the lid on the cooker. Press the BEAN button and cook for 28 minutes.
5. Next, remove the lid according to the manufacturer's directions.
6. Serve warm and enjoy!

Turkey Chili

(Prep + Cook Time: 55 minutes | Servings: 4)

Ingredients:

- 1 tbsp olive oil
- 1 medium yellow onion, diced
- 2 green bell peppers, seeded and diced
- 2 fresh cayenne peppers, chopped (seeds included)
- 4 cloves garlic, chopped
- 1 tsp ground cumin
- ½ tsp dried oregano leaves
- 1 pound ground turkey
- ¼ cup your favorite hot sauce
- 1 (15-oz) can fire-roasted diced tomatoes
- 1 (15-oz) can kidney beans, including their liquid
- Salt and pepper to taste

  To serve:
- 1 cup grated Monterey Jack cheese
- ¼ cup chopped cilantro

Directions:

1. Set the Instant Pot to its SAUTE setting and add the oil. Add the onions, peppers, and garlic, and sauté until the onions soften and begin to brown, about 10 minutes.
2. Add the cumin and oregano and sauté two more minutes, until aromatic.
3. Add the ground turkey, breaking it up with a spoon or spatula. Sauté until opaque and cooked through, about 5 minutes.
4. Add the hot sauce, canned tomatoes and kidney beans and stir to combine. Cover the pressure cooker, then set it to the BEAN/CHILI setting.
5. When the pressure cooker is done the cooking and has depressurized, remove the lid, then ladle chili into bowls and serve hot.
6. Top with grated cheese and cilantro, and serve with rice or cornbread, if desired.

Thanksgiving Turkey Casserole

(Prep + Cook Time: 45 minutes | Servings: 4)

Ingredients:
- 4 turkey breasts, boneless (about 2 pounds), or chicken breasts
- 2 small-sized cans cream of mushroom soup
- 1 stalk celery
- 1 onion, sliced
- 1 cup chicken broth
- 1 bag Pepperidge farms stuffing cubes
- 1 bag frozen mixed veggies

Directions:
1. Put the turkey breasts in the Instant Pot. Add the broth, mixed vegetables, celery, and onion.
2. Cover and lock the lid. Turn the steam valve to SEALING. Press the MANUAL key, set the pressure to HIGH, and set the timer for 25 minutes.
3. When the Instant Pot timer beeps, turn the steam valve to VENTING to quick release the pressure. Unlock and carefully open the lid. Add the stuffing cubes in the pot on top of the cooked mix.
4. Pour in the cream of mushroom soup. Press the SAUTÉ key and cook for 8 minutes.
5. Press CANCEL to stop the sauté function.
6. Shred the turkey breast right in the pot. Serve.

Turkey Drumsticks

(Prep + Cook Time: 45 minutes | Servings: 6)

Ingredients:
- 6 turkey drumsticks
- 2 tsp brown sugar, packed tight
- ½ tsp garlic powder
- ½ cup water
- ½ cup soy sauce
- 1 tsp black pepper, fresh ground
- 1 tbsp kosher salt

Directions:

1. In a small-sized bowl, combine the garlic powder, pepper, brown sugar, and salt, breaking any clump of sugar. Season the turkey drumsticks with the seasoning mix.
2. Pour the water in the Instant Pot. Add the soy sauce. Add the seasoned drumsticks with any remaining seasoning mix. Cover and lock the lid. Turn the steam valve to SEALING. Press the MANUAL key, set the pressure to HIGH, and set the timer for 25 minutes.
3. When the Instant Pot timer beeps, let the pressure release naturally for 15 minutes. Turn the steam valve to VENTING to release remaining pressure. Unlock and carefully open the lid.
4. Using tongs, carefully transfer the drumsticks into a serving plate – be very careful because the drumsticks are cooked to fall-off-the-bone tender. If you have time, pour the cooking liquid into a fat strainer. Let the fat float to the top.
5. Pass the defatted cooking liquid at the table as a sauce.

Stuffed Bell Peppers
(Prep + Cook Time: 50 minutes | Servings: 6)

Ingredients:

- 1 pound turkey meat, ground
- 1 cup water
- 2 green onions, chopped
- 5 oz canned green chilies, chopped
- 1 jalapeno pepper, chopped
- 2 tsp chili powder
- ½ cup whole wheat panko

For the chipotle sauce:
- Zest from 1 lime
- Juice from 1 lime
- ½ cup sour cream
- 2 tbsp chipotle in adobo sauce
- 1/8 tsp garlic powder

- 1 tsp garlic powder
- 1 tsp cumin, ground
- Salt, to taste
- 4 bell peppers, tops and seeds discarded
- 4 pepper jack cheese slices
- 1 avocado, chopped
- Crushed tortilla chips
- Pico de gallo

Directions:

1. In a bowl, mix the sour cream with chipotle in adobo sauce, lime zest and juice, and garlic powder.
2. Stir well, and keep in the fridge. In a bowl, mix turkey meat with green onions, green chilies, bread crumbs, jalapeno, cumin, salt, chili powder, and garlic powder.
3. Stir very well and stuff your peppers with this mix.
4. Add 1 cup water in your Instant Pot, then add peppers in the steamer basket, cover, and cook at HIGH pressure for 15 minutes.
5. Release the pressure naturally for 10 minutes, then transfer bell peppers to a pan, and sprinkle cheese on top.
6. Cook in a preheated broiler just until cheese is browned.
7. Divide bell peppers on plates, top with chipotle sauce you made earlier, and serve.

Ducks Legs in Orange Sauce

(Prep + Cook Time: 60 minutes | Servings: 4)

Ingredients:

- 4 duck legs
- 3 chopped garlic cloves
- ½ cup dry white wine
- ¼ cup chopped celery
- ¼ cup chopped shallots
- ¼ cup chopped carrot
- ¼ cup triple sec
- 2 tbsp chopped parsley
- 2 tbsp sherry vinegar Juice and zest from
- 1 orange
- ½ tbsp olive oil
- ½ tsp salt
- ⅛ tsp sage
- ⅛ tsp thyme
- Salt and pepper to taste

Directions:

1. Rinse the duck legs before patting dry and seasoning with pepper. Turn your Instant Pot to SAUTE and add oil.
2. When hot, brown legs all over, starting with the skin first. When golden, plate legs for now.
3. Get rid of any extra duck fat before adding celery, garlic, shallots, and carrot to the pot.
4. Cook for just a few minutes before pouring in triple sec, white wine, salt, sage, and thyme.
5. Sprinkle in ⅓ of the orange zest.

6. When the liquid is boiling, return the duck legs. Close and seal the lid. Select MANUAL and cook on HIGH pressure for 45 minutes.
7. When the beeper sounds, turn off the cooker and use a quick pressure release.
8. Take out the legs and tent to keep them warm.
9. Add the rest of the zest to your pot and using a hand blender, puree the contents.
10. Pour in orange juice, vinegar, and salt and pepper.
11. Add parsley and serve!

Duck Fat Risotto

(Prep + Cook Time: 20 minutes | Servings: 4)

Ingredients:

- 4 cups warm chicken broth
- 2 cups Arborio rice
- ½ cup white wine
- 8 oz sliced white mushrooms
- 4 oz chopped prosciutto
- 3 tbsp duck fat
- 2 tbsp chopped shallot
- 2 minced garlic cloves
- 1 tbsp orange zest
- 1 tbsp chopped parsley
- Salt and pepper to taste

Directions:

1. Turn your Instant Pot to SAUTE and melt the duck fat until it's fragrant.
2. Add shallot and cook for 3 minutes before adding garlic. Cook for another 30 seconds before tossing in mushrooms.
3. When they have softened a bit (it should take around 4 minutes), add the rice and stir. Keep stirring until the rice has become toasty.
4. Pour in the wine and stir until the wine is almost all evaporated.
5. Add broth and (still) keep stirring until well-combined. Close and seal the pressure cooker lid. Select MANUAL and cook on HIGH pressure for 5 minutes. When the timer beeps, hit CANCEL and use a quick pressure release.
6. Take off the lid and hit SAUTE again. Keep stirring for 3-5 minutes until the liquid is absorbed into the rice.
7. Serve with orange zest, parsley, prosciutto, salt, and pepper.

Limy-Duck

(Prep + Cook Time: 55 minutes | Servings: 4)

Ingredients:

- 2 large whole duck
- 8 cups water
- 6 large oranges
- 6 lemons
- 16-20 key limes
- 2 jar (32 oz.) orange marmalade with peel
- ½ cup orange juice
- 2 tbsp brown sugar
- 2 tsp ground cinnamon
- 2 tsp ground cloves
- sprinkle of paprika
- sprinkle of pepper

Directions:

1. In the Instant Pot, add 8 cup water, 2 oranges (sliced), 2 lemons (sliced), cloves and cinnamon. Cover, and cook on HIGH pressure for 25 minutes.
2. Uncover when steam is released naturally and the duck is done. Mix the orange marmalade, oranges juices, lemon juice, lemon zest, and brown sugar.
3. Pour this glaze (reserve some of the glaze) on cooked duck. Keep the duck in an oven for 15 minutes at 400 degrees F.
4. Now brush the rest of the glaze on the duck.
5. Now cook it for additional 15 minutes to make it crispy.
6. Slice and serve hot.

Duck Chili

(Prep + Cook Time: 1 hour 25 minutes | Servings: 4)

Ingredients:

- 1 pound northern beans, soaked and rinsed
- 1 yellow onion, cut into half
- 1 garlic head, top trimmed off

For the duck:

- 1 pound duck, ground
- 1 tbsp vegetable oil
- 1 yellow onion, minced
- 2 carrots, chopped
- Salt and black pepper, to taste

- Salt, to taste
- 2 whole cloves
- 1 bay leaf
- 6 cups water

- 4 ounces canned green chilies and their juice
- 1 tsp brown sugar
- 15 oz canned tomatoes and their juices, chopped
- A handful cilantro, chopped

Directions:

1. Put the beans in your Instant Pot.
2. Add the whole onion, garlic head, cloves, bay leaf, the water, and salt. Stir, cover, and cook at HIGH pressure for 25 minutes.
3. Release the pressure, uncover the pot, discard solid veggie pieces and spices, and transfer beans to a bowl.
4. Heat up a pan with the oil over medium high heat, add carrots and chopped onion, season with salt and pepper, stir and cook for 5 minutes.
5. Add duck, stir, and cook for 5 minutes.
6. Add the chilies and tomatoes, bring to a simmer, and take off the heat.
7. Pour this into your Instant Pot, cover and cook at HIGH for 5 minutes.
8. Release pressure naturally for 15 minutes, then uncover the pot, add more salt and pepper, beans, and brown sugar.
9. Stir and divide among plates.
10. Serve with cilantro on top.

Spicy Shredded Duck
(Prep + Cook Time: 40 minutes | Servings: 8)

Ingredients:
- 1/3 cup red wine
- ½ cup chicken stock
- 1 tsp onion powder
- 14 oz. duck fillet
- 1 tsp red chili
- 1 tsp cayenne pepper
- 1/3 cup fresh dill
- 1 tsp salt
- 1 tsp ground black pepper
- 1 tbsp sour cream
- 1 tbsp tomato puree
- ¼ tsp minced garlic

Directions:
1. Combine the red wine and chicken stock together.
2. Stir the mixture. Pour the chicken stock mixture in the Instant Pot and preheat it for 1 minute at the sauté mode.
3. Meanwhile, combine the onion powder, red chili pepper, cayenne pepper, salt, ground black pepper, and minced garlic together.
4. Stir the mixture and sprinkle the duck fillet with the spice mixture. Then place the duck fillet in the Instant Pot and close the lid.
5. Cook the dish at the PRESSURE mode for 25 minutes.
6. When the time is over – remove the dish from the Instant Pot and chill it little.
7. Shred the duck fillet with the help of the fork.
8. Leave the 1/3 of all liquid in the Instant Pot and place the shredded duck fillet there.
9. Then add tomato puree and sour cream. Chop the fresh dill and sprinkle the dish with it. Stir it gently and close the lid.
10. SAUTE the dish for 2 minutes more.
11. When the time is over – transfer the hot dish in the serving plate.
12. Serve the dish immediately.

Beef & Broccoli

(Prep + Cook Time: 50 minutes | Servings: 6)

Ingredients:

- 1 small onion
- 3 cloves garlic
- 1.5 pounds thinly sliced steak
- 3 tbsp sesame oil
- 3 tbsp olive oil
- ⅓ cup soy sauce
- ¾ cup beef broth
- ⅓ cup brown sugar
- Fresh or frozen Broccoli
- 1 tbsp cornstarch

Directions:

1. Place oil and meat on SAUTE in your Instant Pot. Until meat is brown.
2. Add in onions and garlic continue to sauté until onions are tender.
3. Add in beef broth and soy sauce. Stir in brown sugar and stir until dissolved.
4. Place on 10 minutes high pressure and do a natural release (10 minutes).
5. Mix 2 tablespoons water with 1 tablespoon cornstarch and add to your mixture.
6. Meanwhile, steam your broccoli and cook your rice according to directions (in this book).
7. Stir in the broccoli and serve over rice.

Russian Beef

(Prep + Cook Time: 40 minutes | Servings: 4)

Ingredients:

- 2 pounds flank steak, cut into 1/4" strips
- 1 tbsp vegetable oil
- 4 cloves garlic, minced or pressed
- ½ cup soy sauce
- ½ cup water
- 2/3 cup dark brown sugar
- ½ tsp minced fresh ginger
- 2 tbsp cornstarch
- 3 tbsp water
- 3 green onions, sliced into 1-inch pieces

Directions:

1. Season beef with salt and pepper. Put oil in the cooking pot and select SAUTE. When oil begins to sizzle, brown meat in batches until all meat is browned - do not crowd. Transfer meat to a plate when browned.
2. Add the garlic and Sauté 1 minute. Add soy sauce, ½ cup water, brown sugar, and ginger. Stir to combine.
3. Add browned beef and any accumulated juices. Select High Pressure. Set timer for 12 minutes.
4. When beep sounds turn pressure cooker off and use a quick pressure release. When valve drops carefully remove the lid.
5. Combine the cornstarch and 3 tablespoons water, whisking until smooth. Add cornstarch mixture to the sauce in the pot stirring constantly.
6. Select SAUTE and bring to a boil, stirring constantly until sauce thickens. Stir in green onions. Serve.

Korean Beef

(Prep + Cook Time: 65 minutes | Servings: 4)

Ingredients:

- 2 pounds beef stew meat
- ½ cup water
- ½ cup soy sauce
- ½ cup brown sugar
- ¼ cup sesame oil
- 1 thinly-sliced green onion
- 1-2 tbsp red pepper flakes
- ½ tbsp onion powder
- ½ tbsp garlic powder
- 1 tsp ginger powder
- Juice from one orange

Directions:

1. In a bowl, mix water, soy sauce, sesame oil, garlic, onion, ginger, pepper flakes, and brown sugar.
2. When the brown sugar has dissolved, add stew meat and marinate for a half-hour.
3. Pour everything from the bowl into the Instant Pot. Add orange juice.
4. Close and seal the lid. Select MEAT/STEW and keep the default time of 35 minutes. .
5. When time is up, hit CANCEL and use a quick pressure release. Top beef with green onions and serve with rice.

Italian Beef
(Prep + Cook Time: 60 minutes | Servings: 4)

Ingredients:
- 2 bell peppers
- 1 tbsp cayenne pepper
- ¼ cup garlic
- 1-pound beef
- 1 tbsp butter
- 1 cup chicken stock

- 1 onion
- 1 cup Italian greens
- 1 tsp salt
- 1 tsp sugar
- 1/3 cup tomato paste
- 1 tbsp oregano

Directions:
1. Peel the garlic and slice it. Remove the seeds from the bell peppers and chop them into the tiny pieces.
2. After this, combine the sliced garlic with the chopped bell pepper.
3. Sprinkle the mixture with the salt, sugar, Italian greens, tomato paste, and oregano.
4. Mix up the mixture. After this, place the beef in the tomato mixture and mix it up carefully. Leave the mixture for 10 minutes.
5. Then place the beef mixture in the Instant Pot and add chicken stock and butter. Sprinkle the meat with the cayenne pepper.
6. Close the Instant Pot lid and cook the dish at the MEAT mode for 35 minutes.
7. When the time is over – remove the beef from the instant. Serve.

Chili Con Carne
(Prep + Cook Time: 25 minutes | Servings: 6)

Ingredients:
- 1 can (28 ounce) ground and peeled tomatoes
- 1 can (14 ounce) kidney beans, rinsed and drained
- 1 can (14 ounce) black beans, rinsed and drained
- 1 ½ pounds ground beef
- 1 ½ tsp ground cumin
- 1 ½ tsp salt
- 1 ½ cups onion, large diced
- 1 tablespoon chili powder
- 1 tbsp Worcestershire Sauce
- 1 tsp dry oregano
- ½ cup fresh water
- ½ cup sweet red bell pepper, large dice
- ½ tsp freshly ground black pepper
- 1-2 jalapeños, medium-sized, stems and seeds removed, finely diced
- 2 tbsp garlic, minced
- 3 tbsp extra-virgin olive oil

Directions:
1. Press the SAUTE button. Let the Instant Pot heat. Put the oil in the pot.
2. Add the ground beef, sauté, breaking up using a wooden spoon, until the beef is slightly brown. Remove excess fat. Add the onions, jalapenos, and bell pepper.
3. Sauté for 3 minutes. Add the garlic, chili powder, cumin, oregano, salt, and pepper. Sauté for 1 minute.
4. Add the beans, tomatoes, water, and Worcestershire sauce. Stir to combine. Close and lock the lid. Turn the steam valve to SEALING.
5. Set the pressure to HIGH and set the timer for 10 minutes.
6. When the timer beeps, let the pressure release for 10 minutes.
7. Turn the steam valve to VENTING to release remaining pressure.
8. Serve immediately or simmer on less SAUTÉ for a thicker chili.

Marinated Steak

(Prep + Cook Time: 60 minutes | Servings: 4)

Ingredients:
- 2 pounds flank steak
- 2 tbsp onion soup mix
- ½ cup olive oil
- 1 tbsp worcestershire sauce
- ¼ cup apple cider vinegar

Directions:
1. Set the Instant Pot to the SAUTE function. Pour in the olive oil and add the steak. Sauté each side of the steak until browned.
2. Pour in the Worcestershire sauce, vinegar, and soup mix. Lock down the lid and seal the steam nozzle.
3. Place the Instant Pot on the MEAT/ STEW setting or set it manually for 35 minutes.
4. Naturally release the pressure for five minutes, and quick release the remainder of the pressure.

Beef Stifado

(Prep + Cook Time: 50 minutes | Servings: 8)

Ingredients:
- 2-pound beef rump
- 2 tbsp tomato paste
- 1 tsp salt
- 1 cup onion
- 3 tbsp olive oil
- ½ cup red wine
- 2 oz. bay leaf
- 1 tsp black peas
- 1 tbsp ground ginger
- 1 tsp thyme
- 1 tbsp cayenne pepper
- 4 tbsp lemon juice
- 1 tsp cilantro
- 1 tsp oregano
- 1 tsp minced garlic

Directions:
1. Chop the beef rump and sprinkle it with salt. Mix up the mixture carefully. Peel the onions and slice them.
2. Combine the sliced onions with the olive oil and stir the mixture.

3. Then combine the red wine, bay leaves, black peas, ground ginger thyme, cayenne pepper, lemon juice, cilantro, oregano, and minced garlic together.
4. Toss the sliced onion mixture in the Instant Pot and SAUTE it for 10 minutes. Stir the onions frequently. After this, add the chopped beef rump and marinade.
5. Mix up the mixture gently and close the Instant Pot lid. Cook the dish at the MEAT/STEW mode for 40 minutes.
6. When the time is over – release naturally the remaining pressure, open the Instant Pot lid and mix up the dish gently.
7. After this, transfer the dish in the serving bowls.
8. Serve the dish immediately.

Beef Steak

(Prep + Cook Time: 50 minutes | Servings: 4)

Ingredients

- 1-pound beef steak
- 1 tsp salt
- 1 tbsp lemon juice
- 1 tsp paprika
- 3 tbsp fresh rosemary
- 3 tbsp balsamic vinegar
- 1 tbsp olive oil
- 1 tsp ground black pepper
- 1/3 cup red wine
- 1 tbsp minced garlic
- 1 onion

Directions:

1. Combine the salt, paprika, fresh rosemary, ground black pepper, and minced garlic together in the mixing bowl.
2. Peel the onion and chop it. Place the chopped onion and spice mixture in the blender.
3. Add lemon juice, balsamic vinegar, olive oil, and red wine. Blend the mixture until it is smooth.
4. Then combine the beef steak with the spice mixture and leave it in the fridge for 15 minutes.
5. Then transfer the marinated steak in the Instant Pot and sauté the meat for 10 minutes. Stir the mixture frequently. After this, close the Instant Pot lid and cook the dish at the HIGH pressure for 15 minutes more.
6. When the dish is cooked – release the remaining pressure and open the Instant Pot lid.
7. Serve the beef steak immediately.

Hot Chili Beef Stew

(Prep + Cook Time: 55 minutes | Servings: 8)

Ingredients:
- 1-pound stewing beef
- 1 jalapeno pepper
- 1 chili pepper
- 1 cup tomato juice
- ½ cup cream
- 1 tsp salt
- 1 tbsp olive oil
- ½ cup dill
- 9 oz. sweet potatoes
- 3 yellow onions
- 1 tsp paprika
- 1 tsp dry oregano
- 1 tsp turmeric
- 8 oz. sweet corn
- 1 cup green beans
- 1 bell pepper
- 3 cups beef stock
- 1 tsp cilantro

Directions:
1. Chop the beef roughly. Peel the sweet potatoes and chop them roughly too.
2. Combine the chopped beef and sweet potatoes together.
3. Sprinkle the mixture with the salt, olive oil, paprika, dry oregano, turmeric, and cilantro.
4. Mix up the mixture and transfer it to the Instant Pot. Sauté the mixture for 2 minutes. Stir it frequently.
5. Meanwhile, chop the dill and peel the onions. Dice the onions roughly.
6. Sprinkle the Instant Pot mixture with the diced onion and chopped dill.
7. Add cream, tomato juice, sweet corn, and green beans. Chop the jalapeno pepper, chili pepper, and bell pepper.
8. Add the chopped vegetables in the Instant Pot and mix up the mixture with the help of the spoon.
9. Close the Instant Pot lid and cook the dish at the MEAT/STEW mode for 35 minutes.
10. When the dish is cooked – serve it immediately.

Beef Ragout
(Prep + Cook Time: 50 minutes | Servings: 10)

Ingredients:
- 2-pound beef brisket
- 2 carrots
- 4 white onion
- 1 tsp sugar
- 3 cups water
- 1 cup cherry tomatoes
- 1 tbsp fresh thyme
- ¼ cup fresh dill
- ½ cup fresh parsley
- 1 cup cream
- 1 cup tomato juice
- 5 oz. fennel
- 11 tsp fresh rosemary
- 1 tbsp butter

Directions:
1. Wash the fresh thyme, fresh dill, and parsley. Chop the greens. After this, chop the beef brisket roughly. Wash the cherry tomatoes and cut them into the halves.
2. After this, chop the fennel. Peel the onions and carrots and chop them roughly.
3. Place all the ingredients in the Instant Pot. Add water, sugar, cream, tomato juice, fresh rosemary, and butter in the Instant Pot.
4. Mix up the mixture gently with the help of the spoon. Then close the Instant Pot lid and cook the beef ragout for 35 minutes at the MEAT/STEW mode.
5. When the dish is cooked – remove it from the Instant Pot and chill little. Serve the chilled dish immediately.

Texas Coffee Beef Ribs
(Prep + Cook Time: 50 minutes | Servings: 8)

Ingredients:
- 1 tbsp chili powder
- 1 tsp ancho chile powder
- 1 tsp garlic powder
- ½ tsp cinnamon
- ½ tsp nutmeg
- 1 tbsp dark cocoa powder
- 1 tbsp espresso powder
- 1 tsp salt
- 1 tsp coarsely ground black pepper
- 1 tbsp whiskey
- 1 tbsp olive oil
- 2 pounds beef ribs
- 1 ½ cups beef broth
- Cooked rice for serving, optional

Directions:

1. In a bowl, combine the chili powder, ancho chile powder, garlic powder, cinnamon, nutmeg, dark cocoa powder, espresso powder, salt, and coarsely ground black pepper.
2. Add the whiskey and the olive oil to the bowl and whisk it together until a thick paste is formed.
3. Liberally brush the paste over the ribs and place them in the Instant Pot.
4. Turn the Instant Pot to the SLOW cook setting and add the beef stock. Cover and cook for 40 minutes.
5. Slowly release the steam using the natural release method and serve with cooked rice, if desired.

Delicious Beef Casserole
(Prep + Cook Time: 25 minutes | Servings: 10)

Ingredients:

- 1 lb cooked ground beef
- 2 medium onion, chopped
- 8 eggs
- 2 cups milk
- 2 cups mozzarella cheese

Directions:

1. Spread the cooked beef in a greased bowl. Sprinkle chopped onion and cheese on top.
2. Beat the eggs and whisk with milk, salt and pepper.
3. Pour this egg mixture over the beef and cheese in the bowl.
4. Cover the bowl with a foil and then place it inside the Instant Pot cooker.
5. Pour required amount of water in the cooker and lock the lid. Cook on MANUAL setting for 22 minutes and then let the pressure release instantly with the help of quick release button.
6. Bring out the casserole dish and serve by slicing into desired sizes.

Mongolian Beef

(Prep + Cook Time: 60 minutes | Servings: 4)

Ingredients:

- 1 ½ lbs sliced flank steak
- ¼ cup arrowroot
- ½ cup grated carrot
- ¾ cup honey
- ¾ cup water
- ¾ cup coconut aminos
- 2 tbsp olive oil
- ½ tsp fresh ginger
- 1/3 cup scallion (green onion)

Directions:

1. Peel and mince the ginger. Cover the steak with the arrowroot powder.
2. Mix the honey, water, coconut aminos, ginger, olive oil, green onions, and carrots; add it all to the inner pot.
3. Lock the lid and seal the steam nozzle. You can manually set the Instant Pot for 35 minutes or use the MEAT/ STEW function.
4. Naturally release the pressure for five minutes and quick release the remainder of the pressure.

Moroccan Beef with Vegetables

(Prep + Cook Time: 1 hour 15 minutes | Servings: 6)

Ingredients:

- 1.5-pounds beef (stew meat)
- 2 tbsp olive oil
- ½ a diced onion
- 2 medium garlic cloves
- 4 tbsp finely chopped fresh parsley
- 1 tbsp tomato paste
- 1 cauliflower (1 head)
- 1 beef bouillon cube
- 1 tsp cumin
- ½ tsp salt
- ½ tsp black pepper
- ½ tsp ginger
- ¼ tsp turmeric

Directions:

1. First, remove the green leaves from the cauliflower. Cut off the bottoms of the cauliflower.
2. Break the cauliflower into large chunks and then rinse. Place the rinsed chunks in a bowl and set aside.

3. Heat the oil in your pressure cooker. Brown the meat on all sides.
4. Then, add enough water to cover the beef. You can now add all the remaining ingredients, except for the cauliflower.
5. Close the lid and bring to HIGH pressure. Cook for 15 minutes. Allow the pressure to drop naturally.
6. Open the lid and add the cauliflower. Stir gently to coat the cauliflower.
7. Close the lid and cook for another 5 to 7 minutes.
8. Allow the pressure to drop and serve.

Garlic Teriyaki Beef
(Prep + Cook Time: 55 minutes | Servings: 6)

Ingredients:
- 1 piece (2 pounds) flank steak
- 2 cloves garlic, finely chopped

For the teriyaki sauce:
- 2 tbsp fish sauce
- ¼ cup maple syrup, preferably organic grade B or higher
- ¼ cup coconut aminos OR soy sauce instead
- 1 tbsp raw honey
- 1 ½ tsp ground or fresh ginger, optional

Directions:
1. Slice the flank steak into 1/2-inch strips.
2. In a bowl, put all of the teriyaki sauce and mix until combined.
3. Put the steak strips and the sauce in the Instant Pot – there is no need to brown the meat. Cover and lock the lid. Turn the steam valve to SEALING.
4. Press the MANUAL key, set the pressure to HIGH, and set the timer for 40 minutes. Wait for the pressure to come down naturally.
5. Serve.

Chinese Beef Stew

(Prep + Cook Time: 60 minutes | Servings: 4)

Ingredients:

- 2 lbs. beef round, cubed into one inch pieces
- 1 tbsp soy sauce
- 2 tsp rice wine or sherry
- ½ tsp sugar
- 2 medium onions sliced
- 1-2 tbsp oil
- 1-2 tsp corn starch slurry if needed
- 1-2 tsp (to taste) fresh ginger chopped finely
- 1 can of mushrooms (optional)
- 1 tbsp Worcestershire sauce
- ½ cup broth, preferably beef
- Salt and pepper, to taste
- 1-2 tsp (to taste) garlic powder
- Pinch of smoked paprika
- 2 tsp corn starch

Directions:

1. Select the SAUTE function. Wait until it indicates hot before adding the oil and onion.
2. Sauté until onion is translucent and then add the sugar, soy sauce and rice wine. Cook for 30 seconds and then stir in the Worcestershire sauce and beef broth and then close the lid and click on the SOUP option.
3. After the 30 minutes, allow the pressure to release. Check the meat to see if it is ready. You can cook for a few minutes more n the stew setting if needed.
4. Add ginger, mushrooms, seasoning and corn-starch to make the soup thicker and cook for 1 more minute if you wish.
5. Serve with vegetables or rice.

Beef and Tomato Gravy

(Prep + Cook Time: 45 minutes | Servings: 4)

Ingredients:

- 3 oz. meat, cut into small pieces
- 1 cup tomato puree
- 1 onion, chopped
- 1 tsp garlic paste
- 1 tsp salt
- ½ tsp chili powder
- ½ tsp cumin powder
- ½ tsp cinnamon powder
- ¼ tsp turmeric powder
- 2 tbsp olive oil
- 1 tsp parsley, chopped

Directions:

1. Heat oil in Instant Pot on SAUTE mode and fry garlic with onion for 1 minute.
2. Add tomato puree, salt, chili powder, and turmeric powder and fry again for 4-5 minutes.
3. Add in boiled meat and fry well on high heat for 10-15 minutes.
4. Let cook with a few splashes of water for few minutes.
5. Sprinkle cumin powder, cinnamon powder and mix well.
6. Transfer to serving the dish and sprinkle parsley on top.
7. Serve and enjoy.

Beef with Beans (S&F)

(Prep + Cook Time: 130 minutes | Servings: 4)

Ingredients:

- 1 can red beans
- 2 oz. beef, pieces
- 2 tomatoes, slices
- 1 cup spring onion, chopped
- 1 tsp salt
- 1 tsp chili powder
- 1 tsp garlic powder
- 2 tbsp olive oil
- 3 cups vegetables broth

Directions:

1. Add all ingredients into the Instant Pot and toss well.
2. Cook on low heat for 2 hours on slow cook mode.
3. Serve and enjoy.

Beef Stroganoff

(Prep + Cook Time: 40 minutes | Servings: 6)

Ingredients:

- 2 cups beef stock
- 2 pounds beef sirloin, sliced
- 1 pound mushrooms, sliced
- 1 tsp fennel seeds
- 3 tbsp vegetable oil
- 2 cloves garlic, peeled and crushed
- 1 onion, peeled and finely chopped
- 2 bay leaves
- 1 teaspoon dried thyme
- ½ tsp dried rosemary
- ¼ cup Mozzarella cheese

Directions:
1. Choose the MEAT functions. Warm the oil in the Instant Pot; sear the beef for 5 minutes.
2. Add the rest of the ingredients, except the cheese.
3. Place the lid on the pot; lock the lid. Push the STEW key and cook for 20 minutes.
4. When the steam is completely released, carefully open the lid.
5. Add cheese and stir.
6. Serve and enjoy.

Spicy Barbacoa
(Prep + Cook Time: 40 minutes | Servings: 4)

Ingredients:
- 2-3 pounds beef chuck roast
- 3 bay leaves
- 3 chipotle peppers + 1 tbsp adobo sauce from can
- 1 cup beef broth
- Juice of ½ lime
- ⅓ cup apple cider vinegar
- 2 tbsp cooking fat
- 1 ½ tbsp ground cumin
- 1 ½ tbsp salt
- 1 tbsp black pepper
- 1 tbsp tomato paste
- 2 tsp oregano
- 1 tsp onion powder
- 1 tsp cinnamon
- ¼ tsp ground cloves

Directions:
1. Turn your Instant Pot to SAUTE.
2. Trim the beef and dry with a paper towel.
3. Season with ½ tablespoon salt and ½ tablespoon of pepper. Put the fat in the pot and melt.
4. Add beef and sear all over.
5. In a blender, mix vinegar, peppers, adobo, lime juice, cumin, salt, pepper, tomato paste, onion powder, cloves, oregano, and cinnamon until smooth.
6. Pour the puree in the pot so the meat is covered. Toss in the bay leaves and pour in broth.
7. Secure the lid and press MANUAL, and then 50 minutes on HIGH pressure.
8. When time is up, press CANCEL and wait for the pressure to come down naturally.
9. When the pressure is gone, open the pot and shred the meat.
10. Serve with the cooking liquid as a sauce.

Classic Corned Beef and Cabbage

(Prep + Cook Time: 1 hour 40 minutes | Servings: 8)

Ingredients:
- 4 cups water
- 3 pounds corned beef
- 3 pounds cabbage, cut into eight wedges
- 1 ½ pounds new potatoes
- 1 pound peeled and cut carrots
- 1 quartered onion
- 1 quartered celery stalk
- 1 corned beef spice packet

Directions:
1. Rinse the beef. Put in the Instant Pot along with onion and celery. Add in the spice packet and pour in water.
2. Close and seal the lid. Press MANUAL and cook for 90 minutes on HIGH pressure.
3. When time is up, hit CANCEL and very carefully quick-release the pressure.
4. Plate beef and keep celery and onion in the pot.
5. Add potatoes, carrots, and cabbage - in that order - in the pot. Close and seal lid again. Select MANUAL and cook for just 5 minutes.
6. When time is up, turn off cooker and quick-release.
7. Move veggies to plate with the corned beef. Pour pot liquid through a gravy strainer.
8. Serve beef and veggies with a bit of broth on top, and the rest in a gravy boat.

Homemade Pastrami

(Prep + Cook Time: 1 hour 25 minutes | Servings: 8)

Ingredients:
- 3-4 pounds corned beef
- 2 cups water
- 3 tbsp black pepper
- 2 tbsp ground coriander
- 1 tbsp kosher salt
- 1 tbsp onion powder
- 1 tbsp garlic powder
- 1 tbsp brown sugar
- 2 tsp paprika
- ¼ tsp cloves
- ¼ tsp ground allspice
- Vegetable oil

Directions:
1. Take out the beef and rinse.

2. Pour 1 cup of water in your cooker and lower in the trivet. Put the meat, fatty side up, on the trivet and close and seal the lid.
3. Hit MANUAL and cook for 45 minutes on HIGH pressure. When time is up, hit CANCEL and wait for a natural pressure release.
4. When that's done, take off the lid and wait another 20 minutes.
5. When cool, take out the meat and throw out the water.
6. Pat dry and coat with veggie oil. In a bowl, mix the spices and press on the meat.
7. Store in a fridge wrapped in plastic wrap at least for the night, or as long as a few days.

Beef and Noodles
(Prep + Cook Time: 70 minutes | Servings: 4-6)

Ingredients:
- 3 pounds boneless beef chuck roast
- 8 oz egg noodles
- 1 cup water
- 1 chopped onion
- 2 minced garlic cloves
- 2 tbsp veggie oil
- Salt and pepper to taste

Directions:
1. Cube roast into bite-sized pieces. Add oil to your Instant Pot, and turn to the SAUTE setting.
2. Brown meat before adding garlic, onion, salt, and pepper. Pour in water and seal the lid. Select MANUAL and cook for 37 minutes on HIGH pressure.
3. When time is up, hit CANCEL and wait for a natural pressure release.
4. Take out the meat. Pour another cup of water into the cooker and turn back to SAUTE. Bring liquid to a boil.
5. Add the noodles and cook, lowering the SAUTE heat if possible to thicken the liquid into a gravy.
6. When noodles are done, add meat, and stir.
7. Serve.

Autumn Vegetable Beef Stew

(Prep + Cook Time: 1 hour 50 minutes | Servings: 4)

Ingredients:

- 2 -3 pounds lean stew beef meat (cubed)
- 4 cups beef broth
- 4 strips bacon (chopped)
- 10 medium potatoes (diced)
- 4 ribs celery (thinly sliced)
- 4 medium carrots (thinly sliced)
- 3 cups rutabaga (chopped)
- 2 large onions (chopped)
- 2 bay leaves
- Freshly ground pepper to taste
- Salt to taste
- 1 tsp dried rosemary (crushed)
- 4 tbsp flour mixed with 1/2 cup water
- A handful parsley (chopped to garnish)

Directions:

1. Preheat the Instant Pot by choosing the option to SAUTE. Add onions, bacon, and beef and sauté for a few minutes until the beef is not pink any more.
2. Add rest of the ingredients except the flour mixture.
3. Stir, cover and cook on LOW pressure for about 2 hours. Add flour mixture stir well. Cook on HIGH pressure for 15-20 minutes.
4. When the timer goes off, use the quick release mechanism to release the pressure.
5. Uncover the pot and stir, taste and adjust the seasonings if necessary.
6. Serve in individual soup bowls garnished with parsley.

Country Beef Hash

(Prep + Cook Time: 20 minutes | Servings: 6)

Ingredients:

- 1/3 cup chicken broth
- 2 ½ tbsp butter
- 2 red bell peppers, sliced
- 3 cloves garlic, minced
- ½ cup leek, chopped
- 1 ¼ pounds potatoes, diced
- 1 ½ pounds cooked deli corned beef, diced
- 1 tsp celery seeds
- ½ tsp ground black pepper, or more to taste
- 1 tsp salt
- 1 tsp fennel seeds

Directions:

1. Melt the butter in the cooker turned to the SAUTE function. Sauté the leeks, stirring often, until softened.
2. Add the corned beef and garlic and cook for 5 minutes longer.
3. Stir in the remaining ingredients; stir until everything is well combined. Lock the lid onto the pot.
4. Cook for 14 minutes under HIGH pressure. Afterwards, use the quick-release function.
5. Serve warm.

Beef and Green Bean Soup

(Prep + Cook Time: 20 minutes | Servings: 6)

Ingredients:

- 20 oz green beans, trimmed and cut into small pieces
- 3 medium parsnips, finely chopped
- 2 onions, chopped
- 4 cloves garlic, minced
- 25 oz canned tomatoes, diced
- 1 ½ pounds boneless beef bottom round, diced
- 1 cup carrots, diced
- 4 ½ cups beef broth
- 1/3 tsp ground black pepper
- 1 tsp salt
- 1 tsp dried marjoram

Directions:

1. First, combine the broth, tomatoes, beef, garlic, onion, parsnip, carrots, marjoram, salt, and black pepper in a cooker.

2. Lock the lid onto the pot. Cook for 16 minutes under HIGH pressure.
3. Use the quick-release method to drop the pressure.
4. Unlock and open the pot. Stir in the green beans.
5. Then, seal the lid and wait for 4 minutes to warm up and blanch the beans.
6. Serve hot with croutons of choice.

Beef Brisket with Tomatillo Sauce
(Prep + Cook Time: 75 minutes | Servings: 6)

Ingredients:
- 1 (2-pound) beef brisket
- 1 ¼ cups water
- 20 oz canned whole tomatillos, drained
- 10 oz canned chipotle peppers in adobo sauce
- 1 tbsp olive oil
- 1 ¼ cups tomato sauce
- 4 cloves garlic, chopped
- ½ cup onion, chopped
- ½ tsp black pepper, to taste
- 1 tsp sea salt

Directions:
1. Press the SAUTE key on the Instant Pot
2. Place the tomato sauce, tomatillos, chipotle peppers, water, salt, and black pepper in the bowl of a food processor; blend until smooth.
3. Heat the olive oil in your Instant Pot over medium heat; then, sauté the onion and garlic for about 4 minutes.
4. Add the beef brisket to the cooker; sear it on all sides. Pour the reserved tomatillo mixture over the brisket; bring to a boil.
5. Cover with the lid and cook for 1 hour and 10 minutes.
6. Allow the cooker to release the pressure naturally.
7. Serve with tomatillo sauce on the side.

Beef Bourguignon

(Prep + Cook Time: 110 minutes | Servings: 4)

Ingredients:

- 1 pound steak, stewing or flank
- 1 cup red wine
- 1 red onion, large-sized, peeled and sliced
- 1 tbsp avocado oil OR olive oil
- 1 tbsp maple syrup
- ½ cup beef broth or stock
- ½ pound bacon tips OR rashers
- 2 cloves garlic, minced
- 2 sweet potato, large-sized, white, peeled and cubed
- 2 tbsp parsley, dried or fresh
- 2 tbsp thyme, dried or fresh
- 2 tsp ground black pepper
- 2 tsp rock salt
- 5 carrots, medium-sized, cut into sticks

Directions:

1. Press the SAUTE key on the Instant Pot. Add 1 tablespoon oil and heat.
2. Pat the beef dry and season. Cooking in batches, sauté the beef until browned, and set aside.
3. Slice the bacon into thin strips. Put into the pot with the onion and sauté until browned.
4. Return the browned beef into the pot. Add the remaining ingredients. Set the pot to HIGH pressure and the timer to 30 minutes.
5. Allow the cooker to release the pressure naturally. Serve.

Beefy Lasagna

(Prep + Cook Time: 30 minutes | Servings: 6)

Ingredients:

- 2 pounds ricotta cheese
- 1 pound of ground beef
- 24 oz pasta sauce
- 8 oz of no-boil lasagna noodles
- 1 package shredded mozzarella cheese
- 2 big eggs
- ¼ cup water
- ⅓ cup grated Parmesan
- 1 diced onion
- 1 tbsp olive oil
- 2 tsp minced garlic
- 1 tsp Italian seasoning
- Salt and pepper to taste

Directions:

1. Pour olive oil in your Instant Pot and heat until it starts to smoke. Quickly add the ground beef, onions, salt, and pepper.
2. When the meat is brown and onions clear, pour in the water and pasta sauce. Stir before pouring out into a bowl.
3. In a separate bowl, mix the ricotta, garlic, Italian seasoning, eggs, Parmesan, salt, and pepper together.
4. Fill the pressure cooker with ¼ inch of water.
5. Layer ⅕ of the beef mixture into the bottom before adding the noodles.
6. Pour in ⅓ of the ricotta mixture, and then more beef sauce.
7. Top with noodles, and keep going until you've used everything. The last layer should be beef sauce.
8. Close the Instant Pot lid. Select MANUAL and cook 7 minutes on HIGH pressure.
9. When the beep sounds, hit CANCEL and quick-release the pressure.
10. Open the lid and sprinkle on the mozzarella.
11. Cool for a few minutes before serving.

Beef in Pepper Sauce

(Prep + Cook Time: 60 minutes | Servings: 4)

Ingredients:

- 2-pounds boneless sirloin steaks – cut into strips
- ½ cup of baby carrots
- 8 oz tomato sauce
- 2 garlic cloves
- 2 tsp ground ginger
- 1 green bell pepper (a red bell pepper can be used as a replacement)
- 1 tsp turmeric
- 1 tsp salt
- ½ tsp black pepper
- 1 tsp cayenne pepper
- ½ tsp ground cardamom
- 2 tbsp olive oil
- 1 cup water
- ½ tsp paprika
- ½ tsp cumin
- 1 sliced onion
- 1 sliced green bell pepper

Directions:

1. First, you will need to remove one tablespoon of tomato sauce from the can. This will be used later in the recipe.

2. Then, blend the remaining ingredients, except for the oil, meat, cumin, and paprika. You should blend using a food processor, so that there are no chunks in the mixture.
3. Place the oil in your pressure cooker. Season the beef with salt and pepper. Brown all sides of the meat in the pressure cooker. This should only take a few minutes.
4. After browning the meat, add the water, the tablespoon of tomato sauce, paprika, and cumin.
5. Close the lid of the pressure cooker and cook on HIGH pressure. After the cooker begins to hiss, cook for 10 minutes. Allow the pressure to drop naturally. Point the steam vent away from your face. Carefully open the lid.
6. Place all the ingredients together in the pressure cooker. Combine everything and stir thoroughly.
7. Close the lid and simmer for 30 minutes or bring to high pressure and cook for 7 minutes.
8. If you bring the pressure back up, allow the pressure to reduce naturally. Check the ingredients.
9. The vegetables and meat should be tender.
10. Otherwise, continue cooking for a few more minutes.
11. Serve and enjoy.

Teriyaki Short Ribs

(Prep + Cook Time: 30 minutes | Servings: 6)

Ingredients:
- 4 big beef short ribs
- 1 cup water
- ¾ cup soy sauce
- 1 big, halved orange
- ½ cup brown sugar
- 1 full garlic bulb, peeled and crushed
- 1 large thumb of peeled and crushed fresh ginger
- ½ tbsp sesame oil
- Dried pepper flakes
- A bunch of chopped green onions

Directions:
1. In a Ziploc bag, mix water, sugar, and soy sauce. Squish around until the sugar has dissolved.
2. Add the orange juice and stir, before adding the orange slices as well.

3. Lastly, throw in the garlic, ginger, onions, and dried pepper flakes. Stir before adding the ribs.
4. Stir one last time and marinate in the fridge for at least 4 hours.
5. When ready to cook the ribs, coat the bottom of the Instant Pot with olive oil and heat.
6. Remove the ribs from the bag (save the liquid!) with tongs and quickly sear for 2-3 minutes on both sides.
7. Pour in the marinade and close the lid. Select the MEAT/STEW setting and select 30 minutes.
8. When time is up, hit CANCEL and quick-release the pressure.
9. Serve.

Teriyaki-Garlic Flank Steak

(Prep + Cook Time: 60 minutes | Servings: 6)

Ingredients:

- 2 pounds of flank steak
- 2 finely-chopped garlic cloves
- ¼ cup soy sauce
- ¼ cup maple syrup
- 2 tbsp
- Red Boat fish sauce
- 1 tbsp honey
- 1 ½ tsp ground ginger

Directions:

1. Slice the steak into ½-inch strips. Mix soy sauce, syrup, fish sauce, honey, and ginger together in the Instant Pot.
2. Add the meat and garlic, and stir to coat.
3. Secure the lid. Hit MANUAL and cook on high pressure for 40 minutes.
4. When time is up, unplug the cooker and let it depressurize naturally for just 5 minutes.
5. Quick-release the remaining pressure.
6. Serve the meat with lots of sauce and rice.

Beef Taco Pie

(Prep + Cook Time: 15 minutes | Servings: 4)

Ingredients:
- 1 package of flour or corn tortillas
- 1 pound lean ground beef
- 12 oz Mexican-style cheese
- ¼ cup refried beans
- 1 package taco seasoning
- Taco toppings (lettuce, tomatoes, sour cream, etc.)

Directions:
1. Follow the directions on the pack of the taco seasoning packet for how to prepare the beef.
2. Take a springform pan, and lay 1 tortilla at the bottom.
3. Cover in a layer of beans, then cheese. Top with another tortilla. Repeat with beans, beef, and cheese.
4. When all the ingredients are used up, put the pan in the Instant Pot. Pour 1 cup of water in the cooker (not the pan).
5. Close and seal lid. Select MANUAL and cook for 10 minutes on HIGH pressure.
6. When time is up, hit CANCEL and quick-release.
7. Carefully remove springform pan and remove it.
8. Serve and enjoy.

Beef and Vegetable Chowder

(Prep + Cook Time: 30 minutes | Servings: 4)

Ingredients:
- ½ pound beef stew meat
- 2 cups frozen mixed vegetables
- ½ 14 ounce can stewed tomatoes
- 2 potatoes (cubed)
- 2 stalks celery (chopped)
- 1 tbsp canola oil
- ¼ tsp dried basil
- 4 cups vegetable stock, divided
- ½ cup instant rice
- 1 tbsp worcestershire sauce
- Salt and pepper to taste

Directions:
1. Heat oil in the Instant Pot and cook the beef in it till it has browned. Set the beef aside in a bowl.

166

2. Next sauté onions in the Instant Pot. When the onions have become translucent add tomatoes, garlic and the stock.
3. Add all the remaining ingredients and mix. Season with the sauce, salt and pepper and stir thoroughly.
4. Cover the pot and cook for 15-20 minutes under HIGH pressure.
5. When the timer goes off, let the pressure release naturally.
6. When the valve drops, uncover the pot and serve hot.

Beef and Yogurt Curry (S&F)

(Prep + Cook Time: 35 minutes | Servings: 4)

Ingredients:

- 1 cup zucchini, peeled and diced
- 1 ½ tbsp vinegar
- A pinch of cinnamon powder
- ½ tsp ground allspice
- 1 ½ cups beef stock
- ½ cup onion, chopped
- ½ cup parsnip, chopped
- 1 cup carrot, chopped

- 3 cloves garlic, peeled and minced
- 1 cup turnip, peeled and chopped
- 1 ½ tbsp red curry paste
- ¾ pound beef, cut into pieces
- ½ tsp black pepper, to your liking
- 1 tsp salt
- 1 cup natural yogurt

Directions:

1. Simply place all the ingredients, except for yogurt, into your Instant Pot.
2. Cover with the lid and press the MEAT button; cook for 30 minutes.
3. While the curry is still hot, pour in natural yogurt. Stir until everything is well combined.
4. Serve over rice.

Beef and Red Wine Sauce

(Prep + Cook Time: 2 hours 20 minutes | Servings: 4)

Ingredients:
- 4 diced purple carrots
- 2 crushed garlic cloves
- 2 beef cheeks
- 1 diced onion
- 3 2/3-pound diced Italian tomatoes
- 1 tsp fresh thyme Half of a
- 1.5-militer bottle of red wine
- 1 tbsp tomato paste
- 1 tsp olive oil
- 1.1-pounds of pasta

Directions:
1. Start by heating the oil in a large pressure cooker.
2. Add the beef and onions.
3. Brown the beef, which should take a few minutes. The onions should be soft and translucent. Add the garlic and continue cooking until the garlic begins to brown.
4. Next, add the wine and continue cooking until the liquid is reduced by about 50 percent.
5. Add the tomatoes, tomato paste, carrots, and thyme.
6. Close the lid on your cooker and bring to HIGH pressure over high heat. Lower the heat to low and stabilize the pressure. Cook for about 90 minutes.
7. Though, cooking for 120 minutes will make the meat softer and easier to shred. Allow the pressure to release naturally.
8. Remove the meat from the cooker and place in a large bowl. Use two forks to shred the meat.
9. Place the shredded meat back in the cooker. Continue cooking with the lid open until the sauce thickens.
10. The liquid should reduce as you stir occasionally.
11. Meanwhile, you can cook the pasta according the directions on the package. Stir the heated noodles into the sauce. Serve and enjoy.

Cuban-Style Braised Beef

(Prep + Cook Time: 55 minutes | Servings: 4)

Ingredients:

- 1 ½ pounds of crosswise-cut flank steak, three pieces
- 3 ½ cups crushed tomatoes
- 2 chopped red bell peppers
- 2 minced garlic cloves
- 1 sliced onion
- 1 jalapeno
- 2 tbsp chopped cilantro
- 2 tsp oregano
- 1 tsp cayenne pepper
- 1 tsp cumin
- 1 sliced avocado
- One small bunch of chopped cilantro
- Crumbled cotija

Directions:

1. Season your steak with the salt and pepper.
2. Turn your pressure to SAUTE and brown the steak on all sides.
3. In a bowl, mix the crushed tomatoes, jalapeno, garlic and spices.
4. Pour over the steak. Select MANUAL and cook on high pressure for 35 minutes. Hit CANCEL or unplug when the timer goes off.
5. Wait 10 minutes before quick-releasing the remaining pressure.
6. Serve with chopped cilantro, cotija cheese, and avocado.

Spaghetti with Bacon and Beef Sauce

(Prep + Cook Time: 20 minutes | Servings: 6)

Ingredients:

- ½ tbsp butter, softened
- 3 slices bacon, chopped
- 1 pound ground beef
- ½ tsp ground black pepper, to taste
- 1 tsp sea salt
- 1 cup onion, peeled and chopped
- 2 tbsp olive oil
- 3 garlic cloves, peeled and crushed
- ½ tsp dried marjoram
- 1 tsp dried basil
- 1 ½ tsp Dijon mustard
- 1 ½ pounds pasta sauce
- 2 ½ cups dried spaghetti

Directions:
1. Select the SAUTE button; warm the olive oil and butter; sauté the onion, garlic, beef, and bacon, stirring frequently, until they are tender for about 6 minutes.
2. Add the remaining ingredients.
3. Cook for 10 minutes.
4. Serve at once.

Pulled BBQ Beef

(Prep + Cook Time: 65 minutes | Servings: 6)

Ingredients:
- Non-stick cooking spray
- 1 ½ cups beef stock
- 1 ½ pounds frozen beef roast
  For the BBQ sauce:
- 1/3 cup water
- 1/3 cup ketchup
- ¼ tsp ground black pepper
- ½ tsp kosher salt
- ½ tsp paprika
- 1 tbsp honey

Directions:
1. Lightly oil your Instant Pot with a cooking spray.
2. Put beef roast and stock into the pot. Put the lid on, choose the MEAT key and set to 1 hour 5 minutes.
3. Meanwhile, combine together the BBQ sauce ingredients in a mixing bowl. Turn the pot off. Next, use a quick pressure release.
4. Now, pull the cooked meat apart into the chunks.
5. Add the beef back to the Instant Pot; pour the BBQ sauce over it.
6. Assemble the sandwiches and serve.

Herbed Mustard Roast

(Prep + Cook Time: 75 minutes | Servings: 6)

Ingredients:
- 1 tbsp olive oil
- 2 cups beef broth
- 1 ½ tsp Dijon mustard
- ½ cup scallions, chopped
- 3 pounds rump roast
- 1 tsp salt
- ½ tsp cayenne pepper
- ¼ tsp freshly cracked black pepper
- 1 bay leaf
- ½ tsp dried marjoram, crushed
- 2 sprigs dried rosemary, crushed

Directions:
1. Pat the rump roast dry and rub with rosemary, marjoram, Dijon mustard, salt, black pepper, and cayenne pepper.
2. Warm the olive oil in the cooking pot and select SAUTE on the Instant Pot.
3. Then, brown the meat on both sides.
4. Remove your roast from the pot; add the scallions, beef broth, and bay leaves; add the water to cover the ingredients.
5. Add the roast back to the cooking pot.
6. Select HIGH pressure and cook 1 hour 5 minutes.
7. Afterwards, use the quick-release function. Serve warm.

Roast & Gravy
(Prep + Cook Time: 1 hour 30 minutes | Servings: 6)

Ingredients:
- 6 cloves of garlic, peeled
- 4 carrots, peeled or scrubbed
- 2 parsnips, peeled
- 4 three inch sprigs thyme
- 1 3-inch sprig of rosemary
- 2 tsp of fish sauce
- 2 tbsp of balsamic vinegar
- 1½ cups of beef broth
- Black pepper, freshly ground
- A good pinch of salt
- 4 pounds of chuck roast cut into
- 4 pieces Parsley, chopped

Directions:
1. First season the meat with salt and pepper and put it in an Instant Pot.
2. Put the rest of the ingredients in the cooking pot, lock the lid in place, and set the timer to 1 hour.
3. Cook under HIGH pressure then natural release for about 15 minutes. Remove the roast from the pot and set on a plate. Discard the thyme and rosemary stems.
4. Pour the liquid from the Instant Pot into a measuring cup or a large jar.
5. When the fat rises to the pot, use a small ladle or large spoon to remove it.
6. Pour the rest of the liquid into a blander that has veggies and puree until smooth.
7. If need be, season the mixture with salt and pepper. Using two forks, shred the meat and pour gravy on it.
8. Alternatively, you can stir gravy into the roast.
9. Serve the roast with mashed or roasted potatoes, cauliflower mash or other roasted or mashed root veggie.

Juicy Pork Belly

(Prep + Cook Time: 50 minutes | Servings: 6)

Ingredients:

- 1/3 cup dry white wine
- 2 ½ cups water
- 3 whole cloves
- 1 cup shallots, peeled and chopped
- 3 cloves garlic, crushed
- ¼ tsp brown sugar
- 2 ½ pounds pork belly, sliced

Directions:

1. Choose the SAUTE button on your Instant Pot.
2. Sear the pork belly on both sides.
3. Add the rest of the above ingredients.
4. Next, choose the MEAT button and cook until the meat is almost falling apart, for 25 minutes.
5. Serve warm.

Barbeque Pork Roast

(Prep + Cook Time: 80 minutes | Servings: 8)

Ingredients:

- 3 pounds pork butt roast
- 14 oz barbeque sauce
- 1 tsp sea salt
- 1 tsp garlic powder
- 1 tsp onion powder
- ¼ tsp black pepper

Directions:

1. Season the pork with the onion and garlic powder; sprinkle with salt and pepper; then place into the cooker.
2. Fill the cooker with enough water to cover. Close the lid and bring up to HIGH pressure. Cook for 1 hour 5 minutes.
3. Use the quick-release method to drop the pressure.
4. Next, drain off juices, reserving about 1½ cups. Shred the pork and combine with barbeque sauce, adding reserved liquid.
5. Serve at once.

Pork Sausage Gravy

(Prep + Cook Time: 20 minutes | Servings: 6)

Ingredients:

- 1 cup beef stock
- ½ tsp celery seeds
- ½ tsp ground black pepper
- 1/3 tsp grated nutmeg
- 1/3 tsp red pepper flakes, crushed
- 1 sprig thyme
- 1 tsp salt
- 2 pounds lean ground pork sausage
- 5 tbsp all-purpose flour
- 2 cups low-fat milk

Directions:

1. Crumble the ground pork into the Instant Pot turned to the SAUTE function; cook, occasionally stirring, until browned, approximately 4 minutes.
2. Stir in the thyme, red pepper, black pepper, nutmeg, salt, and celery seeds; cook for one more minute, until fragrant.
3. Pour in the beef stock. Lock the lid onto the pot. Cook for 5 minutes under HIGH pressure.
4. Afterward, use the quick-release method and open the cooker.
5. Then, bring the gravy to a simmer, stirring continuously.
6. Whisk the milk and flour in a mixing bowl or a measuring cup until the flour dissolves; add the mixture to the simmering gravy.
7. Continue cooking for about 3 minutes.
8. Serve at once.

Pork Rice

(Prep + Cook Time: 30 minutes | Servings: 2)

Ingredients:

- 2 tbsp canola oil, divided
- 1 medium onion, chopped finely
- 2 small carrots, skin peeled and chopped finely
- 1 cup of thin pork loin chops, cut into 1 inch pieces
- Kosher salt
- Black pepper powder
- 2 cups water
- ¾ cup long grain rice
- 1 medium egg
- ½ cup peas
- 4 tbsp soy sauce

173

Directions:

1. Select SAUTE and preheat your Instant Pot. Pour oil; once hot, add carrots and onions and sauté for 4 minutes or until fragrant.
2. Rub salt and some pepper on the pork pieces and add meat to pot. Cook for 8 minutes or until pork gets cooked. Cancel cooking.
3. Transfer carrots, pork and onions to a bowl. Pour water into the pot, and scrape the bottom to get bits mixed with water.
4. Add rice and salt. Secure the lid. Select MANUAL and cook for 20 minutes. Cancel cooking.
5. Uncover the lid. Spread rice towards the corner, making the center of the pot vacant. Select SAUTE and reheat the pot.
6. Pour oil into the center, and add beaten egg onto the hot oil.
7. Once egg is almost cooked, add peas, carrots, pork, and onions and stir well.
8. Combine rice and everything well and serve hot.

Pork Teriyaki

(Prep Time: 2 hours to marinate | Cook Time: 25 minutes | Servings: 2)

Ingredients:

- 1 ½ pounds pork loin roast
- ¼ cup low sodium soy sauce
- ¼ cup pineapple juice
- 1 ¾ tbsp brown sugar
- 5 garlic cloves, mashed and divided
- 1 tbsp grated fresh ginger
- 2 tbsp canola oil
- 2 medium red onions, sliced thin
- 2 tbsp rice vinegar

Directions:

1. Mix pork, pineapple juice, half the garlic, brown sugar, ginger and soy sauce in a zip lock bag and mix well.
2. Marinade overnight or for at least 2 hours. Next, take out the meat and roast to a golden brown on all sides in a skillet and keep aside.

3. Select SAUTE and preheat your Instant Pot. Pour oil; add onions and sauté until golden brown.
4. Toss the rest of the garlic; add marinade juices and pork roast. Pour ¾ cups water and secure the lid.
5. Use MANUAL and cook on High for 25 minutes.
6. Cancel cooking and release pressure naturally. Add vinegar to pork and simmer on Sauté option for 8 minutes.
7. Slice and serve.

Pulled Pork Flavorful
(Prep + Cook Time: 60 minutes | Servings: 2)

Ingredients:
- 1 pound pork roast, boneless, no fat
- 1 tbsp brown sugar
- ½ tbsp chili powder
- 1 tsp smoked paprika
- 1 ½ tsp cumin powder
- 1 cup water
- 1 tbsp apple cider vinegar
- 4 tbsp tomato sauce or ketchup
- 4 hamburger buns
- Kosher salt

Directions:
1. Slice pork against the grain into 4 portions. In a bowl mix chili powder, brown sugar, cumin, paprika, pepper and salt and then rub on the pork portions.
2. Heat the Pot on SAUTE, add meat and pour vinegar, water and the ketchup over the pork. Secure the lid.
3. Cook on MANUAL and HIGH for 50 minutes. Release pressure naturally and transfer pork to a plate.
4. Shred with two forks once you can handle the meat.
5. Slice off the excess fat and also skim any fat in the pot in the hot liquid. Sauté and simmer so that the juices thicken.
6. Check seasonings and add accordingly.
7. Pour additional sauce over the shredded.

Pork Carnitas
(Prep + Cook Time: 55 minutes | Servings: 4)

Ingredients:
- 4 pounds pork roast
- 4 cloves garlic, minced
- 2 tsp Himalayan salt
- 2 tbsp cumin
- 2 tbsp chili powder
- 1 tsp black pepper
- 1 tbsp oregano
- 1 tbsp ghee OR coconut oil
- 1 orange, cut in half
- 1 onion, chopped
- 1 jalapeno pepper, deseeded and diced
- Small gluten-free OR corn tortillas

Directions:
1. Press the SAUTE key of the Instant Pot and wait until hot. Combine the chili powder, cumin, oregano, pepper, and salt to make a rub.
2. Rub the pork the spice rub mix, coating all the surface of the meat and using all the seasoning.
3. Put the oil in the pot and add the pork. Sear each side of the pork for a couple of minutes until all the sides are beginning to get crispy. Add the rest of the ingredients into the pot.
4. Gently mix and spread out the ingredients with a spoon. Squeeze the orange juice over the pork and add the orange back in in the pot to cook with the meat.
5. Press the CANCEL key. Cover and lock the lid. Turn the steam valve to SEALING. Press the MANUAL key, set the pressure to HIGH, and set the timer for 50 minutes.
6. When the Instant Pot timer beeps, release the pressure naturally for 10 minutes to let the meat absorb the flavor. Turn the steam valve to VENTING to release remaining pressure. Unlock and carefully open the lid.
7. Shred the pork carnitas and serve on quesadillas, tortillas, burritos, or top of a salad.
8. If serving on tortillas, top with avocado and sprinkle with cilantro and a dash of paprika.

Pork and Potatoes

(Prep + Cook Time: 75 minutes | Servings: 6)

Ingredients:

- 2-3 lbs. boneless pork loin roast
- 2 tbsp white wine vinegar
- 1 cup of apple juice
- ½ cup of beef or chicken broth
- 6 potatoes medium, peeled and cut in half
- 1 tsp of caraway seeds
- 1 tsp dry marjoram seasoning
- 1 tbsp of brown sugar
- 16 ounces of kraut with most of the juice squeezed out
- 1 tsp minced garlic
- 1 small onion chopped
- 1 tbsp of lard or oil
- Kosher salt or sea salt, pepper and paprika (to taste)

Directions:

1. Season the pork with salt, paprika and pepper and set aside. Select the SAUTE option and once the Instant Pot is hot add the oil or lard and brown the pork on both sides.
2. Once ready, remove the meat and set aside. Add onions and cook until translucent and then add the garlic and continue cooking for 1 more minute. You can add more oil if needed.
3. Add the liquids and use a wooden spoon to scrape the bottom of the Instant Pot.
4. Add kraut, marjoram, brown sugar and caraway seeds and then potatoes and meat on top and close the lid.
5. Click the MEAT option and set time for 50 minutes.
6. Once ready, allow for natural pressure release followed by a quick release. Serve and enjoy.

Milk-Braised Pork

(Prep + Cook Time: 50 minutes | Servings: 4)

Ingredients:

- 2 pounds of pork loin roast, tied together with kitchen string
- 2 ½ cups milk
- 2 tbsp olive oil
- 2 tbsp butter
- 1 bay leaf
- 2 tsp salt
- 2 tsp ground pepper

Directions:

1. Melt the butter in your Instant Pot on SAUTE.
2. Add oil. Put in the meat, fatty-side down, and brown all over. Sprinkle in salt, pepper, bay leaf, and pour in milk.
3. The roast should be half-covered. Close and seal the lid. Hit MANUAL and cook for 30 minutes.
4. When time is up, hit CANCEL and wait for the pressure to come down. After 10 minutes, quick-release leftover pressure.
5. Transfer roast to a dish and tent with foil.
6. Wait for the sauce to cool in the pot, and then skim off the fat. Pick out the bay leaf.
7. Turn the pot to SAUTE and reduce if you want it to be thicker.
8. If there are milk clusters and you don't want them, whisk in a little bit of milk to smooth.
9. Serve roast slices with sauce poured on top.

Pork Ragu

(Prep + Cook Time: 40 minutes | Servings: 6)

Ingredients:

- 2 lbs. cubed stew meat, pork
- ¼ cup diced pancetta
- 1 diced yellow onion
- 1 diced carrot
- 1 cup red wine
- 3 minced garlic cloves
- 1 can tomato sauce
- 1 bay leaf
- 2 tsp Italian seasoning
- Salt and pepper to taste

Directions:

1. Take out the Instant Pot and turn to SAUTE. Brown up the pork and the pancetta. When they are done, you can drain out any extra fat before adding the garlic, carrots, and onions. Cook these for 2 minutes.
2. After this time, you can stir the wine in and then boil so half of it evaporates.
3. Scrape up the brown bits from the cooker before adding the pepper, salt, and Italian seasoning. Pour the tomato sauce over the meat.
4. Place the lid on top, without locking it, and then bring the cooker to a HIGH pressure. When it reaches the pressure, reduce the heat a bit and then cook the meal for 8 minutes.
5. Turn the heat off and let the pressure naturally go down. When the pressure is done, you can take the lid off and let the steam escape.
6. Take out the bay leaf and then stir the meal.
7. Break the meat up with a spoon and then serve this over polenta, pasta, and rice.

Pork and Egg Fried Rice

(Prep + Cook Time: 40 minutes | Servings: 4)

Ingredients:

- 3 cups + 2 tbsp water
- 2 cups long-grain white rice
- 1 beaten egg
- 1 finely-chopped onion
- 1 peeled and finely-chopped carrot
- ½ cup frozen peas
- 8 oz sliced pork loin chop (½-inch pieces)
- 3 tbsp soy sauce
- 3 tbsp veggie oil
- Salt and pepper to taste

Directions:

1. Preheat the cooker to SAUTE function and add 1 tablespoon of oil. Stir the onion and carrot for about 2 minutes.
2. Add pork after seasoning with salt and pepper. Cook for 5 minutes or until the meat is cooked all the way through.
3. Hit CANCEL and take out the onion, carrot, and pork. Pour in water and deglaze, scraping up any bits.

4. Pour in rice, salt, and seal the lid. Hit RICE and cook for whatever the default time is.
5. When time is up, hit CANCEL and wait 10 minutes for a natural release.
6. Quick-release any leftover steam.
7. Create a hole in the rice, and pour in the rest of the olive oil before hitting SAUTE. Add egg and scramble.
8. When the egg is just about ready, add the peas, onion, carrot, and pork.
9. Keep stirring for a few minutes until everything is mixed in well.
10. Serve with soy sauce!

Northern Pork Roast with White Beans
(Prep + Cook Time: 60 minutes | Servings: 6)

Ingredients:
- 1 tbsp olive oil
- 2 pounds pork roast
- ½ tsp salt
- 1 tsp black pepper
- ¼ cup shallots, diced
- 3 cups cannellini beans, cooked and rinsed
- 4 cups chicken stock
- 2 cups sweet potatoes, cubed
- 6 cups spinach, torn
- 1 tbsp crushed red pepper flakes
- 1 tsp nutmeg
- 1 tbsp white vinegar
- 1 tbsp pure maple syrup

Directions:
1. Set the Instant Pot to the SAUTE setting and add the olive oil. Season the pork with salt and black pepper.
2. Once the oil is hot, add the seasoned pork and the shallots. Cook until the roast is browned on all sides.
3. Add the cannellini beans and the chicken stock. Cover the machine and cook on HIGH pressure for 45 minutes.
4. Quickly release the steam using the quick release option and carefully open the top.
5. Stir in the sweet potatoes, spinach, crushed red pepper flakes, nutmeg, white vinegar, and pure maple syrup.
6. Replace the top and cook for an additional 10 minutes, or until the sweet potato is tender.
7. Use the natural release method to release the steam.

Carrots with Pancetta, Butter, and Leeks

(Prep + Cook Time: 20 minutes | Servings: 6)

Ingredients:

- 1 pound baby carrots
- 4 oz diced pancetta
- 1 sliced leek
- ¼ cup sweet white wine
- 2 tbsp chopped butter
- Black pepper to taste

Directions:

1. On the cooker's SAUTE setting, cook pancetta until crisp. Add the white and green parts of the leek and wait for 1 minute.
2. Pour in the wine and deglaze the pot. Add carrots and a dash of pepper before stirring. Pour pot contents into a 1-quart baking dish.
3. Nestle in pats of butter. Put a piece of parchment paper on top of the dish followed by foil, which you should seal over the dish.
4. Carefully wipe out the cooker and add 2 cups of water.
5. Lower in a trivet and then put the dish on top. Seal the lid. Select MANUAL and adjust time to 7 minutes.
6. When time is up, quick-release the pressure.
7. Carefully take out the dish and stir before serving.

BBQ Baby Back Ribs

(Prep + Cook Time: 40 minutes | Servings: 2)

Ingredients:

- 1 ½ pounds baby back ribs
- 1 tsp kosher salt
- 1 tbsp brown sugar
- ½ tsp chili powder
- ½ tsp paprika
- ½ tsp garlic powder
- ½ tsp cayenne
- ½ tsp black pepper powder
- ½ cup tap water or beef broth

Barbeque sauce:

- Kosher salt to taste
- ¾ tsp brown sugar
- ¼ tsp chili powder
- ¼ tsp paprika
- ½ tsp garlic powder
- ¼ tsp cayenne
- ½ tsp black pepper powder

Directions:

1. Take a large mixing bowl and mix the meat ingredients together.
2. Rub onto the ribs and set aside.
3. Select SAUTE and preheat the Instant Pot.
4. Pour in the broth. Place ribs and secure the lid.
5. Select Manual and on HIGH pressure for 40 minutes.
6. Release pressure manually.
7. Bake your oven at 425 F.
8. Pull out the ribs with tongs and place on a baking sheet lined with foil.
9. Mix together the barbeque sauce ingredients and coat the ribs.
10. Bake until crispy. Cut into individual ribs and serve.

Juicy BBQ Pork

(Prep + Cook Time: 55 minutes | Servings: 8)

Ingredients:

- 2 ½ pounds pork butt roast
- 20 oz BBQ sauce
- 1 tsp sea salt
- 1 ½ tsp cayenne pepper
- ½ tsp freshly ground black pepper, to taste
- 1 ½ tsp garlic powder

Directions:

1. Generously season the pork with garlic powder, cayenne pepper, salt, and black pepper; place the seasoned pork roast in your Instant Pot.
2. Fill with enough water to cover the meat. Close the lid and cook on HIGH pressure for 55 minutes.
3. Use the quick-release function.
4. Reserve about 1½ cups of the pot juices.
5. Shred the pork with two forks and mix with BBQ sauce, adding reserved juice.
6. Serve warm over mashed potatoes.

Orange Short Ribs

(Prep + Cook Time: 40 minutes | Servings: 4)

Ingredients:

- ¾ cup water
- 1 cup soy sauce
- 2 tbsp sweetener
- ½ cup blood orange, squeezed
- ½ head of garlic, peeled and crushed
- ¾ cup scallions, chopped
- 1 tsp salt
- ½ tsp ground black pepper
- 1 pound beef short ribs
- 1 tbsp sesame oil

Directions:

1. Combine together the water, soy sauce, sweetener, and orange juice in a mixing bowl.
2. Add the garlic, scallions, salt, and ground black pepper; mix thoroughly. Place the ribs in the bowl and let them marinate at least 3 hours.
3. Heat sesame oil in a large skillet.
4. Sear your ribs for about 4 minutes on each side. Transfer the seared short ribs to the Instant Pot.
5. Next, choose the MEAT/STEW mode, and cook for 35 minutes. To release pressure, use natural release method.
6. Serve warm.

Cranberry BBQ Pulled Pork

(Prep + Cook Time: 55 minutes | Servings: 10)

Ingredients:

- 3-4 pounds pork shoulder or roast, boneless, fat trimmed off

For the sauce:

- 3 tbsp liquid smoke
- 2 tbsp tomato paste
- 2 cups fresh cranberries
- ¼ cup buffalo hot sauce
- 1/3 cup blackstrap molasses
- ½ cup water
- ½ cup apple cider vinegar
- 1 tsp salt, or more to taste
- 1 tbsp adobo sauce
- 1 cup tomato puree
- 1 chipotle pepper in adobo sauce, diced

Directions:
1. Cut the pork against the grain in halves or thirds and set aside. Press the SAUTE key of the Instant Pot.
2. When the pot is hot, add the cranberries and the water. Let simmer for about 4 to 5 minutes or until the cranberries start to pop. Add the remaining sauce ingredients in the pot and continue simmering for 5 minutes more.
3. Add the pork in the pot. Press the CANCEL key to stop the sauté function. Cover and lock the lid. Turn the steam valve to SEALING. Press the MANUAL key, set the pressure to HIGH, and set the timer for 40 minutes.
4. When the Instant Pot timer beeps, unlock and carefully open the lid. With a fork, pull the pork apart into shreds.
5. Serve the pork with plenty of sauce on rolls or bread or over your favorite greens.

Coconut Pork Curry (S&F)
(Prep + Cook Time: 35 minutes | Servings: 4)

Ingredients:
- 1 pound pork, cut into pieces
- 2 bell peppers, chopped
- 1 ½ cups vegetable stock
- 3 potatoes, peeled and diced
- 1 ½ tbsp green curry paste
- 2 lemon grass stalks
- ½ cup parsnip, chopped
- 1 cup onions, chopped
- 4 cloves garlic, minced
- 1 cup carrots, chopped
- ½ cup coconut milk
- 1 ½ tsp sweet paprika
- ½ tsp ground black pepper
- 1 tsp salt

Directions:
1. Place all the ingredients, except coconut milk, in your Instant Pot. Stir to combine.
2. Close and lock the lid; use MEAT option and cook approximately 25 minutes.
3. While your curry is still hot, add ½ cup of coconut milk.
4. Stir again to combine well.
5. Garnish with the fresh coriander if desired, and serve warm.

Milk-Braised Pork

(Prep + Cook Time: 50 minutes | Servings: 4)

Ingredients:

- 2 pounds of pork loin roast, tied together with kitchen string
- 2 ½ cups milk
- 2 tbsp olive oil
- 2 tbsp butter
- 1 bay leaf
- 2 tsp salt
- 2 tsp ground pepper

Directions:

1. Melt the butter in your Instant Pot on SAUTE. Add oil. Put in the meat, fatty-side down, and brown all over. Sprinkle in salt, pepper, bay leaf, and pour in milk.
2. The roast should be half-covered. Close and seal the lid. Hit "manual" and cook for 30 minutes.
3. When time is up, hit CANCEL and wait for the pressure to come down. After 10 minutes, quick-release leftover pressure.
4. Transfer roast to a dish and tent with foil. Wait for the sauce to cool in the pot, and then skim off the fat. Pick out the bay leaf.
5. Turn the pot to SAUTE and reduce if you want it to be thicker.
6. If there are milk clusters and you don't want them, whisk in a little bit of milk to smooth.
7. Serve roast slices with sauce poured on top.

Chinese Pork Belly

(Prep + Cook Time: 40 minutes | Servings: 4)

Ingredients:

- 2 pounds of pork belly sliced into 5-inch pieces
- 2 cups water
- ½ cup soy sauce
- 6 sliced garlic cloves
- 5 slices fresh ginger
- 4 star anise
- 3 tbsp Chinese cooking wine
- 2 tsp cane sugar
- 1 tsp ground white pepper

Directions:

1. Turn on your Instant Pot to SAUTE and add a little oil.
2. When shiny, sear the pork belly slices on both sides, which should take about 2 minutes per side.

3. Throw in the garlic and ginger. Cook and stir for another 5 minutes.
4. Add in the rest of the ingredients and lock the pressure cooker.
5. Select MANUAL and then cook for 30 minutes.
6. Press CANCEL and quick-release the pressure when the timer goes off.
7. The pork belly should be extremely tender.
8. Serve with rice and veggies.

Pork Stew
(Prep + Cook Time: 45 minutes | Servings: 6)

Ingredients:
- 1-pound pork chop
- 3 yellow onions
- 4 oz beetroot
- 4 cups beef broth
- 1 tsp salt
- 1 tsp paprika
- 1 tsp chili powder
- 1 cup sweet corn
- ½ tsp brown sugar
- 1 tbsp ground celery

Directions:
1. Peel the onions and slice them. Chop the pork chop. Combine the pork chop with the salt, paprika, and chili powder. Mix up the mixture.
2. Then peel the beetroot and cut it into the strips. Place the all the prepared ingredients in the Instant Pot.
3. Add beef broth, sweet corn, brown sugar, and ground celery. Mix up the mixture and close the Instant Pot lid.
4. Cook the dish at the MEAT/STEW mode for 35 minutes.
5. When the time is over – remove the stew from the Instant Pot.
6. Serve the stew hot or preheated.

Citrus-Garlic Shredded Pork

(Prep + Cook Time: 55 minutes | Servings: 8)

Ingredients:

For the marinade/ rub:
- 4 pounds cubed, boneless pork shoulder roast
- 3 tbsp olive oil
- 2 tsp salt
- 1 ½ tsp ground cumin
- 1 tsp black pepper
- 1 tsp ground chipotle chili pepper

Other
- 2 quartered onions
- 2 cups fresh orange juice
- ¾ cup fresh lime juice
- 5 minced garlic cloves
- 2 cinnamon sticks
- 2 tsp dried oregano

Directions:
1. Mix the marinade/rub ingredients together and rub on the pork.
2. Stick in the fridge for 2 hours.
3. Turn the Instant Pot to SAUTE. Brown the pork evenly. When golden, add in all the "other" ingredients and cook until the onions have softened and garlic is fragrant.
4. Lock the Instant Pot lid. Select MANUAL and cook on high pressure for 30 minutes.
5. When time is up, unplug the cooker or hit cancel.mLet the pressure come down by itself.
6. Open the cooker and put the pork on a cookie sheet lined with parchment paper.
7. Stick in the broiler for 5 minutes.
8. Shred with two forks. Put back in the cooker and stir in the juices. Serve.

Honey Pork Chops

(Prep + Cook Time: 20 minutes | Servings: 4)

Ingredients:
- 2 pounds pork chops, boneless
- 2 tbsp Dijon mustard
- ¼ tsp cloves, ground
- ¼ tsp black pepper
- ¼ cups honey
- ½ tsp sea salt
- ½ tsp fresh ginger, peeled and minced
- ½ tsp cinnamon
- ½ tbsp maple syrup

Directions:
1. Sprinkle the pork chops with pepper and salt. Put the seasoned pork in the pot.
2. Press the SAUTE key and brown both sides of the pork chops in the pot.
3. In a bowl, combine the honey with the maple syrup, Dijon mustard, cloves, and cinnamon.
4. Pour the mix over the pork chops. Press the CANCEL key to stop the sauté function. Cover and lock the lid. Turn the steam valve to SEALING.
5. Press the MANUAL key, set the pressure to HIGH, and set the timer for 15 minutes.
6. When the Instant Pot timer beeps, release the pressure naturally or quickly.
7. Unlock and carefully open the lid. Serve.

Apple Cider Pork

(Prep + Cook Time: 50 minutes | Servings: 4)

Ingredients:
- 2 pounds pork loin
- 2 cups apple cider
- 2 tbsp extra virgin olive oil
- Salt and black pepper, to taste
- 1 yellow onion, chopped
- 2 apples, chopped
- 1 tbsp dry onion, minced

Directions:
1. Set your Instant Pot to SAUTE mode, add the oil, and heat it up. Add pork loin, salt, pepper, and dried onion.
2. Stir and brown meat on all sides, and transfer to a plate. Add onion to pot, stir, and cook for 2 minutes.
3. Return meat to pot, and add cider, apples, more salt, and pepper. Stir, cover, and cook at HIGH pressure for 20 minutes.
4. Release the pressure, uncover the pot, transfer pork to a cutting board, slice it and divide between plates.
5. Add sauce mixture from the pot on the side and serve.

Hawaiian Pork
(Prep + Cook Time: 2 hours | Servings: 8)

Ingredients:
- 5 pounds bone-in pork roast
- 6 minced garlic cloves
- 1 cup water
- 1 quartered onion
- 1 ½ tbsp red Hawaiian coarse salt
- Black pepper

Directions:
1. Cut the meat into 3 pieces.
2. Put in the Instant Pot. Add in garlic, onion, and salt. Season with black pepper.
3. Pour in the water and lock the lid. Hit MANUAL and cook for 1 ½ hours on HIGH pressure.
4. When time is done, hit CANCEL, and wait for the pressure to decrease naturally.
5. Before serving, shred the pork with two forks.

Asian Pork Chops

(Prep + Cook Time: 30 minutes | Servings: 4)

Ingredients:
- 4 cups frozen broccoli
- 4, ½-inch thick pork chops
- 6 medium scallions
- 2 tbsp brown sugar
- 1 ½ tbsp toasted sesame oil
- 1 tbsp rice vinegar
- ½ cup chicken broth
- ¼ cup soy sauce
- 1 tsp minced garlic

Directions:
1. Turn your Pot to SAUTE and heat the sesame oil.
2. Brown the pork chops until they just start to become golden.
3. Add the garlic and onion. Cook for 1 minute.
4. Pour in the broth, soy sauce, vinegar, and brown sugar. Mix.
5. Close the Instant Pot lid and choose MANUAL, and then 10 minutes on HIGH pressure.
6. When time is up, hit CANCEL and quick-release. Toss in the frozen broccoli and close the lid again.
7. Let the broccoli cook in the leftover heat for 8-10 minutes.
8. Serve and enjoy.

Parmesan Honey Pork Roast

(Prep + Cook Time: 40 minutes | Servings: 6)

Ingredients:
- ½ cup honey
- ½ tsp salt
- 2 tbsp dried basil
- 2 tbsp garlic, minced
- 2 tbsp olive oil
- 2/3 cup Parmesan cheese, grated
- 2-3 pounds pork roast, boneless
- 3 tbsp soy sauce

For the gravy:
- ¼ cup cold water
- 2 tbsp cornstarch

190

Directions:

1. Grease the Instant Pot with nonstick cooking spray. Put all of the ingredients into a 4-quart Instant Pot.
2. Cover and lock the lid. Press the MEAT/ STEW key and cook on preset cooking time of 35 minutes.
3. When the Instant Pot timer beeps, press the CANCEL key. Let the pressure release naturally for 10-15 minutes or until the valve drops.
4. Using an oven mitt or a long handled spoon, turn the steam valve to VENTING to release remaining pressure. Unlock and carefully open the lid.
5. Remove the roast from the pot and transfer into a serving platter. Cover with foil to keep warm. Press the SAUTE key of the Instant Pot. Combine the cornstarch with water until slurry and smooth.
6. Gradually stir in the cornstarch mixture into the sauce in the pot, stirring frequently, for about 2 minutes or until thick.
7. Press the CANCEL key to stop the sauté function and unplug the pot.
8. Slice the meat and serve with the gravy.

Collard Greens and Bacon

(Prep + Cook Time: 15 minutes | Servings: 4)

Ingredients:

- 1 ½ pounds chopped collard greens, with their stems removed
- ½ cup chicken broth
- 4 oz diced slab bacon
- 1 chopped yellow onion
- 3 tbsp balsamic vinegar
- 2 tbsp tomato paste
- 1 tbsp dark brown sugar
- 2 tsp minced garlic

Directions:

1. Turn your Instant Pot to SAUTE and cook the bacon until crispy.
2. Add onion and cook, stirring, for about 2 minutes or until it becomes clear.
3. Add garlic, stir, and then add the greens. Stir for about 2 minutes before adding broth, vinegar, brown sugar, and tomato paste. Stir until dissolved.

4. Close and seal the lid. Select MANUAL and cook on high pressure for 6 minutes.
5. When time is up, hit CANCEL and quick-release.
6. Stir before serving.

Mexican Pulled-Pork Lettuce Wraps
(Prep + Cook Time: 1 hour 35 minutes | Servings: 4-6)

Ingredients:
- 4 pounds pork roast
- 1 head washed and dried butter lettuce
- 2 grated carrots
- 2 tbsp oil
- 2 lime wedges

For Marinade :
- 1 chopped onion
- 1 tbsp salt
- 1 tbsp unsweetened cocoa powder
- 2 tsp oregano
- 1 tsp red pepper flakes
- 1 tsp garlic powder
- 1 tsp white pepper
- 1 tsp cumin
- ⅛ tsp cayenne
- ⅛ tsp coriander

Directions:
1. Marinate the pork the night before by mixing all the ingredients in the second list and rubbing into the pork. Store in the fridge.
2. The next day, turn your Instant Pot to SAUTE. When warm, brown roast all over.
3. Pour in 2-3 cups, so the roast is almost totally submerged. Close and seal the lid.
4. Select MANUAL and cook on HIGH pressure for 55 minutes.
5. When time is up, hit CANCEL and wait for the pressure to decrease naturally. When ready, take out the meat and pull with two forks.
6. Turn the Instant Pot back to SAUTE and reduce the liquid by half. Strain and skim off any excess fat.
7. If you want crispy pork, fry in a pan with some oil until it becomes light brown.
8. Mix pork with the cooking liquid before serving in the lettuce with grated carrots, a squirt of lime, and any other toppings.

Four Ingredient Pulled Pork

(Prep + Cook Time: 1 hour 30 minutes | Servings: 6)

Ingredients:

- 2 lb pork shoulder
- 3-4 slices of uncooked bacon
- 8 oz Not Your Father's Root Beer (non-alcoholic Root Beer could also be used)
- 1 cup Barbeque Sauce (more or less to taste)
- Toasted hamburger buns (optional)

Directions:

1. Place pork in the Instant Pot insert. Lay 3-4 slices of uncooked bacon over the pork.
2. Add approximately half a bottle of Not Your Father's Root Beer, or 8 oz of non-alcoholic root beer to the insert.
3. Lock the lid select MANUAL, and adjust time to 90 minutes.
4. When finished, use a natural release to allow the pressure to come down on its own.
5. After the pin has dropped (pressure has fully released), drain the pork and shred with a fork.
6. Add your favorite barbeque sauce, and enjoy on a toasted hamburger bun, or dig right in!

Carnitas

(Prep + Cook Time: 65 minutes | Servings: 8)

Ingredients:

- 3 pounds pork shoulder roast, boneless, cut into
- 2-inch chunks
- 3 cloves garlic, smashed with the flat part of a knife
- 2 tsp kosher salt
- 2 tsp dried oregano
- 2 tbsp olive oil
- ½ tsp chipotle or ancho chili powder
- ½ tsp black pepper
- ½ cup fresh squeezed lime juice, strained
- 1 tsp ground cumin
- 1 onion, sliced
- 1 cinnamon stick (3-inch)
- 1 ½ cups fresh orange juice, strained

Directions:

1. In a large-sized bowl, whisk the oil with the cumin, salt, pepper, and chili powder. Add the pork in the oil mixture and toss to coat.
2. Press the SAUTE key of the Instant Pot and press the MORE option for high heat. Add the pork and cook until browned.
3. When the pork is browned, stir in the garlic, oregano, onion, and cinnamon stick. Add the lime and orange juice.
4. Press the CANCEL key to stop the sauté function. Cover and lock the lid. Turn the steam valve to SEALING. Press the MANUAL key, set the pressure to HIGH, and set the timer for 35 minutes.
5. When the Instant Pot timer beeps, press the CANCEL key and unplug the Instant Pot. Let the pressure release naturally for 10-15 minutes or until the valve drops.
6. Using an oven mitt or a long handled spoon, turn the steam valve to VENTING to release remaining pressure.
7. Unlock and carefully open the lid. Transfer the pork into the baking sheet. Put an oven rack 6 inches from the heat source and preheat the broiler.
8. While the broiler is heating, decrease the cooking liquid from the pot using a fat separator; discard the fat. Using 2 forks, shred the pork on the baking sheet.
9. Pour a cup of the cooking liquid over the pork. Broil for about 10 minutes or until the meat begins to crisp. Stir and then broil for 5 minutes more.
10. Remove from the oven and serve with avocado, tortillas, queso fresco, salsa Verde, and remaining of the cooking liquid.

Sausage and Peppers

(Prep + Cook Time: 30 minutes | Servings: 8)

Ingredients:
- 1-2 pounds of sweet sausage
- 2 sliced sweet bell peppers
- 1 Vidalia onion
- 3 ½ cups crushed tomatoes
- 1 cup of tomato sauce
- 1 tbsp Italian seasoning
- Salt and pepper to taste

Directions:
1. Cut the sausage into thirds, and prepare the veggies. Cut the onion into rings.
2. Pour the tomatoes, tomato sauce, and Italian seasoning into your Instant Pot.
3. Put the cut sausage on top (without stirring), before adding the onions and peppers. Season.
4. Close the Instant Pot lid, select MANUAL, and cook on HIGH pressure for 25 minutes.
5. When time is up, press CANCEL and quick-release the pressure.
6. Serve with some Parmesan cheese.

Creamy savoy cabbage with bacon

(Prep + Cook Time: 20 minutes | Servings: 4)

Ingredients:

- 1 chopped, medium-sized head of Savoy cabbage
- 2 cups bone broth
- 1 cup diced bacon
- 1 chopped onion
- 1 bay leaf
- ½ can of full-fat coconut milk
- 2 tbsp parsley flakes
- ¼ tsp nutmeg
- Salt to taste

Directions:

1. Prep your Instant Pot by inserting a round piece of parchment paper sized to fit the bottom of the pot. Don't put it in just yet.
2. Preheat the cooker and add onion and bacon. Cook until the onions are browning and the bacon is crisp.
3. Pour in broth and deglaze. Add the bay leaf and cabbage.
4. Put the parchment paper on top to cover the food. Close and seal the lid. Select MANUAL and cook for just 4 minutes on HIGH pressure.
5. When time is up, hit CANCEL and quick-release.
6. Remove the parchment and turn the pot to SAUTE.
7. When boiling, pour in the coconut milk and add nutmeg.
8. Let the food simmer for 5 minutes.
9. Serve with parsley flakes on top!

Turnip Greens with Bacon

(Prep + Cook Time: 45 minutes | Servings: 4)

Ingredients:

- 1 bag (1-pound) turnip greens
- ½-1 cup smoked ham hocks or necks
- 3-4 slices bacon, cut into small pieces
- 2 cups chicken broth
- ½ cup onion, diced (I use frozen)
- Splash extra-virgin olive oil
- Salt and pepper, to taste

Directions:

1. Set the Instant Pot to SAUTE. Pour a splash of olive oil.
2. Add the bacon, the smoked ham, and onion. Season with salt and pepper and sauté until the fat is rendered and the meat is cooked.
3. Add the broth and the greens. Close and lock the lid. Set to pressure and cook on HIGH for 30 minutes.
4. When the timer beeps, quick release the pressure and serve warm.

Barbecue Meatballs
(Prep + Cook Time: 20 minutes | Servings: 6)

Ingredients:

- 18 oz BBQ Sauce
- 1 (48 oz) bag fully cooked frozen meatballs
- 18 oz grape jelly

Directions:

1. Pour one cup of water into the Instant Pot.
2. Put the steamer basket in and add the meatballs (still frozen). Set the timer for five minutes using the HIGH pressure setting.
3. After the beep, discharge the pressure with the quick release function.
4. Remove the basket and meatballs. Discard the water and add the jelly and BBQ sauce to the Instant Pot.
5. Choose the SAUTE function— stirring frequently until the jelly melts, and the sauce is creamy smooth. Add the meatballs and stir.
6. Place the pot on the keep warm setting and enjoy.

Lamb and Feta Meatballs

(Prep + Cook Time: 15 minutes | Servings: 6)

Ingredients:

- 1 ½ pounds ground lamb
- 4 minced garlic cloves
- One, 28 oz can of crushed tomatoes
- 6 oz can of tomato sauce
- 1 beaten egg
- 1 chopped green bell pepper
- 1 chopped onion
- ½ cup crumbled feta cheese
- ½ cup breadcrumbs
- 2 tbsp chopped parsley
- 2 tbsp olive oil
- 1 tbsp chopped mint
- 1 tbsp water
- 1 tsp dried oregano
- ½ tsp salt
- ¼ tsp black pepper

Directions:

1. In a bowl, mix lamb, egg, breadcrumbs, mint, parsley, feta, water, half of the minced garlic, pepper, and salt.
2. With your hands, mold into 1-inch meatballs. Turn your Instant Pot to SAUTE and add oil.
3. When hot, toss in the bell pepper and onion. Cook for 2 minutes before adding the rest of the garlic.
4. After another minute, mix in crushed tomatoes with their liquid, the tomato sauce, and oregano. Sprinkle in salt and pepper.
5. Put the meatballs in and ladle over the sauce before sealing the cooker lid. Select MANUAL and adjust time to 8 minutes on high pressure.
6. When time is up, hit CANCEL and carefully quick-release.
7. Serve meatballs with parsley and more cheese!

Lamb Curry

(Prep + Cook Time: 65 minutes | Servings: 4)

Ingredients:

- 2 pounds lamb meat, with bone
- 2 cans (14 oz) diced tomatoes, preferably organic
- ½ pound potatoes, cut into halves
- 1 ½-inch knob fresh ginger, minced
- 1 bay leaf
- 1 tbsp coriander powder
- 1 tsp cumin powder
- 1 tsp garam masala, add more to taste
- 1 tsp kashmiri chili powder(if using cayenne use a little less)
- 1 tsp paprika
- 1 tsp turmeric powder
- ½ cup water
- 2 onions, diced
- 2 tbsp avocado oil
- 2 tsp salt, or to taste
- 3 cloves garlic, minced
- 4 cardamom pods
- 4 whole cloves

Directions:

1. Press the SAUTE key of the Instant Pot. Add the oil and the lamb meat. Cook until the lamb starts to brown. Add the garlic, onion, and spices. Stir-fry for about 2 to 3 minutes.
2. Pour in the water, potatoes, and diced tomatoes. Press the CANCEL key to stop the sauté function. Cover and lock the lid. Press the MEAT/ STEW key set the timer for 45 minutes.
3. When the Instant Pot timer beeps, release the pressure naturally for 10-15 minutes or until the valve drops.
4. Turn the steam valve to VENTING to release remaining pressure. Unlock and carefully open the lid.
5. If you want a thicker sauce, press the SAUTE key and cook until the liquid is reduced. Serve.

Half-Hour Rosemary Lamb

(Prep + Cook Time: 30 minutes | Servings: 6)

Ingredients:

- 4 pounds cubed, boneless lamb
- 1 ½ cups veggie stock
- 1 cup sliced carrots
- 4 minced garlic cloves
- 4-6 rosemary sprigs
- 3 tbsp flour
- 2 tbsp olive oil
- Salt and pepper to taste

Directions:

1. Preheat your cooker with oil, using the SAUTE setting.
2. Season the lamb with salt and pepper. Put in the Instant Pot along with minced garlic. Cook until the lamb has browned all over.
3. Whisk the flour in quickly before slowly pouring in the stock.
4. Add rosemary and carrots. Seal the lid closed. Select MANUAL and adjust time to 20 minutes on HIGH pressure.
5. When the timer beeps, hit CANCEL and quick-release the pressure.
6. Open up the lid and pick out the rosemary stems.
7. Serve lamb with plenty of sauce.

Garlic Lamb Shanks

(Prep + Cook Time: 70 minutes | Servings: 4)

Ingredients:

- 4 pounds lamb shanks
- 1 cup chicken broth
- 1 cup port pine
- 20 peeled, whole garlic cloves
- 2 tbsp tomato paste
- 2 tbsp butter
- 2 tsp balsamic vinegar
- 1 tsp dried rosemary
- Salt and pepper to taste

Directions:

1. Trim any fat you don't want from the lamb and season generously with salt and pepper.
2. Heat oil in your Instant Pot on the SAUTE setting, and when hot, add the lamb. Brown all over.

3. When the lamb is golden, add garlic and stir until they've browned. Pour in port and stock, and stir in tomato paste and rosemary.
4. When the tomato paste has dissolved, close and seal the lid. Select MANUAL and cook on high pressure for 32 minutes.
5. When time is up, hit CANCEL and wait for a natural pressure release. Carefully remove lamb.
6. Turn the pot back to SAUTE to boil the cooking liquid. Boil for 5 minutes to reduce it down and thicken. Mix in butter, and then vinegar.
7. Serve with sauce poured over the lamb.

Lamb Shanks With Figs and Ginger
(Prep + Cook Time: 1 hour 50 minutes | Servings: 4)

Ingredients:
- 2 tbsp coconut oil
- 4 pieces (12 oz) lamb shanks
- 1 onion, large-sized, sliced thinly pole-to-pole
- 2 tbsp fresh ginger, minced
- 2 tbsp coconut aminos
- 2 tbsp apple cider vinegar
- 2 tsp fish sauce
- 2-3 cloves garlic, finely minced
- 1 ½ cups bone broth
- 10 dried figs, stems cut off and cut lengthwise into halves

Directions:
1. Press the SAUTE key of the Instant Pot. When hot, put in 1 tablespoon coconut oil in the pot.
2. Put 2 pieces lamb shanks in the pot and cook until all sides are browned, occasionally turning the meat. Transfer into a bowl or a plate. Repeat the process with the remaining tablespoon coconut oil and lamb shanks.
3. Put the ginger and the onion in the pot. Cook, stirring often, for about 3 minutes or until the onion is soft. Stir in the garlic, fish

sauce, vinegar, and coconut aminos. Stir in the broth and scrape the browned bits off from the bottom of the pot.

4. Add the figs as return the brown shanks, along with the meat juices collected in the bowl/ plate, in the pot.
5. Make sure that the meaty part of the shanks are at least partially submerged in the cooking liquid. Press the CANCEL key to stop the sauté function. Cover and lock the lid.
6. Press the MANUAL key, set the pressure to HIGH, and set the timer for 1 hour.
7. When the Instant Pot timer beeps, turn off and release the pressure naturally for 10-15 minutes or until the valve drops. Turn the steam valve to VENTING to release remaining pressure.
8. Unlock and carefully open the lid. Transfer the shanks into a serving platter.
9. Skim the fat off from the surface of the sauce and discard.
10. Alternatively, you can pour the sauce in a fat separator. Ladle the de-fatted sauce over the shanks.
11. Serve with cauliflower rice or white rice.

Mediterranean Lamb

(Prep + Cook Time: 1 hour 30 minutes | Servings: 4)

Ingredients:
- 6 pound lamb leg, boneless
- 2 tbsp extra virgin olive oil
- Salt and black pepper, to taste
- 1 bay leaf
- 1 tsp marjoram
- 1 tsp sage, dried
- 1 tsp ginger, grated
- 3 garlic cloves, minced
- 1 tsp thyme, dried
- 2 cups veggie stock
- 3 pounds potatoes, chopped
- 3 tbsp arrowroot powder mixed with
- 1/3 cup water

Directions:
1. Set your Instant Pot to SAUTE mode, add the oil, and heat it up.

2. Add the lamb leg and brown on all sides. Add salt, pepper, bay leaf, marjoram, sage, ginger, garlic, thyme, and stock. Stir, cover the pot, and cook at HIGH pressure for 50 minutes.
3. Release the pressure quickly, then add potatoes, arrowroot mixture, and more salt and pepper if needed. Stir, cover again, and cook at HIGH pressure for 10 minutes.
4. Release the pressure again, uncover the pot, and divide Mediterranean lamb on plates and serve.

Mexican Lamb

(Prep + Cook Time: 1 hour 15 minutes | Servings: 4)

Ingredients:
- 3 pounds lamb shoulder, cubed
- 19 oz enchilada sauce
- 3 garlic cloves, minced
- 1 yellow onion, chopped
- 2 tbsp extra virgin olive oil
- Salt, to taste
- ½ bunch cilantro, finely chopped
- Corn tortillas, warm for serving
- Lime wedges, for serving
- Refried beans, for serving

Directions:
1. Put enchilada sauce in a bowl, add the lamb meat, and marinate for 24 hours.
2. Set your Instant Pot to SAUTE mode, add the oil, and heat it up. Add onions and garlic, stir and cook for 5 minutes.
3. Add lamb, salt, and all the marinade. Stir, bring to a boil, cover the pot, and cook at HIGH pressure for 45 minutes.
4. Release the pressure naturally, take meat out, and put on a cutting board to cool down for a few minutes.
5. Shred meat and put in a bowl. Add the cooking sauce to the meat, and stir.
6. Divide meat between the tortillas, sprinkle cilantro on each, add beans, squeeze lime juice, roll, and serve.

English Lamb Shanks
(Prep + Cook Time: 45 minutes | Servings: 4)

Ingredients:

- 4-6 lamb shanks
- 4 tbsp flour
- 3 thickly sliced carrots
- 1 chopped onion
- 1 crushed garlic clove
- 1 tbsp freshly chopped oregano
- 1 tsp grated lemon rind
- 6 oz red wine
- 4 tbsp vegetable stock
- 8 tsp cold water – helps thicken the gravy
- Salt and pepper to taste

Directions:

1. First, peel the potatoes and cut into quarters.
2. Then, coat the shanks in flour. The easiest way to coat the shanks is to add flour to a large freezer bag. Place the shanks in the bag and shake. Shake to remove any excess flour.
3. Heat half of the oil in the bottom of your Instant Pot.
4. Then, brown the shanks. You should be able to add two shanks at a time. After browning the shanks, set them aside.
5. Add the remaining oil to the bottom of your pressure cooker.
6. Next, add the onions, garlic, and carrots. Sauté the vegetables for 5 minutes while stirring occasionally.
7. Add the tomatoes, oregano, and lemon rind. Then, stir in the wine and stock.
8. Bring the mixture to a boil while stirring. Boil for a few minutes. Place the lamb shanks back in the cooker and season with salt and pepper.
9. Use a spoon to spoon some of the liquid and veggies over the lamb shanks.
10. Close the lid to your pressure cooker and bring to HIGH pressure. Cook for 25 minutes. Allow the pressure to release naturally and then check the meat.
11. It should be very tender and falling off the bone. If needed, you can cook for a few more minutes.
12. If the gravy is too thin, you can thicken it by adding more flour and stirring until smooth.
13. Serve while still hot. You can serve the gravy on the side or pour it over the dish.

Lamb Stew

(Prep + Cook Time: 50 minutes | Servings: 6)

Ingredients:

- 2 lbs. lamb stew meat (you could substitute beef or goat), cut into 1" cubes
- 1 acorn squash
- 3 large carrot
- 1 large yellow onion
- 1 sprig rosemary (2 if it's small)
- 1 bay leaf
- 6 cloves garlic, sliced
- 3 tbsp broth or water
- ¼- ½ tsp salt, to taste (more if using water, less if using broth)

Directions:

1. Peel, seed and cube acorn squash. A nice trick is to microwave the whole squash for 1 minute.
2. This makes it easier to cut, seed and peel. Slice the carrots into thick circles. Peel the onion, cut in half, and then slice into half-moons.
3. Depending on whether you like your veggies softer or firmer in your stew, you can cut the pieces bigger (for firmer) or smaller (for softer).
4. Place all of the ingredients in your pressure cooker (yes, it's that easy).
5. Cook use the SOUP/STEW setting for 35 minutes.
6. Carefully release the pressure naturally before unlocking the lid.
7. Serve.

Fish with Orange & Ginger Sauce
(Prep + Cook Time: 17 minutes | Servings: 4)

Ingredients:
- 4 white fish fillets
- Juice and zest from 1 orange
- Thumb size piece of ginger, chopped
- 3 to 4 spring onions
- 1 tbsp olive oil
- Salt and pepper to taste
- 1 cup of fish stock or white wine

Directions:
1. Take your fish fillets and dry them with a paper towel.
2. Rub olive oil onto them and season lightly.
3. Add fish stock or white wine, spring onions, ginger, orange zest and juice into your pressure cooker.
4. Place fish into the steamer basket, pop the lid on, bring up to pressure and cook for 7 minutes.
5. Serve on top of an undressed garden salad, the sauce will dress it beautifully.

Mediterranean Tuna Pasta
(Prep + Cook Time: 30 minutes | Servings: 6)

Ingredients:
- 1 tbsp olive oil
- ½ cup chopped red onion
- 1 cup egg pasta (uncooked)
- 2 cup diced tomatoes
- 1 tbsp basil
- 1 tbsp garlic
- 1 tsp oregano
- 1 ½ cup water
- Salt and pepper to taste
- 7 oz tuna fish
- 7 oz marinated artichoke
- Crumbled feta cheese
- Fresh chopped parsley

Directions:
1. SAUTE the red onion for about 2 minutes.

2. Add the dry noodles, tomatoes, water, salt, and pepper then set your Instant Pot to SOUP for 10 minutes.
3. Turn off the warm setting and add tuna, artichokes and your reserved liquid from the artichokes and sauté on normal while stirring for about 4 more minutes till hot.
4. Top with a little feta cheese and parsley for your taste.

Tuna and Pasta Casserole

(Prep + Cook Time: 10 minutes | Servings: 2)

Ingredients:
- 1 can cream of mushroom soup
- 1 cup cheddar cheese, shredded
- 1 cups frozen peas
- 2 cans tuna
- 2 ½ cups macaroni pasta
- ½ tsp salt
- ½ tsp pepper
- 3 cups water

Directions:
1. Mix the soup with the water in the Instant Pot. Except for the cheese, add the rest of the ingredients. Stir to combine.
2. Lock the lid and turn the steam valve to SEALING. Press MANUAL, set the pressure to HIGH, and set the timer for 4 minutes.
3. When the timer beeps, turn the steam valve to VENTING to quickly release the pressure.
4. Unlock and open the lid. Sprinkle the cheese on top.
5. Close the lid and let sit for 5 minutes or until the cheese is melted and the sauce is thick.

Tuna and Capers Tomato Pasta

(Prep + Cook Time: 20 minutes | Servings: 2)

Ingredients:
- 1 can (15 ounces) fire-roasted diced tomatoes
- 1 can (3.5 ounces) solid tuna packed in vegetable oil
- 2 cups pasta, your choice (I used Orecchiette)
- 2 garlic cloves, sliced
- 2 tbsp olive oil
- 2 tbsp capers Grated parmesan
- Red wine (just enough to fill ½ of the tomato can)
- Salt and pepper
- Seasonings (I use oregano and dried chilies)

Directions:

1. Set the Instant Pot to SAUTE and wait until hot.
2. Add the garlic and sauté until fragrant. Add the pasta, seasonings, and tomatoes.
3. Fill the empty can of tomatoes with red wine until ½ full and then pour enough water into the can until full.
4. Pour the wine mix in the Instant Pot. Lock the lid and turn the steam valve to SEALING. Press the MANUAL key and set the timer for 6 minutes.
5. When the timer beeps, turn the steam valve to VENTING to quick release the pressure.
6. Carefully open the capers and tuna. Gently toss to combine.
7. Divide the pasta into serving bowls.

Steamed Fish Fillet

(Prep + Cook Time: 20 minutes | Servings: 4)

Ingredients:

- 4 white fish fillets
- 1.1 lb cherry tomatoes, sliced
- 1 cup olives
- 1 clove of garlic, crushed
- a large pinch of fresh thyme
- 1 tbsp olive oil
- Salt and pepper to taste

Directions:

1. Heat the Instant Pot and add a cup of water.
2. Put the fish fillets in a single layer in the steaming basket fitted for the pressure cooker.
3. Place the sliced cherry tomatoes and olives on top of the fillets. Add the crushed garlic, a few sprigs of fresh thyme, a dash of olive oil, and a little salt.
4. Put the steaming basket inside the pressure cooker. Seal the lid of the cooker properly.
5. Once it reaches pressure, reduce heat. Cook the fillets for 7-10 minutes on low pressure (or 3-5 minutes on high pressure).
6. When finished, release pressure through the normal release method.
7. Serve the fillets in separate bowls, sprinkled with the remaining thyme, pepper, and little amount of olive oil.

Teriyaki Salmon

(Prep + Cook Time: 20 minutes | Servings: 4)

Ingredients:

- 1 ½ cups boiling water
- 5 salmon fillets
- 2 oz dried mushrooms
- 4 washed and halved bok choy
- 3 sliced spring onions
- ¼ cup soy sauce
- 2 tbsp sweet rice wine
- 1 tbsp sesame oil
- 1 tbsp sugar

Directions:

1. Pour the boiling water over the mushrooms to rehydrate them.
2. Put the bok choy in your Instant Pot. Add everything else (minus the salmon) and mushrooms/ water on top.
3. Put the salmon on top. Close and seal the lid. Select MANUAL and cook for 4 minutes on HIGH pressure.
4. When time is up, press CANCEL and wait 10 minutes before quick-releasing.
5. Serve.

Salmon Steaks with Yogurt Tartar Sauce

(Prep + Cook Time: 10 minutes | Servings: 4)

Ingredients:

Tartar sauce:

- ¾ cup mayo
- ¾ cup plain Greek yogurt
- ⅓ cup dill pickle relish
- ¼ cup chopped green onions
- 3 tbsp chopped parsley

Salmon:

- 4 skin-on salmon steaks
- 1 cup water
- ¾ cup dry white wine
- 1 peeled and sliced onion

- 3 tbsp rinsed and chopped capers
- 3 tbsp lemon juice
- 1 tsp Dijon mustard
- Pinch of turmeric
- Pinch of black pepper

- 1 sliced lemon
- 1 wedge-cut lemon
- 1 tsp dried dill
- Salt and pepper to taste

Directions:

1. You want to make the tartar sauce first. Mix everything in the first ingredient list.

2. Store in the fridge for at least an hour before eating, so the flavors can blend really well.
3. Put the trivet and steamer basket in your Instant Pot.
4. Put onion slices in the basket, so they overlap like a mosaic on the bottom. Add steaks. Pour wine over the fish and add dill. Season with salt and pepper.
5. Put the slices of lemon on top and pour in water. Turn cooker on to SAUTE and bring the cooker to a boil for 1 minute.
6. Close and seal the lid. Select MANUAL and cook for 4 minutes on HIGH pressure.
7. When time is up, hit CANCEL and quick-release.
8. Remove the lemon slices and move salmon.
9. You can eat the onions if you want.
10. Serve with the tartar sauce and lemon wedges.

Salmon Al Cartoccio
(Prep + Cook Time: 35 minutes | Servings: 4)

Ingredients:
- 4 salmon fillets, fresh or frozen
- 3 tomatoes, sliced
- 1 lemon, sliced
- 1 white onion, shaved
- 4 sprigs of parsley
- 4 sprigs of thyme
- Olive oil
- Salt and pepper to taste

Directions:
1. Lay the ingredients on the parchment paper in this order: a swirl of oil, a layer of potatoes, salt, pepper and oil, fish fillets, salt, pepper and oil, herbs, onion rings, lemon slices, salt, and oil.
2. Fold the packet. Wrap the packet snugly in tinfoil.
3. Pour two cups of water in the pressure cooker. Place the steamer basket in position and lay the packet on the steamer.
4. Cook two fillets at a time.
5. Close the pressure cooker top. Turn to HIGH heat, and let it reach pressure. Then, turn down the heat to the lowest setting.
6. Cooking time should be between 12 to 15 minutes, after which you can release the vapor but do NOT open the top just yet.

7. Let the packets of fish sit inside the locked pan for another 5 minutes.
8. Open the top and take out the packets. Take off the tinfoil and serve.

Curried Fish Coconut Dish

(Prep + Cook Time: 30 minutes | Servings: 4)

Ingredients:

- 1 tbsp olive oil
- ½ pound fish fillets (e.g. cod)
- 1 sliced green chili
- 1 diced tomato
- 1 diced onion
- 1 minced garlic clove
- 3 curry leaves
- ½ tbsp grated ginger
- 1 tsp cumin
- ½ tsp turmeric
- ½ tsp chili powder
- 1/2 tbsp coriander
- ½ tsp ground fenugreek
- ½ cup coconut milk, unsweetened
- 1 tsp salt juice from
- ½ lemon

Directions:

1. Pour a bit of olive oil into your Instant Pot, and place the setting on medium-low heat. Ensure you keep the lid off at this time.
2. Add the curry leaves to the oil, and fry them until they're slightly golden. This should take one minute.
3. Next, add the garlic, ginger, and onion. Sauté well, stirring occasionally, until the onion is nearly clear.
4. Add the listed spices to the Instant Pot, stirring all the time, until the "flavor" of them reaches the air. You should be able to smell the richness of the spices.
5. Add the coconut milk to the Instant Pot to de-glaze, ensuring that nothing sticks to the bottom of the Instant Pot.
6. Add the tomatoes, the green chilies, and the pieces of fish. Stir well, coating the fish.
7. Place the lid on the Instant Pot. Set the pressure level to low. The moment the pressure reveals it has reached this low pressure, turn the pressure up to high.
8. When the Instant Pot reaches this high pressure, lower the heat back to low. Set the timer for five minutes at this time.

9. After five minutes, release the Instant Pot pressure with the normal method, by pushing out the vapor through the Instant Pot's valve.
10. Spritz the fish curry with lemon juice and salt, and serve.

Lemony Fish Fillets
(Prep + Cook Time: 30 minutes | Servings: 4)

Ingredients:
- 4 fish fillets
- 2 tbsp extra-virgin olive oil
- 1 tsp fine sea salt
- 1 tsp black pepper
- Lemon wedges, for serving
- 2 tbsps lemon juice

Directions:
1. Sprinkle salt and pepper on fish.
2. Drizzle lemon juice and oil, rub all over fish.
3. Place it into greased Instant Pot and let to cook for 15 minutes on pressure cooker.
4. Serve with lemon wedges.

Mediterranean Whitefish
(Prep + Cook Time: 15 minutes | Servings: 4)

Ingredients:
- 2 cups cherry tomatoes, halved
- 2 cloves garlic, crushed and minced
- 1 pound whitefish fillets
- ½ tsp sea salt
- 1 tsp coarsely ground black pepper
- 1 tsp oregano
- 1 cup onion, sliced
- 1 cup artichoke hearts, quartered
- 2 tbsp capers
- 1 tbsp olive oil

Directions:
1. Pour 1 ½ cups of water in the Instant Pot and place the steaming basket/ shelf inside the machine.
2. Lay out a large piece of parchment paper and fold over the edges to create a type of basket.

3. Combine the cherry tomatoes and garlic together, and lay them out on the parchment paper.
4. Place the fish on top and season it with salt, pepper, and oregano. Top the fish with the onion, artichoke hearts, and capers.
5. Drizzle the fish with the olive oil. Lower the parchment paper into the pot. Close the lid, turn MANUAL button and cook on HIGH pressure.
6. Cook for 8 minutes and then use the ten minute natural release method to dissipate the steam before serving.

Seafood Gumbo

Gumbo is like the Holy Grail. It's full of shrimp, crab, and oysters, and flavored with smoky sausage, peppers, onion, and garlic.

(Prep + Cook Time: 85 minutes | Servings: 6)

Ingredients:
- 6 cups fish stock
- 1 pound crab meat
- 1 pound peeled and cleaned shrimp
- 24 shucked oysters
- 2 chopped smoked sausages
- 3 chopped celery stalks
- 2 chopped red bell peppers
- 1 chopped onion
- ½ cup flour
- ½ cup chopped green onions
- ½ cup veggie oil
- ¼ cup chopped parsley
- 2 tbsp dried thyme
- 2 tbsp minced garlic cloves
- Salt and pepper to taste

Directions:
1. Turn on your Instant Pot to SAUTE and pour in 2 tablespoons of vegetable oil.
2. Add red pepper, celery, garlic, and onions.
3. When the veggies are browned, pour in the fish stock and add sausages, pepper, and thyme.
4. Close the Instant Pot lid and hit MANUAL and then 10 minutes. 5. When time is up, hit CANCEL. Quick-release.
5. In another skillet, heat up the rest of the oil and mix in the flour to make a roux.

6. Stir constantly until the flour becomes golden.
7. Take the skillet off the heat and mix in a bowl with some fish stock.
8. Pour into the Instant Pot and stir until the gumbo thickens.
9. Throw in the shrimp, oysters, and crab.
10. Lock the lid again and cook for just 1 minute on high pressure.
    12. Quick-release.
11. Serve the gumbo with greens onions, parsley, and rice.

Seafood Cranberries Plov
(Prep + Cook Time: 35 minutes | Servings: 4)

Ingredients:
- 1 package (16 ounces) frozen seafood blend, (I used Trader Joe's)
- 1 lemon, sliced
- 1 onion, large-sized, chopped
- 1 ½ cups basmati rice, organic
- 1 pepper, red or yellow, sliced
- ½ cup dried cranberries
- 2-3 tbsp butter
- 3 cups water
- 3-4 big shredded carrots
- Salt and pepper, to taste

Directions:
1. Press the SAUTE key of the Instant Pot and wait until the word HOT appears on the display. Put the butter in the pot.
2. Add the onion, carrots, pepper, and cook stirring for about 5-7 minutes.
3. Stir in the rice, seafood blend, and cranberries. Season generously and add 3 cups water. Press RICE and lock the lid.
4. Just before servings, squeeze fresh squeezed lemon juice over the dish.

Scallop Chowder
(Prep + Cook Time: 25 minutes | Servings: 4)

Ingredients:

- 2 pounds cut Yukon Gold
- 1 ½ pounds bay scallops
- 3 thin bacon slices
- 2 chopped celery stalks
- 1 chopped yellow onion
- 2 cups chicken broth
- 1 cup heavy cream
- 1 cup clam juice
- ½ cup dry white wine
- ¼ cup chopped parsley
- 2 bay leaves
- 2 tbsp butter
- 2 tbsp minced chives
- 1 tbsp fresh thyme leaves

Directions:

1. Fry the bacon in your Instant Pot on the SAUTE setting.
2. Move to a plate.
3. Add butter to the pot and melt.
4. Toss in celery and onion. Cook until soft.
5. Pour in clam juice, broth, and wine.
6. Deglaze.
7. Add potatoes, thyme, and bay leaves.
8. Secure and lock the lid.
9. Select HIGH pressure for 7 minutes.
10. When time is up, hit CANCEL and quick-release.
11. Open the lid.
12. Stir and turn to the SAUTE setting.
13. Crumble the bacon and add scallops, cream, chives, and parsley. Cook for 2 minutes while stirring the whole time.
14. Pick out bay leaves.
15. Serve and enjoy.

White Fish with Beer and Potatoes (S&F)
(Prep + Cook Time: 50 minutes | Servings: 6)

Ingredients:

- 1 pound white fish (like cod or pollock)
- 4 peeled and diced potatoes
- 1 cup beer 1 sliced red pepper
- 1 tbsp sugar
- 1 tbsp oil
- 1 tbsp oyster sauce
- 1 tsp salt

Directions:

1. Put everything in the Instant Pot.
2. Secure the lid.
3. Push BEAN.
4. Cook for 40 minutes.
5. When time is up, quick-release.
6. Serve and enjoy.

White Fish with Orange Sauce

(Prep + Cook Time: 40 minutes | Servings: 4)

Ingredients:

- 4 white fish fillets
- 4 spring onions, chopped
- A drizzle of extra virgin olive oil
- A small piece of ginger, chopped
- Salt and black pepper, to taste
- Juice and zest from
- 1 orange
- 1 cup fish stock

Directions:

1. Pat the fish fillets dry, then season with salt and pepper, and rub them with the olive oil.
2. Put the stock, ginger, orange juice, orange zest, and onions in your Instant Pot.
3. Put the fish fillets in the steamer basket, cover the pot, and cook at HIGH pressure for 7 minutes.
4. Quick release the pressure, divide fish between plates, and drizzle the orange sauce on top.
5. Serve.

Spanish Style Fish (S&F)

(Prep + Cook Time: 15 minutes | Servings: 4)

Ingredients:

- 4 fillets cod fish
- 1 pound cherry tomatoes, cut in halves
- 1 cup Taggiesche olives
- 2 garlic cloves, crushed
- 2 tbsp pickled capers
- 2 tbsp olive oil
- Couple sprigs fresh thyme
- Salt and black pepper to taste

216

Directions:
1. Take the large heatproof bowl that fits your Instant Pot. Place halved cherry tomatoes and Taggiesche olives at the bottom of the bowl.
2. Add a bunch of fresh thyme. Place the cod on top of the tomatoes.
3. Add the crushed garlic, sprinkle with the olive oil and a season with salt and black pepper.
4. Put the bowl inside the pressure cooker and cook at LOW pressure for about 5-7 minutes.
5. When the cooking time is up, use the natural release method to lower the pressure.
6. Serve in individual plates. Garnish with more cherry tomatoes and herbs on top.

Healthy Fish with Savory Sauce (S&F)
(Prep + Cook Time: 20 minutes | Servings: 4)

Ingredients:
- 4 white fish fillets
- Zest and juice from 1 orange
- Thumb size piece of ginger, chopped or grated
- 4 spring onions, chopped
- 2 tbsp olive oil
- Salt and freshly ground black pepper
- 1 cup of fish stock or white wine

Directions:
1. Rinse the fish fillets and dry them with kitchen towels.
2. Rub fillets with the olive oil and season them with salt and pepper lightly. In the large mixing bowl combine fish stock or white wine, spring onions, ginger, orange zest and juice.
3. Pour the mixture in the Instant Pot. Lay the fish fillets into the steamer basket secure the lid and cook at HIGH pressure for 6-7 minutes.
4. Using natural method, release pressure and open the lid.
5. Serve with fresh vegetables, garden salad and sauce which you like.

Salmon Fillets in Mayonnaise Sauce

(Prep + Cook Time: 15 minutes | Servings: 4)

Ingredients:

- ¼ cup mayonnaise
- 2 tbsp fresh lemon juice
- ½ tsp salt
- ½ tsp cayenne pepper
- 2 tbsp fresh parsley
- ¼ tsp ground black pepper, or more to taste
- 2 sprigs rosemary
- 2 sprigs thyme
- 1 pound salmon filets

Directions:

1. Sprinkle the salmon filets with cayenne pepper, salt, and ground black pepper.
2. Choose SAUTE mode and brown your filets on all sides for 5 minutes.
3. Place the rack at the bottom of your cooker. Add about 1 cup of water to the pot. Lay the browned salmon fillets on the rack.
4. Seal the cooker's lid and select the STEAM setting; cook for 4 minutes.
5. In the meantime, prepare the sauce.
6. Mix the remaining ingredients in a mixing bowl.
7. Then, pour the sauce over the filets.
8. Serve and enjoy.

Dijon Salmon

(Prep + Cook Time: 5 minutes | Servings: 2)

Ingredients:

- 2 pieces firm fish fillets or steaks, such as salmon, scrod, cod, or halibut
- 1 cup water
- 1 tsp Dijon mustard per fish fillet
- Steamer basket or trivet

Directions:

1. On the fleshy portion of the fish fillets, spread 1 teaspoon of Dijon mustard over. Pour 1 cup of water into the Instant Pot.
2. Set the steamer basket or trivet in the pot. With the skin side faced down, put the fish fillets in the steamer basket/ trivet.

3. Cover and lock the lid. Turn the steam valve to SEALING. Press MANUAL and set the timer according to the thickest fish fillet.
4. When the timer beeps, turn the steam valve to VENTING to quick release the pressure.
5. Serve.

Mustard Crusted Salmon

(Prep + Cook Time: 10 minutes | Servings: 4)

Ingredients:

- 1¼ lb salmon fillets, cut into four equal portions
- ¼ cup reduced fat sour cream
- 2 tbsp stone-ground mustard
- 2 tsp lemon juice
- Salt and pepper to taste

Directions:

1. Heat the Instant Pot and place the salmon fillets in the pot. Remember to keep the fish with the skin side down.
2. Make a paste with all the other ingredients and spread the mixture with a spoon over the fish fillets.
3. Close the pot and cook on HIGH pressure for 5 minutes. Let the pressure release naturally before removing the lid.
4. Serve the fish by garnishing with lime wedges.

Five-Spicer Tilapia

(Prep + Cook Time: 10 minutes | Servings: 4)

Ingredients:

- 1 lb tilapia fillets
- 1 tsp Chinese five-spice powder
- ¼ cup soy sauce
- 3 tbsp brown sugar
- 3 scallions, thinly sliced

Directions:

1. Sprinkle five-spice powder generously on both sides of the fish fillets and keep them aside. Blend soy sauce and brown sugar in a bowl and keep ready for use.

2. Heat some oil in the Instant Pot cooker and cook the tilapia fillets in the oil for some time.
3. Make sure that the sides of the fish fillets turn opaque and then turn over the fillets.
4. Pour in the sauce mixture and close the lid. Cook on HIGH pressure for 5 minutes and then let the pressure release naturally.
5. Open the lid and add the scallions.
6. Serve the fish warm.

Cod with Mango Salsa

(Prep + Cook Time: 40 minutes | Servings: 2)

Ingredients:

For the marinade:
- 2 frozen cod fillets
- 1 cup coconut milk
- 1 tbsp Thai green curry paste
- 1 tbsp fresh minced ginger
- 1 tbsp fish sauce
- 2 tsp brown sugar
- 1 tsp minced garlic
- Zest of one lime
- Juice of ½ lime

For the salsa:
- ¾ cup of diced mango
- 1 minced jalapeno chile
- 1 chopped scallion
- Juice of 1 lime

Directions:

1. Mix the marinade ingredients together and pour into a bag with the fillets. Store in the fridge for 30 minutes.
2. In the meantime, make the mango salsa. Pour 2 cups of water into the Instant Pot and lower in the steamer basket.
3. Wrap the fish tightly in foil (with a few lime slices) and put into the steamer.
4. Close the lid. Select MANUAL and cook on HIGH pressure for 10 minutes.
5. In the meantime, bring the marinade from the fish to a simmer in a saucepan on the stove.
6. When the timer goes off, hit CANCEL and quick-release.
7. Serve with mango salsa, a bit of simmered marinade, and chopped scallions.

Green Chili Mahi-Mahi Fillets

(Prep + Cook Time: 10 minutes | Servings: 2)

Ingredients:

- ¼ cup green chili enchilada sauce, homemade or store-brought
- 2 Mahi-Mahi fillets, thawed
- 2 pats butter
- Salt and Pepper, to taste

Directions:

1. Pour 1 cup water into the Instant Pot and set a steamer rack.
2. Grease the bottom of each mahi-mahi fillet with 1 pat butter, spreading the pat from end to end – this will prevent the fish from sticking to the rack.
3. Put the fillets on the rack. Spread ¼ cup enchilada sauce between each fillet using a pastry brush – cover them well.
4. Top with more enchilada sauce, if desired. Season fillets with salt and pepper. Lock the lid and close the steam valve.
5. Press MANUAL, set the pressure to HIGH, and set the timer for 5 minutes.
6. When the timer beeps, quickly release the pressure and transfer the fillets into serving plates on a bed of greens.

Shrimp Bisque

(Prep + Cook Time: 25 minutes | Servings: 4)

Ingredients:

- 2 pounds chopped shrimp (save shells)
- 4 cups water
- 1 peeled and minced onion
- 1 peeled and minced shallot
- ½ minced celery stalk
- ½ cup heavy cream
- 3 tarragon sprigs
- 2 thyme sprigs
- 3 tbsp flour
- 3 tbsp sherry
- 2 tbsp tomato paste
- Salt and pepper to taste

Directions:

1. Turn on the CHIECKEN/MEAT option on your pot and add butter.
2. Put in the shrimp shells, carrots, shallots, celery, and onion. Stir for 4 minutes.

3. Add tomato paste and flour. After 2 minutes, add everything else except shrimp, sherry, and cream.
4. Simmer for 3-4 minutes until it's thickened.
5. Close and seal the lid. Turn off CHIECKEN/MEAT and press SOUP/STEW. Cook for 10 minutes. When time is up, hit CANCEL and quick-release.
6. Strain out the soup and get rid of the shells and veggies, obviously saving the liquid, which is your soup.
7. Add cream, sherry, and shrimp bits. Turn back to CHIECKEN/MEAT and simmer for 2 minutes.
8. Season to taste before serving.

Shrimp Jambalaya
(Prep + Cook Time: 25 minutes | Servings: 4)

Ingredients:
- 8 oz raw shrimp
- 14 oz chicken broth
- 2 cups instant brown rice
- 16 oz bell pepper and onion mixture, sliced
- 8 oz andouille sausage, thickly sliced

Directions:
1. Press SAUTE button and heat olive oil in the Instant Pot cooker and cook the onion, pepper and sausage slices.
2. Cook till the vegetables become soft and then add chicken broth and rice in the pot.
3. Close the lid and cook on HIGH pressure for 18 minutes. Use the quick release valve to release the pressure and then open the lid.
4. Add the shrimps and close the lid once again.
5. Cook on HIGH pressure for 4 minutes and let the pressure release naturally.
6. Fluff the rice with a fork and serve warm.

Shrimp Creole

(Prep + Cook Time: 17 minutes | Servings: 4)

Ingredients:

- 1 can (28 ounces) crushed tomatoes
- 1 pound jumbo shrimp, frozen, peeled and deveined
- 1 onion, medium-sized, chopped
- 1 tsp thyme
- ¼ tsp cayenne pepper
- 2 cloves garlic, minced
- 2 stalks celery, diced
- 1 bay leaf
- 1 bell pepper, diced
- 1 tbsp tomato paste
- 1 tsp salt
- ½ tsp pepper
- 2 tsp olive oil

Directions:

1. Press the SAUTE key of the Instant Pot. Add the oil and heat.
2. When the oil is hot, add the vegetables and sauté for 3 minutes or until the veggies starts to soften. Add the tomato paste. Stir and cook for 1 minute.
3. Add the crushed tomatoes, shrimp, seasoning, and stir to combine. Lock the lid and close the steam valve.
4. Press MANUAL, set the pressure to HIGH, and set the timer to 1 minute. When the timer beeps, quick release the pressure.
5. Carefully open the lid. If the shrimp is not fully cooked, press the SAUTE key and cook the shrimp for 1 minute, constantly stirring. Serve over rice.

Shrimp Scampi (S&F)

(Prep + Cook Time: 5 minutes | Servings: 4)

Ingredients:

- 1 pound frozen wild-caught shrimp
- 1 cup jasmine rice
- 1 ½ cups water
- 4 minced garlic cloves
- ¼ cup chopped parsley
- ¼ cup butter
- 1 medium, juiced lemon
- 1 pinch saffron
- Salt to taste
- Pepper to taste
- Red pepper flakes

Directions:

1. Mix everything in your pressure cooker, leaving the shells on the shrimp.

2. Close the lid and select MANUAL and cook 5 minutes on HIGH pressure.
3. When time is up, quick-release.
4. When you can touch the shrimp, peel off the shells.
5. Serve with parsley and grated cheese.

Shrimp Paella
(Prep + Cook Time: 25 minutes | Servings: 4)

Ingredients:
- 20 shrimp, deveined
- 1 cup jasmine rice
- ¼ cup butter
- Salt and black pepper, to taste
- ¼ cup parsley, chopped
- A pinch of crushed red pepper
- A pinch of saffron
- Juice of 1 lemon
- 1½ cups water
- 4 garlic cloves, minced
- Melted butter, for serving
- Hard cheese, grated for serving
- Parsley, chopped

Directions:
1. Put shrimp in your Instant Pot. Add rice, butter, salt, pepper, parsley, red pepper, saffron, lemon juice, water, and garlic.
2. Stir, cover, and cook at HIGH pressure for 5 minutes.
3. Release pressure, uncover pot, take out shrimps, and peel them.
4. Return to pot, stir well and divide into bowls.
5. Add melted butter, cheese and parsley on top and serve.

Shrimp Curry
(Prep + Cook Time: 50 minutes | Servings: 4)

Ingredients:
- 1 pound big shrimp, peeled and deveined
- 1/3 cup butter
- 2 bay leaves
- 1 cinnamon stick
- 10 cloves
- 3 cardamom pods
- 2 red onions, chopped
- 14 red chilies, dried
- 3 green chilies, chopped
- ½ cup cashews
- 1 tbsp garlic paste
- 1 tbsp ginger paste
- 4 tomatoes, chopped
- Salt, to taste
- 1 tsp sugar
- 1 tsp fenugreek leaves, dried
- ½ cup cream

Directions:

1. Set your Instant Pot to SAUTE mode, add butter, and melt it. Add bay leaves, cardamom, cinnamon stick, and onion, stir and cook for 3 minutes.
2. Add red chilies, green chilies, cashews, tomatoes, garlic paste, and ginger paste, and stir.
3. Add salt, then stir, cover and cook at HIGH pressure for 15 minutes. Release the pressure, transfer everything to your blender, and pulse well.
4. Strain into a pan and heat it up over medium high heat.
5. Add shrimp, stir, cover and cook for 12 minutes.
6. Add fenugreek, cream, and sugar, then stir and cook for 2 minutes.
7. Take off heat and divide among plates. Serve.

Shrimp with Rice

(Prep + Cook Time: 35 minutes | Servings: 4)

Ingredients:

- 1 jalapeno chopped pepper
- 2 cups finely chopped tomatoes
- 1 tbsp olive oil
- 1½ pounds peeled and deveined shrimp
- ¼ tsp crushed red pepper flakes
- Pinch of salt
- 1 cup chicken broth
- ¼ cup chopped scallion
- 1 large red bell pepper
- 2 chopped celery stalks
- 2 minced garlic cloves
- 1 cup long grain white rice

Directions:

1. Pour the oil in the Instant Pot and select SAUTE.
2. Then add the shrimp and sprinkle with half the red pepper flakes, a pinch of salt and black pepper. Cook for about 4 minutes.
3. Transfer the shrimp into a bowl.
4. Then add onion, bell pepper and celery, and cook for about 5 minutes. Add garlic, jalapeño, remaining red pepper flakes and black pepper, and sauté for about 1 minute.

5. Select CANCEL and stir in the tomatoes, rice and broth, then mix thoroughly. Set HIGH pressure and cook for about 7 minutes.
6. Select the CANCLE button and carefully do a quick release. Remove the lid and immediately stir in the cooked shrimp.
7. Secure the lid right away and keep aside for about 5 minutes before serving.

Crispy Skin Salmom Fillet
(Prep + Cook Time: 15 minutes | Servings: 2)

Ingredients:
- 2 salmon fillets, frozen (1-inch thickness)
- 1 cup tap water, running cold
- 2 tbsp olive oil
- Salt and pepper, to taste

Directions:
1. Pour 1 cup water in the Instant Pot. Set the steamer rack and put the salmon fillets in the rack. Lock the lid and close the steamer valve. Press MANUAL, set the pressure on LOW, and set the timer for 1 minute.
2. When the timer beeps, turn off the pot and quick release the pressure.
3. Carefully open the lid. Remove the salmon fillets and pat them dry using paper towels.
4. Over medium-high heat, preheat a skillet. Grease the salmon fillet skins with 1 tablespoon olive oil and generously season with black pepper and salt.
5. When the skillet is very hot, with the skin side down, put the salmon fillet in the skillet.
6. Cook for 1-2 minutes until the skins are crispy. Transfer the salmon fillets into serving plates and serve with your favorite side dishes.
7. This dish is great with rice and salad.

Trout Hash

(Prep + Cook Time: 10 minutes | Servings: 4)

Ingredients:

- 1 lb boiled and diced potatoes
- 4 oz smoked trout, flaked
- 2 tbsp whole grain mustards
- 4 cups sliced mustard greens
- 2 tbsp cider vinegar

Directions:

1. You will have to heat olive oil in the Instant Pot and sauté the boiled potatoes till they become golden in color and crispy.
2. Whisk mustard, vinegar along with salt and pepper in a bowl and add it into the pot.
3. Add trout flakes and mustard greens and close the lid of the cooker. Cook on MANUAL setting for 2 minutes and then quick release the pressure.
4. Open the lid and check if the hash is moist enough.
5. You can add 2 tablespoons of water and cook on SAUTE setting without the lid for a minute if the hash seems too dry.
6. Serve the dish warm.

Sausage and Seafood Delight (S&F)

(Prep + Cook Time: 15 minutes | Servings: 6)

Ingredients:

- 2 corn on the cobs, quartered
- 6 medium-sized potatoes, peeled and diced 16 clams
- 3 ½ cups water
- ½ tsp ground black pepper, or more to taste
- 1 tsp salt
- ¾ cup vegetable stock
- 1 bay leaf
- 2 ½ pounds shrimp
- 1 ½ pounds smoked sausage, sliced
- 1 cup fresh chopped chives, as garnish

Directions:

1. Simply place all the ingredients, except for chives, into the inner pot of your cooker.
2. Press the BEANS button; cook for about 16 minutes.
3. Serve sprinkled with chopped chives.

Clam Rolls

(Prep + Cook Time: 5 minutes | Servings: 4)

Ingredients:

- 4 hot dog buns
- 8 romaine lettuce leaves
- 24 scrubbed littleneck clams
- 3 sliced celery stalks
- 1 stemmed, cored, and chopped red bell pepper
- 4 tbsp melted and cooled butter
- ¼ cup plain Greek yogurt
- ¼ cup mayonnaise
- 2 tbsp lemon juice
- ½ tsp black pepper
- ½ tsp dried dill

Directions:

1. Pour 1 ½ cups water into the Instant Pot and add the clams. Close and lock the lid. Select MANUAL and cook for 4 minutes on HIGH pressure.
2. When time is up, hit CANCEL and quick-release.
3. Pour the Instant Pot contents into a colander in a sink. Cool.
4. In a bowl, mix the bell pepper, yogurt, mayo, celery, lemon juice, pepper, dill, and a few dashes of hot sauce.
5. Pull the meat from their shells, chop, and mix into the dressing.
6. Brush the inside of the hot dog buns with butter.
7. Heat a skillet and toast the buns.
8. Fill buns with lettuce and clam salad.

Quick Seafood Paella

(Prep + Cook Time: 30 minutes | Servings: 4)

Ingredients:

- 2 cups short-grain rice
- 1 ¾ cups veggie stock
- 2 cups mixed seafood (shrimp, clams, etc.)
- 1 cup seafood (like scallops and white fish)
- 1 diced green bell pepper
- turmeric
- 1 diced red bell pepper
- 1 diced yellow onion
- 4 tbsp olive oil
- 2 tsp sea salt
- ½ tsp paprika
- ¼ tsp ground

Directions:
1. Heat your Instant Pot on the SAUTE function and heat oil.
2. When the oil is shiny and hot, add peppers and onion. Cook for about 4 minutes, or until the onions have softened.
3. Add saffron, seafood, and rice. Cook for 2 minutes.
4. Pour in stock, salt, and turmeric. Stir before adding the mixed shellfish on top, without stirring it in.
5. Close and seal the lid. Select MANUAL and adjust time to 6 minutes on HIGH pressure.
6. When the timer beeps, hit CANCEL and wait 15 minutes.
7. Release any remaining pressure.
8. Stir and wait 1 minute before serving.

Caramelized Haddock
(Prep + Cook Time: 50 minutes | Servings: 4)

Ingredients:
- 1 pound of haddock
- 3 garlic cloves Just under
- 1 cup of coconut water
- 1 minced red chili
- 1 minced spring onion
- ⅓ cup water
- ¼ cup white sugar
- 3 tbsp fish sauce
- 2 tsp black pepper

Directions:
1. Marinate the fish in garlic, fish sauce, and pepper for at least 30 minutes.
2. Put the sugar and regular water in the Instant Pot and heat on the lowest setting until the sugar has browned into a caramel.
3. Add fish and coconut water to the cooker.
4. Close and seal lid. Click on MANUAL and cook on high pressure for 10 minutes.
5. When time is up, hit CANCEL and wait for the pressure to come down on its own.
6. Serve with chili and onion.

Mustard Trout

(Prep + Cook Time: 10 minutes | Servings: 4)

Ingredients:

- 1¼ lb trout fillets
- ¼ cup reduced fat sour cream
- 2 tbsp stone-ground mustard
- 2 tsp lemon juice
- Salt and pepper

Directions:

1. Heat the Instant Pot and place the trout fillets in the pot.
2. Make a paste with all the other ingredients and spread the mixture with a spoon over the fish fillets.
3. Close the pot and cook on HIGH pressure for 5 minutes.
4. Let the pressure release naturally before removing the lid.
5. Serve the fish by garnishing with lime wedges.

Oysters in the Shell (S&F)

(Prep + Cook Time: 15 minutes | Servings: 6)

Ingredients:

- 36 in-shell oysters
- 6 tbsp melted butter
- Salt and pepper to taste

Directions:

1. Clean the oysters. Toss in the Instant Pot with 1 cup of water.
2. Select MANUAL and cook on high pressure for 3 minutes.
3. When time is up, hit CANCEL and quick-release.
4. Serve right away with melted butter.

Cheesy Tuna

(Prep + Cook Time: 15 minutes | Servings: 6)

Ingredients:

- 1 can (5 ounces) tuna, drained
- 1 cup frozen peas
- ¼ cup bread crumbs (optional)
- 16 oz egg noodles
- 28 oz canned cream mushroom soup
- 3 cups water
- 4 oz cheddar cheese

Directions:

1. Put the noodles in the Instant Pot. Pour in the water to cover the noodles.
2. Add the frozen peas, tuna, and the soup on top of the pasta layer. Cover and lock the lid. Turn the steam valve to SEALING. Press the MANUAL key, set the pressure to HIGH, and set the timer for 4 minutes.
3. When the Instant Pot timer beeps, press the CANCEL key and unplug the Instant Pot.
4. Using an oven mitt or a long handled spoon, turn the steam valve to VENTING to quick release the pressure.
5. Unlock and carefully open the lid. Stir in the cheese.
6. If desired, you can pour the pasta mixture in a baking dish, sprinkle the top with bread crumbs, and broil for about 2 to 3 minutes. Serve.

Crab Legs

(Prep + Cook Time: 20 minutes | Servings: 6)

Ingredients:

- 2 pound of crab legs
- 1 cup of water
- 1 cup of white wine
- Lemon wedges
- Melted butter

Directions:

1. Pour the water and wine into the inner pot
2. Put in the crab legs Set the pot at HIGH pressure and let it cook for 7 minutes.
3. Once done, simply wait for 10 minutes and let the pressure release naturally.
4. Open and top it up with some melted butter and dashes of sherry.

?

Zucchini Soup (VEG)
(Prep + Cook Time: 30 minutes | Servings: 2)

Ingredients:
- 2 tbsp extra virgin olive oil
- 1 large onion - coarsely chopped
- 2 cloves garlic - crushed
- 2 small potatoes (1/2 lb) - cut in 1/2" cubes
- 2 large carrots - cut in 1/2" slices
- 4 large zucchini (2 lbs) - cut in 1" slices
- 4 cups vegetable stock - or bouillon
- 1 tbsp minced fresh basil - or
- 1 tsp dried basil
- Salt and pepper to taste

Directions:
1. Heat the oil in the pressure cooker. Sauté the onions and garlic for 1 minute.
2. Add the potatoes and sauté for another 1 to 2 minutes.
3. Add the remaining ingredients and stir to blend.
4. Lock the lid in place and over high heat bring to high pressure. Adjust the heat to maintain high pressure and cook for 5 minutes.
5. Let the pressure drop naturally or use a quick-release method. Remove the lid, tilting it away from you too and pepper to taste.
6. Serve and enjoy.

Creamy Tomato Soup (VEG)

(Prep + Cook Time: 40 minutes | Servings: 2)

Ingredients:

- 3 tbsp extra virgin olive oil
- 2 medium onions, chopped
- 2 medium carrots, skin peeled and chopped
- 3 large garlic cloves, finely chopped
- 2 cups of chopped ripe tomatoes
- 1 tbsp sugar
- 2 tbsp tomato paste
- 1 cup vegetable broth (or chicken)
- Salt and black pepper, as needed
- ½ cup heavy cream
- 3-4 Fresh basil leaves, as garnish
- ½ cup Parmesan cheese, grated (optional)

Directions:

1. Preheat the pot by selecting SAUTE.
2. Pour in the oil. Once hot, add carrots and onions.
3. Cook for 7 minutes or until onions become tender.
4. Toss in the garlic and stir until fragrant.
5. Pour in tomato paste, chopped tomatoes, broth, sugar, pepper and salt, mix and secure the lid.
6. Select MANUAL and cook on HIGH for about 20 minutes.
7. Once done, release pressure naturally and open lid.
8. Pour in the cream, and puree the mix (using an immersion blender if you have one) to get a creamy soup.
9. Garnish with torn basil leaves and cheese.
10. Serve hot.

Minestrone Soup (S&F)

(Prep + Cook Time: 45 minutes | Servings: 4)

Ingredients:
- 1 ¼ cups cooked beans
- 1 quart beef broth
- 25 ounces canned tomatoes, crushed
- 1 cup carrots, trimmed and thinly sliced
- 2 potatoes, diced
- ½ celery stalks, chopped
- 2 cloves garlic, minced
- 1 cup onions, chopped
- 1 ¼ pounds ground beef
- ¼ tsp ground black pepper
- ½ tsp sea salt

Directions:
1. Add the ingredients to your Instant Pot and stir to combine.
2. Put the lid on; choose MANUAL and HIGH pressure for 25 minutes.
3. Serve warm and enjoy.

Tortilla Soup

(Prep + Cook Time: 45 minutes | Servings: 10)

Ingredients:
- 2 tbsp vegetable oil
- 2 large onions, chopped
- 1 (12 ounce) jar roasted red peppers, drained and chopped
- 1 (4 ounce) can roasted jalapeno peppers, diced
- 1 clove garlic, minced
- 1 tbsp ground black pepper salt to taste
- 4 cups diced tomatoes
- 1 (32 fluid ounce) container chicken stock
- 1 cup heavy whipping cream
- 1 cup chopped fresh cilantro
- 1 (14.5 ounce) package tortilla chips
- 1 cup sour cream (optional)
- 1 (8 oz) package shredded queso quesadilla (white Mexican cheese)

Directions:

1. Heat vegetable oil in Instant Pot over medium heat; cook and stir onions until slightly softened - 5 to 8 minutes.
2. Add red peppers, jalapeno peppers, garlic, black pepper, and salt; cook until garlic is fragrant and onions are softened, about 5 more minutes.
3. Stir tomatoes into onion mixture and cook until warmed, about 1 minute.
4. Transfer tomato mixture to a blender. Cover and hold lid down; pulse a few times before leaving on to blend. Puree in batches until smooth.
5. Transfer tomato puree back to pressure cooker. Stir chicken stock into tomato puree; cook and stir over high heat until just boiling, about 5 minutes.
6. Cover and lock Instant Pot. Cook over high heat until steam begins to build and steadily escapes. Lower heat to medium-low, cook for 20 more minutes.
7. Remove from heat, allow all the steam to release naturally.
8. Remove lid. Bring soup to a boil. Stir in cream and cilantro.
9. Remove from heat. Let cool for 5 minutes.
10. Crush tortilla chips into serving bowls; pour soup over tortilla chips. Top with sour cream and queso quesadilla.
11. Serve and enjoy.

Spanish Bean Soup

(Prep + Cook Time: 85 minutes | Servings: 8)

Ingredients:

- 1 tbsp olive oil
- 1 ½ cups chopped onion
- 5 garlic cloves, minced
- 4 oz Spanish chorizo, diced
- 2 ½ cups water
- 2 ½ cups fat-free, lower-sodium chicken broth
- 1 ½ cups dried beans
- 2 bay leaves
- 6 cups chopped escarole
- 1 tbsp sherry vinegar
- ½ tsp kosher salt
- ½ tsp freshly ground black pepper
- ¼ tsp crushed red pepper

Directions:

1. Heat a 6-quart Instant Pot over medium-high heat. Add oil to pan; swirl to coat.
2. Add onion; sauté 3 minutes.
3. Add garlic and chorizo; sauté 2 minutes.
4. Stir in 2 ½ cups water, broth, garbanzo beans, and bay leaves.
5. Close lid securely; bring to HIGH pressure over high heat. Adjust heat to medium or level needed to maintain high pressure; cook 1 hour.
6. Remove from heat; release pressure through steam vent Remove lid.
7. Discard bay leaves. Add escarole and remaining ingredients, stirring just until escarole.
8. Serve immediately.

Red Pepper Soup
(Prep + Cook Time: 27 minutes | Servings: 6)

Ingredients:
- 6 red bell peppers cut into short, thin strips
- 4 tomatoes cut into short, thin strips
- 1 potato, cut into short, thin strips
- 2 red onions cut into short, thin strips
- 4 clove garlic minced
- 3 cups water
- 3 cups chicken stock
- 1 cup dry white wine
- 3 tbsp olive oil
- Salt and ground black pepper to taste

Directions:
1. Put the inner pot into the Instant Pot. Press the SOUP. Set time to 15 min.
2. Place in the red peppers, garlic and onion. Cook for three-four minutes; add the tomatoes and white wine and cook for two-three minutes more
3. Add the chicken stock, water and potato.

4. Put the lid, close the top and switch the weight discharge valve.
5. Once the clock achieves 0, the cooker will consequently change to KEEP WARM. Press the CANCEL Button. Make sure that all the steam has dissipated from the cooker and the Pressure Release Valve.
6. Open the lid and transfer the soup in a blender. Blend for one-two minutes until smooth and creamy.
7. Serve hot.

Wholesome Tomato Soup
(Prep + Cook Time: 40 minutes | Servings: 2)

Ingredients:
- 3 tbsp extra virgin olive oil
- 2 medium onions, chopped
- 2 medium carrots, skin peeled and chopped
- 3 large garlic cloves, finely chopped
- 2 cups of chopped ripe tomatoes
- 1 tbsp sugar
- 2 tbsp tomato paste
- 1 cup chicken or vegetable broth
- Kosher salt Black pepper, as needed
- ½ cup heavy cream
- 3-4 Fresh basil leaves, as garnish
- ½ cup Parmesan cheese, grated (optional)

Directions:
1. Preheat the pot by selecting SAUTE. Pour in the oil. Once hot, add carrots and onions. Cook for 7 minutes or until onions become tender.
2. Toss in the garlic and stir until fragrant. Pour in tomato paste, chopped tomatoes, broth, sugar, pepper and salt, stir and secure the lid.
3. Select MANUAL and cook on HIGH pressure for about 20 minutes.
4. Once done, release pressure naturally and open lid.
5. Pour in the cream, and puree the mix (using an immersion blender if you have one) to get a creamy soup.
6. Garnish with torn basil leaves and cheese. Serve hot.

Pork ribs soup with peas

(Prep + Cook Time: 60 minutes | Servings: 6)

Ingredients:

- 1 pound pork ribs
- 1 cup peas, soaked
- 1 carrot
- 1 stalk celery
- 2 onions
- 2 potatoes
- 2 cloves of garlic
- 8-10 cups water
- 2 tbsp olive oil
- Salt and pepper, to taste
- fresh parsley, for garnish

Directions:

1. Cut the pork ribs into pieces (along with the bones). Rinse the peas. Peel and cut the potatoes into cubes (3/4"). Peel and grate the carrot, chop the onions and the celery stalk, mince the garlic.
2. Take off the lid of your Instant Pot and press SAUTE button to pre-heat the inner pot of the cooker (use Normal mode).
3. As soon as the words HOT appear on display add the olive oil. In a minute put in the pork ribs and brown them on all sides (it will take about 10 min), then remove the ribs from the cooker to a bowl, leaving the hot oily liquid in the pot.
4. Continue to use SAUTE function, add the onions and the garlic, stir and roast them for 1 min. Add the carrot, the celery, the potatoes, the peas, salt, pepper, and stir.
5. Then put in the ribs and pour in water (hot or warm preferred).
6. Cancel SAUTE function, close and lock the lid, press MANUAL button and set 20 minutes high-pressure cooking time.
7. When time is up, open the cooker using 10-minute Natural Release way and serve warm, garnished with chopped parsley.

Lentil Vegetable Soup (VEG)

(Prep + Cook Time: 60 minutes | Servings: 6)

Ingredients:
- 1 tbsp olive oil
- 1 clove garlic, minced
- 1 small onion, minced
- 1 medium potato (Peeled & Cubed)
- 2 medium carrots (Cubed)
- 1 small sweet potato (Peeled & Cubed)
- 5 cups water
- 1 cup lentil blend
- 1 bay leaf
- 1 tsp marjoram
- 1 tsp thyme
- ¼ tsp rosemary powder
- ½ tsp smoked paprika
- ¼ cup nutritional yeast
- Salt and pepper, to taste

Directions:
1. Turn on the Instant Pot and use the SAUTE function. Heat olive oil, then sauté your onion until translucent.
2. Add garlic and sauté 1 to 2 minutes.
3. Turn off the SAUTE function and add all of your soup ingredients. Put the lid on and make sure the vent is closed. Press the MANUAL button and set to cook for approximately 10 minutes.
4. Once the cooking time is over, allow it to release the pressure naturally.
5. Stir in your yeast, salt, and pepper.
6. Serve and Enjoy.

Chicken Soup (S&F)

(Prep + Cook Time: 40 minutes | Servings: 4)

Ingredients:
- 2-3 pounds chicken, pastured and free roaming
- 2 carrots, roughly chopped
- ¼ turnip OR radish, cut into
- 2-inch cubes
- 2 bay leaves
- 1 tsp freshly ground black pepper
- 1 tbsp sea salt
- 1 tbsp Italian seasoning OR equal mixture of dried
- rosemary, oregano, parsley, and thyme
- 1 stalk celery, roughly chopped
- 1 medium onion, sliced or diced
- 3 cloves garlic, crushed
- Purple onion, thinly sliced OR scallion, finely chopped, to garnish

Directions:

1. In the Instant Pot's inner pot, add the veggies. Top with the chicken and then top the herbs on the chicken.
2. Pour in 4-5 cups of cold water. Close and lock the lid. Turn the steam valve to SEALING.
3. Press SOUP and set the time to 20 minutes. When the timer beeps, let the pressure release naturally for about 20-30 minutes.
4. Turn the steam valve to VENTING to release remaining pressure.
5. Carefully open the lid. Take the chicken out and remove the meat from the bone. Reserve the bone to make bone broth.
6. Return the meat into the pot. Stir to mix. With the back of a spoon, crush the celery and the carrots against the side of the pot.
7. Season to taste with salt and pepper.
8. Garnish with thinly sliced scallions and onions before serving.

Chicken Curry Soup (S&F)

(Prep + Cook Time: 30 minutes | Servings: 4)

Ingredients:

- 1 cup coconut milk
- 3 cups water
- 2 portions curry sauce mix
- 1 tsp ground ginger
- 12 oz mix of frozen broccoli, carrots, water chestnut
- 6 oz frozen okra
- 6 oz cooked chicken breast

Directions:

1. Place all ingredients in the Instant Pot cooker and select SOUP option.
2. After 20 minutes your tasty soup will be ready.
3. Serve and Enjoy.

Chicken Cream Chesse Chili

(Prep + Cook Time: 30 minutes | Servings: 6)

Ingredients:

- 1 can black beans, drained and rinsed (15 ounces)
- 1 can corn, undrained (15.25 ounces)
- 1 can rotel, undrained (10 ounces)
- 1 pound chicken breasts, boneless skinless
- 1 package dry ranch seasoning (1 ounce)
- 2 tsp cumin, or to taste
- 2 tsp chili powder, or to taste

Directions:

1. Put all the ingredients in the Instant Pot. Lock the lid and close the steam valve.
2. Set the pressure to high and set the timer for 20 minutes.
3. When the timer beeps, let the pressure release for 10-15 minutes. Open the steam valve to release any remaining pressure from the pot.
4. Carefully open the lid. Remove the chicken and shred. Break up the cream cheese and stir into the pot. Cover and let the cheese melt.
5. When the cheese is melted, open the lid and return the shredded meat in the pot.
6. Stir everything to mix.

Buffalo Chicken Soup

(Prep + Cook Time: 15 minutes | Servings: 2)

Ingredients:

- 2 boneless skinless chicken breasts
- 3 cups chicken bone-broth
- ½ cup diced celery
- ¼ cup diced onion
- 1 clove garlic, chopped
- 1 tbsp ranch dressing mix
- 2 tbsp butter
- 1/3 cup hot sauce
- 2 cups cheddar cheese, shredded
- 1 cup heavy cream

Directions:

1. Combine all ingredients except cream & cheese.

2. Cook under HIGH pressure for 10 minutes then using a damp towel carefully perform a quick pressure release.
3. Carefully remove chicken with a fork, shred and return to pot.
4. Add heavy cream and shredded cheese, stir to combine.
5. Serve.

Tortilla Chicken Soup
(Prep + Cook Time: 30 minutes | Servings: 4)

Ingredients:
For the soup:
- 3-4 cups chicken broth (or 3-4 cups water + 1 tablespoon Better Than Bouillon)
- 3 chicken breasts (roughly 12-16 ounces)
- 2 tsp chili powder
- 2 tbsp fresh cilantro, chopped
- 2 pieces (6-inch each) corn tortillas, chopped into 1-inch squares
- 2 cloves garlic, minced
- ¼ tsp ground cayenne pepper
- 1 tsp ground cumin
- 1 tbsp olive oil
- 1 ripe tomato, very large, chopped
- 1 onion, medium-sized, chopped
- 1 cup frozen corn
- 1 can (15 ounces) black beans (or equivalent amount cooked beans)
- 1 bay leaf

For serving:
- Canola oil, or other oil for frying
- Corn tortillas, sliced into strips
- Fresh cilantro
- Fresh squeezed lime juice
- Grated cheese

Directions:
1. Press the SAUTE key and set the heat to default (medium) heat. Add olive oil and onion, and cook, frequently stirring, until the onions are soft.
2. Add the garlic, cilantro, and tortilla squares, and stir to combine. Cook for 1 minute.

3. Add the back beans, tomato, corn, chicken breast, 3 cups of broth, and spices.
4. Press CANCEL to stop the SAUTE function. Lock the lid and close the steam valve.
5. Press the SOUP key and adjust the time to 4 minutes. Meanwhile, prepare the toppings.
6. Over medium heat, heat the frying oil in a medium skillet. Heat the oil until hot.
7. To test, put 1 strip tortilla. It should start bubbling. Lightly salt the fried tortillas.
8. Grate the cheese. Wash and then chop the cilantro. Slice the lime wedges. When the timer beeps, release the pressure quickly.
9. Transfer the chicken breast into a plate. Using two forks, shred the meat apart.
10. Return the shredded meat into the pot and stir to combine. Ladle the soup into bowls.
11. Top each serving with cilantro, sprinkle of cheese, and squeeze of lime juice, and crisp tortilla chips.

Fish Soup

(Prep + Cook Time: 30 minutes | Servings: 4)

Ingredients:
- 1 tsp garlic paste
- 2 fish fillets, cut into pieces
- 1 cup cream
- 1 pinch chili powder
- 1 cup milk
- 1 tsp parsley, chopped
- Salt and black pepper to taste

Directions:
1. Heat oil in the Instant Pot and fry garlic with onion for 1 minutes.
2. Add fish and fry well till nicely golden.
3. Season with salt and chili powder.
4. Shred fish with folk and transfer again to Instant Pot.
5. Add in cream and milk; mix to combine.
6. Let to simmer for 10 minutes on low heat.
7. Sprinkle chili powder and parsley on top while serving.

Rice Soup (S&F)

(Prep + Cook Time: 30 minutes | Servings: 4)

Ingredients:
- ½ cups rice, soaked
- 1 carrot, peeled, chopped
- ¼ inch ginger slice
- 2-3 garlic cloves, minced
- 1 tsp black pepper
- 2 tsp salt
- 3 tbsp olive oil
- 4 cups chicken broth

Directions:
1. Add all ingredients in the Instant Pot and mix well
2. Cover with lid and leave to cook for 40-50 minutes on stew mode.
3. Serve and enjoy.

Leek Broccoli Cream Soup

(Prep + Cook Time: 30 minutes | Servings: 2)

Ingredients:
- 3 tbsp butter, divided
- 3 large leeks, cleaned and diced
- 4 garlic cloves, chopped
- 4 cups broccoli florets
- 3 cups vegetable or chicken broth
- 3 Pinches of red pepper flakes
- 4 tbsp all-purpose flour
- 1 cup milk
- ½ cup grated Parmesan cheese or more, as required
- Kosher salt
- Ground black pepper

Directions:
1. Select the SAUTE and heat the pot. Add in 2 tablespoons butter.
2. Once hot and melted, add in garlic, leeks, and sauté for 5 minutes until leeks are soft.
3. Add in broth, broccoli, pepper, salt and red pepper flakes. Stir and close the lid.

244

4. Cook on MANUAL at HIGH pressure for 8 minutes.
5. Add rest of butter in a saucepan, melt and tip flour into saucepan. Once it bubbles, stir well.
6. Remove pressure naturally, spread Parmesan and mix.
7. With an immersion blender, puree the broccoli with broth and now add the milk-flour mix and stir well.
8. Check seasonings, set to SAUTE and reheat the soup before serving.
9. Serve with more Parmesan.

Amazing Beef Soup
(Prep + Cook Time: 30 minutes | Servings: 4)

Ingredients:
- 7 cups beef broth
- 3 tbsp cognac
- 2 meaty beef ribs salt and pepper
- 2 pounds sliced onion
- ¼ tsp all spice
- 1 tbsp potato starch
- 2 tbsp unsalted butter
- 1 tbsp olive oil

Directions:
1. Melt the butter and olive oil in the Instant Pot to the browning setting.
2. Add onion into the Instant Pot and stir it until brown.
3. Add cognac into the mix to make a juice
4. Transfer the onions that are now soaked in the juice over to a bowl. Add all spice, broth, salt and pepper, wine, and beef into the Instant Pot.
5. Close the lid and time it for 45 minutes on HIGH pressure.
6. When the time is up, press the quick release valve to release the pressure.
7. Remove the lid from the Instant Pot and then transfer the ribs over to a cutting board.
8. Chop up the meat and get rid of all of the bones.
9. Place the meat into the Instant Pot and mix it with the onions and juices.
10. Shut the lid and time the ingredients to cook for 5 minutes at a HIGH pressure.

11. Press the SAUTE button on the Instant Pot and bring the food inside to a simmer.
12. Combine one tablespoon of water and potato starch in a bowl and whisk them neatly together.
13. Pour the potato starch into the Instant Pot, and stir it in with the rest of the ingredients while cooking for one to two minutes.
14. Serve and Enjoy.

Smoked Turkey & Black Bean Soup
(Prep + Cook Time: 1 hour 15 minutes | Servings: 6)

Ingredients:
- 1 smoked turkey drumstick
- 2 medium-sized onions, chopped
- 1 medium-sized carrot, chopped
- 1 celery stalk, chopped
- 4 garlic cloves, minced
- 2 cups dried black beans
- 1 tbsp vegetable oil
- 4 tbsp chopped parsley
- 6 cups water
- 2 bay leaves
- Salt and fresh ground black pepper to taste

Directions:
1. Heat the vegetable oil in your Instant Pot using the SAUTE button.
2. Add onions, carrots, celery and parsley in the pressure cooker and cook until fragrant, about 8 to 10 minutes. Add the garlic and cook 1 minute more.
3. Add water, bay leaves, beans, turkey leg, and black pepper and bring to boil. Secure the lid on the Instant Pot. Bring to HIGH pressure and cook beans for 45 minutes.
4. Turn off the cooker and release the pressure using natural method. Remove the lid. Discard bay leaves and remove turkey leg.
5. Remove skin from the turkey leg and cut meat off bone into bite size pieces. Using a blender, puree the beans leaving the soup chunky, or to your desired consistency.

6. Return the beans to the pot after they are pureed. Add the salt and return the turkey to the soup.
7. Ladle in plates, garnish with chopped parsley and serve.

Pork and Hominy Soup
(Prep + Cook Time: 1 hour 10 minutes | Servings: 6)

Ingredients:
1 ¼ pounds pork shoulder, boneless and fat trimmed, cut into 4-inch pieces
2 small onions, chopped
3 garlic cloves, minced
2 tbsp chill powder
4 cups chicken broth
2 cups water
2 cans (15 oz) hominy, drained and rinsed
2 tbsp olive oil
Salt and fresh ground pepper
4 oz diced avocado and lime wedges, for serving
Freshly chopped cilantro for garnish

Directions:
1. Preheat the pressure cooker and add a tablespoon of olive oil in it. Season the pork with salt, and cook until pieces are browned on all sides, about 8 minutes.
2. Then, transfer to a plate. Add one more tablespoon of olive oil, onions, garlic, and chili powder and sauté until soft, 4 minutes.
3. Add broth and water, cook, stirring and scraping up browned bits from the bottom with a wooden spoon. Return pork to the Instant Pot.
4. Clove and lock the lid. Bring to HIGH pressure over medium-high heat; reduce heat to maintain pressure and cook until meat is tender, about 45 minutes.
5. After that, turn off the cooker and lower the pressure using natural pressure release method.
6. Remove the pork to a plate and shred it using two forks, then stir in hominy and heat through.
7. Serve with avocado and lime and garnish with cilantro.

Beef, Tomato and Pasta Soup
(Prep + Cook Time: 45 minutes | Servings: 4)

Ingredients:
- 1 pound lean ground beef
- 4 oz small pasta
- 1 tsp salt
- 1 medium-sized onion, diced
- 1 stalk celery, diced
- 1 medium-sized carrot, diced
- 1 can (28 oz) diced tomatoes
- 32 oz beef broth
- 1-2 bay leaves Grated Parmesan cheese
- Ground black pepper to taste

Directions:
1. Preheat the Instant Pot using the SAUTE button and cook ground beef with salt and black pepper, until brown. Don't forget to break the meat up to small pieces while cooking. When browned, add onions, carrots, celery and sauté another 3-5 minutes, until veggies become tender.
2. Add the tomatoes, beef stock and bay leaves, secure the lid and cook at high using SOUP button. Cook for about 35 minutes.
3. When ready, use quick release to lower the pressure. Open the lid and add pasta. Stir well and cook additionally for 5-6 minutes.
4. Remove bay leaves, ladle to plates, sprinkle with Parmesan cheese and serve!

Beef and Green Bean Soup
(Prep + Cook Time: 30 minutes | Servings: 6)

Ingredients:
- 20 oz green beans, trimmed and cut into small pieces
- 3 medium parsnips, finely chopped
- 2 onions, chopped
- 4 cloves garlic, minced
- 25 oz canned tomatoes, diced
- 1 ½ pounds boneless beef bottom round, diced
- 1 cup carrots, diced
- 4 ½ cups beef broth
- 1/3 tsp ground black pepper
- 1 tsp salt
- 1 tsp dried marjoram

248

Directions:

1. First, combine the broth, tomatoes, beef, garlic, onion, parsnip, carrots, marjoram, salt, and black pepper in a cooker.
2. Lock the lid onto the pot. Cook for 16 minutes under HIGH pressure. Use the quick-release method to drop the pressure.
3. Unlock and open the pot. Stir in the green beans.
4. Then, seal the lid and wait for 4 minutes to warm up and blanch the beans.
5. Serve hot with croutons of choice.

Italian-Style Beef Soup (S&F)

(Prep + Cook Time: 30 minutes | Servings: 4)

Ingredients:

- 4 cups beef broth
- 1 ¼ pounds ground beef
- 3 potatoes, diced
- 1 tsp minced garlic
- 1 cup onions, chopped
- 1 ½ cups cooked beans
- 2 ripe tomatoes, crushed
- ½ cup turnip, finely chopped
- ½ cup celery, finely chopped
- 1 cup carrots, trimmed and thinly sliced
- ½ tsp freshly ground black pepper
- 1 tsp salt

Directions:

1. Add all of the above ingredients to your Instant Pot; give it a good stir.
2. Seal the lid according to manufacturer's directions; choose MANUAL mode and HIGH pressure for 25 minutes.
3. Serve hot and enjoy.

Barley and Beef Soup

(Prep + Cook Time: 1 hour30 minutes | Servings: 8)

Ingredients:
- 1 ½ pounds stew meat
- 1 cup water
- 1 potato, large-sized, shredded using grater or food processor
- ½ tsp dried thyme
- 10 baby bella mushrooms, quartered
- 2 bay leaves
- 2 tbsp oil
- 2/3 cup pearl barley, rinsed
- 3 cups mirepoix (just a combination of chopped onion, celery, and carrots)
- 6 cups beef broth or vegetable broth, low sodium
- 6-8 cloves garlic, minced
- Salt and pepper

Directions:
1. Season the meat with a good pinch of salt and pepper. Press the SAUTÉ key of the Instant Pot.
2. Add 1 tablespoon oil and heat. Put ½ of the beef in the pot and for 2-3 minutes and brown all the sides.
3. Transfer into a plate and repeat the process with the other ½ meat.
4. Add the mushrooms in the pot and cook for 1-2 minutes until browned or until the mushrooms start picking the browned bits in the pot. Transfer the mushrooms into the plate with the browned meat.
5. Add a bit more oil into the pot, if needed. Add the mirepoix mic.
6. Cook the veggies until the onions are soft and translucent, about 4-5 minutes.
7. Add the garlic and cook for 30 seconds. Add the browned meat and the mushrooms into the pot. Add the water, broth, dried thyme, and bay leaves.
8. Press CANCEL to stop the sauté function. Lock the lid and close the steam valve. Cook for 13-16 minutes or more, depending on the size of the meat.
9. When the timer beeps, let the pressure release quickly. Carefully open the lid.

10. Add barley and the potatoes. Press the SLOW COOK and set the time for 1 hour.
11. When the timer beeps, quick release the pressure. If needed, season with more salt.
12. Serve warm garnish with chopped parsley. Serve with crackers or a loaf with crusty bread.

Tasty Shrimp Soup (S&F)
(Prep + Cook Time: 25 minutes | Servings: 4)

Ingredients:
- 1 cup small shrimp, boiled
- 1 tbsp garlic, minced
- Salt and pepper to taste
- 3 cups vegetable broth
- 1 tsp lemon juice

Directions:
1. Put all the ingredients in the Instant Pot cooker and lock the lid.
2. Cook with SOUP setting for 20 minutes and then let the pressure release naturally.
3. Open the lid of the Instant Pot and simmer the soup for another 5 minutes without the lid to get the right consistency of the soup.
4. Serve hot by seasoning with some more pepper and salt.

Quick Matzo Ball Soup

(Prep + Cook Time: 1 hour 25 minutes | Servings: 2)

Ingredients:

- ¾ heaped cup matzo meal
- ¼ tsp baking powder
- 1 tsp Kosher salt
- ½ tsp black pepper
- ¼ tsp ground nutmeg
- 2 medium eggs
- 2 cups water, divided
- 2 tbsp vegetable oil
- 1 chicken breast, bone in, skin on
- 2 bay leaves
- 4 cups chicken broth
- 1 small carrot, chopped
- 2 small celery stalks, chopped

Directions:

1. Mix together the matzo meal, a pinch of salt, pepper, nutmeg and baking powder in a medium bowl.
2. Crack the eggs in another bowl, pour ½ cup water and oil. Whisk well and transfer into the previous bowl of matzo meal.
3. Stir well until it looks like a moist oatmeal mix. (If not, add more meal and stir). Let this mixture chill for 40 minutes.
4. Take your Instant Pot and add chicken, remaining water, broth, a bit salt and cook on MANUAL at HIGH pressure for 8 minutes.
5. Once done, press CANCEL and release naturally (5 minutes).
6. Discard bay leaves and shred the chicken pieces using two forks and remove the bones.
7. Make 1-inch balls out of the chilled matzo mix.
8. Add the balls, carrot, celery, seasonings into the pot, select MANUAL and cook again on HIGH pressure for 10 minutes.
9. Serve.

Cheese soup
(Prep + Cook Time: 60 minutes | Servings: 2)

Ingredients:
- 8 oz broccoli
- ½ cup parsley
- 10 oz beef brisket
- 1 tsp salt
- 1 tbsp sour cream
- 7 cups water
- 1 carrot
- 1 cup green beans
- 10 oz Cheddar cheese
- 1 tsp cilantro
- 1 tsp ground black pepper
- ¼ cup coriander leaves
- 1 tsp lemon juice

Directions:
1. Place the broccoli, beef brisket, green beans, and salt in the Instant Pot. Peel the carrot and chop it.
2. Add the chopped carrot and water in the Instant Pot too. After this, close the lid and cook the dish at the HIGH pressure mode for 30 minutes.
3. Then remove the Instant Pot vessel from the Instant Pot machine carefully to not burn the hands.
4. Discard the beef brisket and blend the mixture until you get smooth mass. Transfer the Instant Pot vessel in the Instant Pot machine again.
5. Add sour cream, cilantro, ground black pepper, and lemon juice. Chop the parsley and coriander leaves and add them to the soup too.
6. Then grate Cheddar cheese. Sprinkle the mixture with the Cheddar cheese and cook the SOUP for 10 minutes more.
7. When the time is over – the cheese should be melted. Mix up the soup carefully until you get a smooth texture.
8. Remove the soup from the Instant Pot and add beef brisket. Ladle the soup into the serving bowls. Serve it.

Simple Potato Frittata

(Prep + Cook Time: 35 minutes | Servings: 2)

Ingredients:

- 1 tbsp coconut oil
- 2 large potatoes, sliced
- 1 white onion, finely sliced
- 1 capsicum, sliced
- 2 cups water
- 2 free-range eggs
- 2 tbsp sour cream
- 4 tbsp cheddar cheese
- Salt and pepper, to taste

Directions:

1. Select SAUTE and preheat your Instant Pot. Pour in the coconut oil.
2. Once hot, add in the potato slices and saute for 3 minutes. Remove from the pot.
3. Throw in the chopped onion and capsicum and cook until fragrant. Remove and turn off the pot.
4. Add in the water and place a steam rack on top. Grease a 6 inch baking dish with cooking spray. Set aside.
5. Take a small mixing bowl and whisk in the egg with sour cream. Sprinkle salt and pepper and mix everything up.
6. Distribute half of the potato-onion-capsicum mixture in the dish. Pour half of the egg-cream mixture on top and spoon in 2 tablespoons of cheese.
7. Repeat this on remaining mixtures. Hit the MANUAL button and cook for 20 minutes on LOW pressure.
8. Once cooked, quick release the pressure and broil in the oven for 2 minutes (optional). Serve.

Potato Soup With Leek and Cheddar (VEG)

(Prep + Cook Time: 25 minutes | Servings: 8)

Ingredients:

- 4 medium gold potatoes, peeled and diced, I used Yukon
- 1 ½ cups cream or half and half
- 1/3 cup cheddar cheese, grated
- 3 tbsp leeks, cleaned and thinly sliced, white and light green (reserve 2 for serving)
- 1 ½ tsp dried oregano
- 1 tsp kosher salt
- 2 bay leaves
- 2 tbsp unsalted butter
- ¾ cup white wine
- 4 cloves garlic, crushed
- 4 sprigs fresh thyme
- 5 cups vegetable broth
- Extra crispy bacon, leeks, and cheese, for topping

Directions:

1. Set the Instant Pot to SAUTE. Put the butter in the pot and melt.
2. When melted, add the leek and season with salt and sauté until soft. Add the garlic and sauté for 30 seconds. Press CANCEL.
3. Reserve a few portion of the leek and set aside for serving.
4. Add the thyme, bay leaves, oregano, broth, white wine, and potatoes into the pot. Stir to mix. Close and lock the lid. Close the steam valve. Set the pressure to HIGH and set the timer to 10 minutes.
5. When the timer beeps, quick release the pressure. Carefully open the pot.
6. Add the cream and with an immersion blender, puree the soup until desired consistency. Press the WARM button and heat the soup through.
7. When the soup is hot, sprinkle with the sautéed leeks, crispy bacon, and sprinkle with cheese. Serve.

Lentil, Potato, and Carrot Soup (VEG)

(Prep + Cook Time: 25 minutes | Servings: 6)

Ingredients:

For the sauté:
- 1 clove garlic, minced
- 1 onion, small-sized, minced
- 1 tbsp olive oil (or dry sauté with no added oil)

For the soup:
- 1 cup lentil blend (pachraya massoor, autumn blend, or mix of red lentils, yellow split peas, brown lentil and Beluga lentils)
- 2 carrots, medium-sized, cubed
- 1 potato, medium-sized, peeled and cubed
- 1 sweet potato, small-sized, peeled and cubed
- 1 tsp marjoram
- 1 tsp thyme
- ½ tsp smoked paprika
- ¼ tsp rosemary powder (OR 1 teaspoon dried whole rosemary)
- 5 cups water
- 1 bay leaf

After cooking:
- ¼ cup nutritional yeast
- Salt and pepper, to taste

Directions:
1. Press the SAUTE key of the Instant Pot. Add the olive oil and heat. Add the onion and sauté until translucent.
2. Add the garlic and sauté for 1-2 minutes. Press CANCEL to turn off the sauté function.
3. Add all the soup ingredients in the pot. Lock the lid and close the steam valve.
4. Press MANUAL and set the timer to 10 minutes. When the timer beeps, let the pressure release naturally.
5. Open the steam valve to release any remaining pressure.
6. Carefully open the lid, stir to mix, and ladle into bowls.
7. Serve with crusty bread.

Easy and Quick Chicken Noodle Soup

(Prep + Cook Time: 20 minutes | Servings: 8)

Ingredients:
- 2-3 cups spinach, chopped
- 2 cups chicken, cooked leftovers, cubed, plus more of a meatier soup
- 2 carrots, large-sized, diced
- 8 oz noodles of your choice, if using spaghetti, break them in half
- 8 cups chicken broth or vegetable broth, homemade broth is preferred
- 5 garlic cloves, minced
- 3 tbsp butter
- 3 stalks celery, diced
- 1 tsp dried thyme
- 1 tsp dried oregano
- 1 tsp dried basil
- 1 onion, medium-sized, diced
- Pepper Salt

Directions:
1. Press the SAUTE key. When the pot is hot, melt the butter in the Instant Pot.
2. Add the onion, celery, carrot, and season with big pinch of salt.
3. Cook for 5 minutes until sweet and soft. Add the basil, oregano, thyme, and garlic, and cook for 1 minute.
4. Add the chicken, broth, and noodles. Press CANCEL to turn of the sauté function. Lock the lid and close the steam valve. Press the MANUAL key and set the time to 4 minutes.
5. When the timer beeps after cooking cycle, open the steam release valve to quick release the pressure.
6. Carefully open the lid.
7. Stir in the spinach until wilted and season with more salt and pepper to taste. Serve warm.

Rainbow Soup (S&F)

(Prep + Cook Time: 25 minutes | Servings: 8)

Ingredients:

- 5 cups veggie broth
- 3 minced garlic cloves
- 3 cups cooked black beans
- 2 diced carrots
- 15 oz can diced tomatoes
- 1 chopped small red cabbage
- 1 chopped onion
- 1 diced jalapeno chile
- 1 chopped yellow bell pepper
- 6 oz quartered mushrooms
- 2 tbsp tomato paste
- 1 tbsp oregano
- 1 tbsp chili powder
- 1 tsp cumin
- Salt to taste

Directions:

1. Mix everything in your pressure cooker, minus the salt.
2. Close the lid, select MANUAL, and cook on HIGH pressure for 6 minutes.
3. When time is up, turn off the cooker and wait 15 minutes.
4. Release any remaining pressure. Salt and serve.

Chicken Stock

(Prep + Cook Time: 2 hours | Liters: 4)

Ingredients:

- 1 chicken carcass
- 1 onion, cut into quarters
- 10-15 whole pieces peppercorns
- 2 bay leaves
- 2 tbsp apple cider vinegar
- Veggie scraps, optional
- Water

Directions:

1. Put the chicken carcass in the Instant Pot. If desired, feel free to add the skin.
2. Add the vegetable scraps, onion, apple cider vinegar, peppercorns, and bay leaves. Fill the pot with water to 1/ 2-inch below the max line. Cover and lock the lid.
3. Turn the steam valve to SEALING. Press the SOUP key and set the timer for 120 minutes.
4. When the Instant Pot timer beeps, press the CANCEL key and unplug the Instant Pot.
5. Let the pressure release naturally for 10-15 minutes or until the valve drops – do not turn the steam valve for at least 30 minutes.
6. Using an oven mitt or a long handled spoon, turn the steam valve to VENTING to release remaining pressure.
7. Unlock and carefully open the lid. Strain out everything else from the stock and discard. Put a funnel over a mason jar.
8. Pour the stock into the mason jar – do not overfill If you are planning to freeze your stock, use 5 mason jars.
9. Let the stock cool and then store in the fridge or freeze within 3 days.

Beef Bone Broth

(Prep + Cook Time: 95 minutes | Servings: 8)

Ingredients:

- 5 oz carrots
- 4-5 sprigs thyme
- 4 cloves garlic
- 3 pounds beef bones (oxtail or neck bones preferred)
- 3 bay leaves
- 1 onion, roughly chopped
- Half head celery, chopped
- Pepper, to taste
- Salt, to taste

ctions:

1. Cut the celery and onion. Add into the Instant Pot. Add the rest of the ingredients into the pot.
2. Fill the pot with water up to the line before the max line of the Instant Pot. Cover and lock the lid. Press the MANUAL key, set the pressure to HIGH, and set the timer for 90 minutes.
3. When the Instant Pot timer beeps, press the CANCEL key and unplug the Instant Pot.
4. Using an oven mitt or a long handled spoon, turn the steam valve to VENTING to quick release the pressure.
5. Unlock and carefully open the lid.
6. Strain the broth and store in freezer.

Bone Broth

(Prep + Cook Time: 2 hours 20 minutes | Servings: 8)

Ingredients:

- 1 tsp unrefined sea salt
- 1-2 tbsp apple cider vinegar
- 2-3 pounds bones (2-3 pounds lamb, beef, pork, or non-oily fish, or 1 carcass of whole chicken)
- Assorted veggies (1/ 2 onion, a couple carrots, a couple stalks celery, and fresh herbs, if you have them on hand)
- Filtered water

Directions:

1. Put the bones in the Instant Pot. Top with the veggies. Add the salt and apple cider vinegar.
2. Pour in enough water to fill the pot 2/3 full.
3. If you have enough time, let the pot sit for 30 minutes to allow the vinegar to start pulling the minerals out of the bones. Cover and lock the lid. Press the SOUP key, set the pressure to LOW, and set the timer for 120 minutes.
4. When the Instant Pot timer beeps, press the CANCEL key and unplug the Instant Pot. Let the pressure release naturally for 10-15 minutes or until the valve drops.
5. Using an oven mitt or a long handled spoon, turn the steam valve to VENTING to release remaining pressure.
6. Unlock and carefully open the lid. Strain the broth. Discard the veggies and bones. Pour the broth into jars.
7. Store in the refrigerator or freeze.

Fish Stock
(Prep + Cook Time: 65 minutes | Servings: 8)

Ingredients:
- 2 salmon heads, large-sized, cut into quarters
- 2 lemongrass stalks, roughly chopped
- 1 cup carrots, roughly chopped
- 1 cup celery, roughly chopped
- 2 cloves garlic
- Handful fresh thyme, including stems
- Oil, for frying the fish heads

Directions:
1. Wash the fish heads with cold water – make sure there is no blood – and then pat them dry.
2. Put the oil in a pan and lightly sear the fish heads – this will minimize the fish meat from falling apart. Slice the vegetables and put them in the Instant Pot. Add the fish and thyme.
3. Pour water in the pot until the level reaches 3 quarts or just cover the fish. Cover and lock the lid. Press the SOUP key, set the pressure to HIGH, and set the timer for 45 minutes.
4. When the Instant Pot timer beeps, press the CANCEL key and unplug the Instant Pot. Let the pressure release naturally for 10-15 minutes or until the valve drops.
5. Using an oven mitt or a long handled spoon, turn the steam valve to VENTING to release remaining pressure.
6. Unlock and carefully open the lid.
7. Strain the fish and vegetable and store the stock.

Vegetable Stock (VEG)
(Prep + Cook Time: 30 mins | Cups: 8)

Ingredients:
- 2 green onions, sliced
- 2 tsp minced garlic
- 4 medium-sized carrots, peeled and chopped
- 4 celery stalks, chopped
- 6 parsley sprigs
- 4 thyme sprigs
- 1,8 liters water
- 2 bay leaves
- 8 black peppercorns
- 1 ½ tsp salt

Directions:
1. Prepare vegetables. In a 6-quarts Instant Pot, pour in water and add all the ingredients except salt.
2. Plug in and switch on the Instant Pot, and secure pot with lid.
3. Then position pressure indicator, press SOUP option, and adjust cooking time to 30 minutes and let cook. Instant Pot will take 10 minutes to build pressure before cooking timer starts.
4. When the timer beeps, switch off the Instant Pot and let pressure release naturally for 10 minutes and then do quick pressure release.
5. Then uncover the pot and pass the mixture through a strainer placed over a large bowl to collect stock and vegetables on the strainer.
6. Stir salt into the stock and let cool completely before storing or use it later for cooking.

Chicken and Beef Bone Broth
(Prep + Cook Time: 2 hours | Liters: 4)

Ingredients:

- Chicken and/or beef bones, enough to fill the pot (put the beef bones first)
- Onions, celery, carrots
- Bay leaf
- Handful peppercorns
- 1 tbsp apple cider vinegar
- Filtered water

Directions:

1. Put all of the ingredients in the Instant Pot.
2. Fill the pot with water, not more than 2/3 full.
3. Cover and lock the lid. Press the MANUAL key, set the pressure to HIGH, and set the timer for 120 minutes.
4. When the Instant Pot timer beeps, press the CANCEL key and unplug the Instant Pot. Let the pressure release naturally for 10-15 minutes or until the valve drops.
5. Using an oven mitt or a long handled spoon, turn the steam valve to VENTING to release remaining pressure.
6. Unlock and carefully open the lid. Strain and store the broth in jars.

Tomato Sauce
(Prep + Cook Time: 55 minutes | Cups: 8)

Ingredients:
- 4,2 pounds tomatoes, cut into halves or quarters, less or more to fill the Instant Pot to the max level
- 1 onion, minced
- 1 tbsp oregano
- 1 tbsp salt
- 1 tbsp sugar
- 2 bay leaves
- 2 tbsp basil, chopped
- 2-3 tbsp parsley, chopped
- Lemon juice (1 tbsp per jar)

Directions:
1. Put all of the ingredients in the Instant Pot. Cover and lock the lid. Press the MANUAL key, set the pressure to HIGH, and set the timer for 30-40 minutes.
2. While the sauce is cooking, sterilize the mason and new lids in a pot of boiling water for 15 minutes.
3. Drain the sterilized jars and lids on a paper towel.
4. When the Instant Pot timer beeps, press the CANCEL key and unplug the Instant Pot. Let the pressure release naturally for 10-15 minutes or until the valve drops.
5. Using an oven mitt or a long handled spoon, turn the steam valve to VENTING to release remaining pressure.
6. Unlock and carefully open the lid. Set a food mill over another pot. Scoop out the tomatoes into the food mill. The tomatoes will mush up quickly and go through the pot, leaving the seeds and the skins behind.
7. Put 1 tablespoon lemon juice or 1/4 teaspoon citric acid on each mason jar and immediately fill the mason jars with the hot sauce.
8. Wipe the rims to ensure that the lids will seal. Put the lids on and screw them down.
9. Put the jars in the boiling water where you sterilized the jars and rims. Sterilize for 30 minutes.
10. Remove the jars and let them cool – make sure that each lid pops and is concave.

Pasta and Spaghetti Sauce

(Prep + Cook Time: 20 minutes | Cups: 6)

Ingredients:
- 2 pounds Italian sausage, casings removed (hot or mild), optional
- 1 can (28 ounces) diced tomatoes
- 1 onion, small-sized, chopped, optional
- 1 tbsp olive oil
- ½ cup red wine (use a cabernet)
- ½ cup water
- ¼ tsp coarse black pepper, fresh ground
- ¼- ½ tsp crushed red pepper flakes
- 2 cans (15 ounces) tomato sauce
- 2 tsp brown sugar
- 2 tsp dried parsley flakes
- 2 tsp fennel seed, crushed
- 2 tsp salt
- 3 tsps basil
- 3-4 cloves garlic, minced
- 6 oz tomato paste
- Parmesan cheese OR a piece of rind, optional

Directions:
1. Press the SAUTE key of the Instant Pot and wait until hot. Put 1 tablespoon olive oil in the pot and add the sausage.
2. Cook until browned, breaking the sausages in the process as you stir.
3. Add the rest of the ingredients in the pot. If you are not using any meat, then start at this step.
4. Press the CANCEL key to stop the sauté function. Cover and lock the lid. Press the MANUAL key, set the pressure to HIGH, and set the timer for 10 minutes.
5. When the Instant Pot timer beeps, press the CANCEL key and unplug the Instant Pot. Let the pressure release naturally for 10-15 minutes or until the valve drops.
6. Using an oven mitt or a long handled spoon, turn the steam valve to VENTING to release remaining pressure.
7. Unlock and carefully open the lid.
8. Serve with your spaghetti or your favorite pasta.

Chipotle Honey BBQ Sauce

(Prep + Cook Time: 20 minutes | Cups: 2)

Ingredients:
- 1 tsp olive oil
- 1 onion, medium-sized, chopped
- ½ tsp cumin
- ¼ cup honey
- 2 chipotles in adobo sauce PLUS
- 1 tablespoon adobo sauce
- 2 tsp apple cider vinegar
- 1 cup ketchup
- 1 tsp chili powder
- 1 tsp paprika
- 1 tsp salt
- ½ tsp pepper
- ¼ cup orange juice
- 2 cloves garlic, chopped

Directions:
1. Press the SAUTE key of the Instant Pot. Put the olive oil in the pot and heat until shimmering.
2. Add the garlic and onion; sauté for about 3 minutes or until soft.
3. While the veggies are sautéing, whisk the ketchup with the orange juice, honey, and apple cider vinegar.
4. Pour the ketchup mix over the veggies. Add the adobo sauce, chipotles, seasoning, and spices.
5. Press the CANCEL key to stop the sauté function. Cover and lock the lid. Press the MANUAL key, set the pressure to HIGH, and set the timer for 8 minutes.
6. When the Instant Pot timer beeps, press the CANCEL key and unplug the Instant Pot.
7. Using an oven mitt or a long handled spoon, turn the steam valve to VENTING to quick release the pressure.
8. Unlock and carefully open the lid.
9. Pour the sauce carefully into a blender and puree.
10. Pour the sauce in a glass jar and store in the refrigerator for up to 1 week.

Cranberry Sauce (VEG, S&F)
(Prep + Cook Time: 20 minutes | Cups: 2)

Ingredients:
- 1 cup dried cranberries
- ¾ cup water
- 1 tsp lemon juice
- ¾ cup cranberry juice

Directions:
1. Put cranberries, water, lemon juice and cranberry juice in your Instant Pot, cover and cook on HIGH pressure for 5 minutes.
2. Release pressure naturally for 10 minutes, transfer the sauce to your blender and pulse a few times.
3. Serve right away or keep in the fridge.

Tabasco Sauce (VEG, S&F)
(Prep + Cook Time: 15 minutes | Cups: 2)

Ingredients:
- 2 tsp smoked salt
- 12 oz hot peppers, roughly chopped
- 1 ¼ cup apple cider vinegar

Directions:
1. In your Instant Pot, mix hot peppers with salt, vinegar and water to cover everything.
2. Cover pot and cook on HIGH pressure for 1 minute.
3. Release pressure naturally for 10 minutes, pour everything in a blender and pulse well.
4. Strain into a bottle and serve when ever you need.

Mushroom Sauce (VEG)

(Prep + Cook Time: 15 minutes | Cups: 2)

Ingredients:

- 10 mushrooms, chopped
- 1 yellow onion, chopped
- 2 garlic cloves, minced
- 1 tsp thyme, dried
- 2 cups veggie stock
- ½ tsp rosemary, dried
- ½ tsp sage
- 1 tsp sherry
- 1 tbsp water
- 1 tbsp nutritional yeast
- 1 tbsp coconut aminos
- Salt and black pepper to the taste
- ¼ cup almond milk
- 2 tbsp rice flour

Directions:

1. Set your Instant Pot on SAUTE mode, add onion and brown for 5 minutes.
2. Add mushrooms and the water, stir and cook for 3 minutes.
3. Add garlic, stir again and cook for 1 minute.
4. Add stock, yeast, sherry, soy sauce, salt, pepper, sage, thyme and rosemary, coconut aminos, stir, cover and cook on HIGH pressure for 4 minutes.
5. Meanwhile, in a bowl, mix milk with rice flour and stir well.
6. Release pressure from the pot, add milk mix, stir well, cover and cook on HIGH for 6 more minutes.
7. Relies pressure again and serve sauce.

Mango Chutney Sauce (VEG)

(Prep + Cook Time: 35 minutes | Cups: 3)

Ingredients:

- 1 shallot, chopped
- 1 tbsp vegetable oil
- ¼ tsp cardamom powder
- 2 tbsp ginger, finely chopped
- A pinch of cardamom
- 2 red hot chili peppers, chopped
- 1 apple, chopped
- 2 mangoes, chopped
- A pinch of salt
- ¼ cup raisins
- 1 ¼ cup raw sugar
- 1 cup white wine sugar

Directions:

1. Set your Instant Pot on SAUTE mode, add the oil and heat it up. Add shallot and ginger, stir and cook for 2 minutes.
2. Add hot peppers, cinnamon and cardamom, stir and cook 1 minute more.
3. Add mangoes, apple, salt, raisins, sugar and vinegar, stir, cover pot and cook on HIGH pressure for 15 minutes.
4. Release pressure naturally for 10 minutes, stir well, transfer to jars and keep until you serve it.

Orange Sauce (VEG)
(Prep + Cook Time: 20 minutes | Cups: 2)

Ingredients:

- 1 tsp ginger paste
- ¼ cup white wine vinegar
- 3 tbsp palm sugar
- 2 tbsp tomato paste
- 1 cup orange juice
- 1 tsp garlic, minced
- 2 tbsp agave nectar
- 1 tsp sesame oil
- 2 tbsp soy sauce
- 1 tsp chili sauce
- 1/3 cup veggie stock
- 2 tbsp cornstarch

Directions:

1. Set your Instant Pot on SAUTE mode, add sesame oil, heat up, add ginger paste and garlic, stir and cook for 2 minutes.
2. Add palm sugar, vinegar, tomato paste, orange juice, agave nectar, soy sauce and chili sauce, stir, cover and cook on HIGH pressure for 3 minutes.
3. Release pressure, add stock and cornstarch, stir, cover and cook on HIGH for 4 more minutes.
4. Release pressure again and serve sauce.

Vegetable Sauce

(Prep + Cook Time: 30 minutes | Cups: 3)

Ingredients:

- 2 medium-sized carrots, peeled and chopped
- 10 oz potatoes, peeled and chopped
- 1 medium-sized white onion, peeled and chopped
- 3 garlic cloves, peeled
- 1 tsp salt
- 1 tsp turmeric powder
- ½ cup nutritional yeast
- 2.5 oz cashews, raw
- 16 fluid ounce water

Directions:

1. Place all the ingredients in a 6-quarts Instant Pot and stir until just mixed.
2. Plug in and switch on the Instant Pot and secure with lid. Then position pressure indicator, select MANUAL option and adjust cooking time on 5 minutes and let cook.
3. When the timer beeps, switch off the Instant Pot and let pressure release naturally for 10 minutes and then do quick pressure release.
4. Uncover the pot and let the mixture cool for 15 minutes.
5. Then transfer mixture into a food processor and pulse for 2 minutes or until mixture is smooth and creamy.
6. Spoon into a clean and air-tight jar and store in the refrigerator for 2 weeks or in the freezer for up to 1 month.

Vegetarian Recipes

Carrot and Pumpkin Stew

(Prep + Cook Time: 70 minutes | Servings: 2)

Ingredients:

- 1 cup pumpkin, chopped
- 1 onion, chopped
- 4 carrots, peeled, chopped
- 1 tsp salt
- 1 tsp black pepper
- ½ tsp cumin powder
- 3-4 garlic cloves, minced
- 2 tbsp olive oil
- 2 cups chicken broth
- 1 cup vegetable broth

Directions:

1. In the Instant Pot add pumpkin, carrots, chicken broth, onion, oil, salt, garlic, cumin powder, vegetable broth, and black pepper. Mix well.
2. Cove pot with lid and leave to cook on SLOW cook mode for 60 minutes.
3. Transfer to blender and blend till puree.
4. Pour stew into serving bowls and serve hot.
5. Serve and enjoy.

Steamed Broccoli (S&F)

(Prep + Cook Time: 3 minutes | Servings: 4)

Ingredients:

- 2 pounds broccoli
- 2/3 cup water
- Salt and pepper to taste

Directions:

1. Place water into the bottom of your Instant Pot, and you can measure it out with the cup provided.
2. Chop your broccoli into florets and place it on the steamer rack.
3. Place the lid on your Instant Pot and set the valve to sealing and press STEAM for 2 minutes.
4. Once it has started, it will beep when done. Once it has cooled down from keep warm mode you can get it out.
5. Serve seasoned with salt and pepper.

Steamed Green Beans

(Prep + Cook Time: 17 minutes | Servings: 4)

Ingredients:
- 1 pound green beans, washed
- 1 cup water, for the pot
- 2 tbsp fresh parsley, chopped, for garnish

For the dressing:
- 1 pinch ground black pepper
- 1 pinch salt
- 2 tbsp white wine vinegar
- 3 tbsp Parmesan cheese, freshly grated
- 3 tbsp olive oil
- 3 cloves garlic, sliced

Directions:
1. Pour the water into the Instant Pot and set the steamer basket. Put the green beans in the basket.
2. Close and lock the lid. Turn the steam valve to SEALING. Press MANUAL, set the pressure to HIGH and the timer to 1 minute.
3. When the timer beeps, turn the valve to VENTNG to quick release the pressure. Transfer the beans into a serving bowl.
4. Toss with the dressing Ingredients and let stand for 10 minutes.
5. Remove the slices of garlic and then garnish with the parsley. Serve.

Lentil and Veggie Soup

(Prep + Cook Time: 5 minutes | Servings: 6)

Ingredients:
- 1 cup diced onions
- 6 small potatoes, diced (see note above)
- 3 large carrots, sliced
- 3 cups chopped broccoli
- 1 cup dry lentils
- 2 quarts of water
- 1 tsp salt
- ½ tsp black pepper
- 1 tsp onion powder
- 1 tsp garlic powder
- ½ tsp paprika
- ½ tsp thyme
- 1 bay leaf

Directions:

1. Add all of the chopped veggies to a large pot on medium heat. I like to do this as I'm cutting them but if you pre-cut them you can do it all at once.
2. Add the dry lentils, careful to sort them for debris. I found a stick in mine.
3. Add the water and all of the seasonings and cover with a lid.
4. Bring to a simmer and allow to simmer for 30 minutes.
5. Check soup, make sure the carrots and potatoes are soft.
6. Remove the bay leaf and serve.

Veggie Spaghetti

(Prep + Cook Time: 18 minutes | Servings: 2)

Ingredients:

- 1 pound (16 oz) spaghetti squash, halved, deseeded, fibrous innards removed
- 1 cup water
- ¼ cup pistachios, shell removed
- 2 tbsp butter
- 2 large garlic cloves, finely chopped
- ½ tbsp lime juice
- 4 tbsp parmesan cheese, grated
- 2 tbsp basil leaves, freshly chopped
- Sea salt and black pepper powder, to taste

Directions:

1. Pour water into the Instant Pot and place the squash halves, cut-side facing up.
2. Secure the lid, select MANUAL and cook for 7 minutes on HIGH pressure.
3. In the meantime, heat a medium skillet on stove top.
4. Once hot, add the pistachios and sauté for 2 minutes or until toasted. Remove from the skillet and aside.
5. Pour 1 tablespoon butter (in the same skillet).
6. Once hot and melted, sauté garlic for about a minute until lightly golden. Turn off the stove and keep aside.

7. Release the pressure of the Instant Pot once it is done cooking.
8. Remove the squash and drain out the water. Carefully separate the squash strands from the peel using a fork.
9. Transfer the strands into a large mixing bowl, mix the cooked garlic, remaining tablespoon butter, lime juice and grated parmesan.
10. Sprinkle salt and pepper, top with toasted pistachios and freshly chopped basil. Serve.

The Green Bowl
(Prep + Cook Time: 10 minutes | Servings: 2)

Ingredients:
- 1 tsp olive oil
- 2 large garlic cloves, minced
- ½ tsp turmeric powder
- 1 medium bunch (~ 4 cups) greens - kale/ collards (thick stems discarded)
- 2 + tbsp water/veggie stock
- 1 tbsp tahini
- 1 tsp tamari
- ½ tsp balsamic vinegar
- Salt and pepper, to taste

Directions:
1. Select SAUTE and preheat your Instant Pot. Pour in the oil.
2. Once hot, add the garlic and turmeric.
3. Sauté for 1 minute. Add the greens and water. (Pour more water if the greens are tough).
4. Secure the lid. Select Manual and cook for 3 minutes on HIGH Pressure.
5. Do a quick pressure release and remove the lid.
6. Mix in the tahini and stir everything up.
7. Transfer the contents to a serving bowl. Sprinkle the soy sauce and vinegar.
8. Adjust the seasonings and serve.

Hawaiian Black Beans

(Prep + Cook Time: 35 minutes | Servings: 4)

Ingredients:

- 2 cups dry black beans, soaked overnight and drained
- 2 tbsp coconut oil
- 1 cup sweet onion, diced
- 2 cloves garlic, crushed and minced
- 1 tbsp jalapeno pepper, diced
- 1 tsp salt
- 1 tsp black pepper
- 1 tsp cumin
- 1 tbsp soy sauce
- 3 cups vegetable stock
- 1 cup pineapple juice
- 1 cup red bell pepper, diced
- 1 cup green bell pepper, diced
- Crushed pineapple for garnish

Directions:

1. Place the coconut oil in a pressure cooker and set to the SAUTE setting.
2. Add the onion, garlic and jalapeno pepper.
3. Sauté for 2-3 minutes, or until highly fragrant.
4. Season with salt, black pepper, cumin and soy sauce.
5. Add the black beans, vegetable stock and pineapple juice. Mix well.
6. Cover and seal the pressure cooker and set to high, Cook for 20 minutes.
7. Use the quick release method to release the steam from the Instant Pot. Add in the red and green bell pepper. Seal the pressure cooker and bring the pressure back up to low.
8. Cook for an additional 3 minutes.
9. Use the natural release method to release the pressure from the pressure cooker.
10. Serve garnished with fresh pineapple, if desired.

Spring Green Risotto

(Prep + Cook Time: 25 minutes | Servings: 4)

Ingredients:

- 2 cup Arborio rice
- 2 tbsp olive oil
- 2 tbsp shallots, diced
- ¼ cup dry white wine
- 2 cups asparagus, cut into 1 inch pieced
- 1 cup leek, sliced
- 1 tbsp fresh tarragon
- 1 tsp salt
- 1 tsp black pepper
- 4 cups vegetable stock
- Fresh chives for serving

Directions:

1. Place the olive oil in the Instant Pot and set to the SAUTE setting. Add in the shallots and sauté for 2 minutes.
2. Add in the rice and sauté, stirring frequently, until lightly toasted, approximately 3-4 minutes.
3. Pour in the white wine and let reduce for 1-2 minutes.
4. Next, add the asparagus and leek. Season with the tarragon, salt and black pepper. Mix well.
5. Close the Instant Pot and set the pressure to HIGH. Cook for 5-7 minutes, or until rice is tender. Use the natural release method to release the steam from the pressure cooker.
6. Open the pressure cooker and stir the risotto. Garnish with fresh chives before serving.

Basil Rice

(Prep + Cook Time: 20 minutes | Servings: 4)

Ingredients:

- 1 cup long grain brown rice
- 1 tbsp olive oil
- 2 cloves garlic, crushed and minced
- 1 tsp salt
- 1 tsp black pepper
- 1 tsp lemon zest
- 2 ½ cups vegetable stock
- ½ cup fresh basil, chopped
- ½ cup fresh parsley, chopped
- 1 cup fresh peas

Directions:

1. Place the olive oil in the Instant Pot and set to the SAUTE setting. Add the garlic and sauté for 1 minute. Add the rice and toast, stirring frequently for 2 minutes.
2. Season the rice with salt, black pepper and lemon zest. Pour in the vegetable stock. Cover and seal the pressure cooker.
3. Set to HIGH and cook for 20 minutes. Use the quick release method to release the steam from the pressure cooker.
4. Stir in the basil, parsley and peas. Cover and bring the pressure to low. Cook for 1 additional minute.
5. Use the natural release method to release the steam from the Instant Pot. Stir in the basil, parsley and peas.
6. Cover and bring the pressure to low. Cook for 1 additional minute.
7. Use the natural release method to release the steam from the pressure cooker before serving.

Spiced Carrot Quinoa
(Prep + Cook Time: 15 minutes | Servings: 4)

Ingredients:

- 2 cups quinoa
- 2 tbsp coconut oil
- 2 cups carrots, shredded
- 2 cloves garlic, crushed and minced
- 1 tbsp fresh grated ginger
- 1 tsp cinnamon
- 1 tsp cumin
- ½ tsp coriander
- ½ tsp smoked paprika
- ½ tsp salt
- 3 cups vegetable stock or water
- Golden raisins for serving

Directions:

1. Place the coconut oil in the Instant Pot and turn to the sauté or brown setting. Add in the carrots, garlic and ginger. Sauté until fragrant, approximately 1-2 minutes.
2. Next, add in the quinoa and season with the cinnamon, cumin, coriander, smoked paprika and salt. Mix well.
3. Add the vegetable stock or water. Cover and seal the pressure cooker. Set the pressure to HIGH and cook for 3-5 minutes.
4. Use the natural release method to release the steam from the Instant Pot.
5. Garnish with golden raisins before serving.

Mexican Rice Mix (S&F)

(Prep + Cook Time: 60 minutes | Servings: 6)

Ingredients:

- 2 cup raw California or Calrose rice
- 1 cup raw white beans
- 5 cup water
- 1 can tomato paste
- 4 cloves garlic, minced
- 1 red onion, diced
- 2 tsp chili powder
- Salt and pepper to taste

Directions:

1. Place all the ingredients into the Instant Pot. Stir before covering and sealing the lid.
2. Press the MANUAL option and cook for 25 minutes.
3. After 25 minutes, leave the Instant Pot for another 10 minutes to let off the pressure.
4. Fluff the rice using spatulas. Serve and enjoy.

Curry Tofu

(Prep + Cook Time: 35 minutes | Servings: 4)

Ingredients:

- 2 cup coconut milk
- 1 tbsp yellow curry powder
- 2 tbsp raw peanut, skin off
- 1 tbsp garam masala
- 2 large green bell peppers, cored and diced
- 1 cup tomato paste
- 1 white onion, diced
- 4 cloves garlic, minced
- 1 pack firm tofu, cubed
- Salt and pepper to taste

Directions:

1. On a non-stick pan, roast the peanuts on low heat. Keep moving the peanuts around to avoid burning them.
2. After 5 minutes, transfer the peanuts to a food processor and turn it into paste.
3. Before removing the peanut paste from the processor, add the other ingredients except for the tofu.

4. Blend these together to form a thick sauce. Place the cubed tofu in the Instant Pot and then pour over the sauce.
5. Cover and seal the lid. Press the MANUAL button and cook for 5 minutes. After 5 minutes, let the Instant Pot release its pressure naturally. Uncover the lid.
6. Serve and enjoy.

Pumpkin Oats with Pecan Pie
(Prep + Cook Time: 40 minutes | Servings: 6)

Ingredients:
- 1 tbsp butter
- 1 cup oats
- 3 cups water
- 1 cup Pumpkin puree
- ¼ cup Maple syrup
- 2 tsp cinnamon
- 1 tsp pumpkin pie spice
- ½ tsp salt

Directions:
1. Add butter to electric pressure cooking pot, select SAUTE. When butter is melted, add the oats and toast, constantly stirring, until they smell nutty, about 3 minutes.
2. Add water, pumpkin puree, maple syrup, cinnamon, pumpkin pie spice, and salt. Select HIGH pressure and 10 minutes cook time.
3. When beep sounds, turn off the pressure cooker, stir oats.
4. Remove cooking pot from the Instant Pot and let oats rest in the cooking pot uncovered for 5 - 10 minutes until oats thicken to desired consistency.
5. Serve warm with pecan pie granola, milk, and maple syrup if desired.

Buttery Braised Cabbage
(Prep + Cook Time: 10 minutes | Servings: 2)

Ingredients:
- 3 bacon slices
- 2 tbsp butter
- 1 small-medium cabbage, cored and quartered and sliced into half inch slices
- 1 cup vegetable broth
- Sea salt and black pepper, to taste

Directions:
1. Select SAUTE and preheat your Instant Pot. Once hot, place the bacon slices and sauté until both sides are crisp and brown.
2. Remove and chop into smaller pieces. Add in the butter.
3. Once melted, add the cabbage strips, vegetable broth and browned bacon. Sprinkle salt and pepper and cover/ secure the lid.
4. Hit MANUAL and cook for 3 minutes on high pressure.
5. Once cooked, do a quick pressure release. Let cool and serve.

Instant Broccoli Mushroom Combo
(Prep + Cook Time: 10 minutes | Servings: 2)

Ingredients:
- 1 tsp olive oil
- 1 medium onion, diced
- 2 large garlic cloves, minced
- 1 tsp minced ginger
- 1 ½ cup sliced mushrooms (cremini)
- 2 ½ cups Chinese broccoli, sliced - stems separated from flowers and leaves
- 2 tbsp water/veggie stock
- 1 tbsp tamari
- 1 tbsp sesame seeds, toasted

Directions:
1. Select SAUTE and preheat your Instant Pot. Pour oil.
2. Once hot, add the chopped onion, garlic and ginger. Saute for 1 minute.

3. Add the sliced mushrooms, broccoli stems, water/ stock and tamari. Stir well. Secure the lid.
4. Select MANUAL and cook for 1 minute on Low Pressure. Do a quick pressure release and remove the lid.
5. Throw in the broccoli flowers and leaves. Quickly put back the lid, select Manual, and cook for 2 minutes on Low Pressure.
6. Do a quick pressure release and remove the lid.
7. Transfer the contents to a serving bowl.
8. Sprinkle toasted sesame seeds on top and serve warm.

Sesame & Napa Cabbage
(Prep + Cook Time: 10 minutes | Servings: 2)

Ingredients:
- 1 tsp sesame oil
- 2 tsp sesame seeds
- 1 ½ cup tap water
- 1 medium head napa cabbage leaves
- Sea salt and black pepper, to taste
- 2 tsp soy sauce

Directions:
1. Pour the water in your Instant Pot. Place the steam rack on top.
2. Place and stack the napa leaves on the rack and cover/ secure the lid. Select MANUAL and cook for 4 minutes on high pressure.
3. Once done, do a quick pressure release.
4. Take a large mixing bowl and transfer the steamed leaves on it.
5. Toss with the mixture of all the listed ingredients – soy sauce, sesame oil, sesame seeds.
6. Sprinkle salt and peppers and mix. Serve.

Cajun Succotash
(Prep + Cook Time: 18 minutes | Servings: 4)

Ingredients:
- 2 tbsp olive oil
- ½ cup red onion, diced
- 2 cloves garlic, crushed and minced
- 1 cup green bell pepper, chopped
- 1 cup butternut squash, cut into small cubes
- 2 cups fresh corn kernels
- 2 cups tomatoes, chopped
- 2 cups frozen lima beans
- 1 tsp salt
- 1 tsp black pepper
- 1 tsp Cajun seasoning
- 1 tsp oregano
- 1 cup vegetable stock or water
- 1 tbsp lime juice
- Scallions, sliced for serving
  .

Directions:
1. Place the olive oil in a pressure cooker and set to the SAUTE setting. Add the onion, garlic and green bell pepper. Sauté for 2 minutes.
2. Add the butternut squash, corn kernels, tomatoes and lima beans.
3. Season with the salt, black pepper, Cajun seasoning and oregano and mix well.   Pour in the vegetable stock or water and lime juice.
4. Cover and seal the pressure cooker. Set to high and cook for 5 minutes.
5. Use the natural release method to release the steam from the pressure cooker. Garnish with scallions before serving, if desired.

Creamy Mushrooms

(Prep + Cook Time: 12 minutes | Servings: 4)

Ingredients:

- 2 tbsp olive oil
- 2 tbsp shallots, diced
- ½ tsp salt
- 1 tsp coarse ground black pepper
- ½ tsp nutmeg
- ¼ cup white wine
- 8 cups mushrooms, quartered
- 2 cups fresh spinach, torn
- ½ cup walnuts, chopped
- 1 cup vegetable stock
- 1 cup coconut milk
- Fresh parsley for garnish
- Fresh parsley for garnish

Directions:

1. Place the olive oil in a pressure cooker and turn on the SAUTE setting.
2. Add the shallots and season with salt, black pepper and nutmeg. Sauté for 2 minutes.
3. Add the white wine and let reduce for 1-2 minutes.
4. Next, add in the mushrooms, spinach, walnuts, vegetable stock and coconut milk. Mix well.
5. Cover and seal the pressure cooker. Set to low and cook for 5 minutes.
6. Use the natural release method to release the steam from the pressure cooker. Garnish with fresh parsley before serving.

Peanut Stew

(Prep + Cook Time: 30minutes | Servings: 4)

Ingredients:

- 2 tbsp peanut oil
- 1 red onion, chopped finely
- 3 cloves garlic, minced
- 1 thumb-size ginger, minced
- 1 small red chili, chopped
- 2 cans diced tomatoes
- 1 ½ cup toasted peanuts
- 2 cup vegan broth
- 1 fist-size taro, washed, peeled, and cubed
- 1 can white beans, washed and drained
- ½ cup green peas

Directions:

1. Using a food processor, blitz the toasted peanuts with a dash of peanut oil until it becomes a puree.
2. Sauté the garlic, onion, chili and ginger in an Instant Pot. After a couple of minutes, place the rest of the ingredients, except the white beans, green peas and corn, in the pot.
3. Cover and seal the lid. Select MANUAL mode and cook for 12 minutes. Leave the Instant Pot for about 5 to 10 minutes or until the pressure naturally seeps through.
4. Add the corn, peas, and beans. Cover the lid and cook for another minute.
5. Quick release the pressure. Transfer to a platter. Serve with a side of bread or quinoa.

Herbed Mashed Potatoes

(Prep + Cook Time: 30 minutes | Servings: 4)

Ingredients:

- 4 large russet potatoes, washed, peeled, and cubed
- 1 cup vegan broth
- 3 tbsp garlic powder
- 1 tbsp onion powder
- ½ cup almond milk
- ½ cup flat leaf parsley, finely chopped
- 1 tbsp coconut butter
- Salt and pepper to taste

Directions:

1. Place the russet potatoes, vegan broth, and 1 tablespoon garlic powder in the Instant Pot.
2. Cover and seal the lid. Select MANUAL and cook for 5 minutes. Remove the lid and drain the potatoes.
3. Mash them using a manual masher for better texture.
4. Place in a bowl and add the remaining garlic powder, onion powder, almond milk, and coconut butter. Mix well.
5. Finally, add the chopped parsley, salt and pepper. Mix well.
6. Serve in a bowl. Enjoy.

Classic Ratatouille

(Prep + Cook Time: 15 minutes | Servings: 2)

Ingredients:

- 1 tbsp olive oil
- ½ cup capsicum, cored, deseeded and diced
- ½ cup onion, finely chopped
- ¼ cup garlic, minced
- 2 tbsp veggie stock
- 1 cup cubed brinjal (eggplant)
- 1 cup zucchini, cut into 1-inch pieces
- 1 cup yellow squash, cut into 1-inch pieces
- ½ cup ripe tomatoes, diced
- 4 tbsp cup finely chopped fresh basil
- 2 tbsp finely chopped fresh cilantro
- 1 tbsp balsamic vinegar
- 1 tsp ground coriander
- Salt and pepper, to taste

Directions:

1. Select SAUTE and preheat your Instant Pot. Pour the oil. Once hot, add the chopped onion and capsicum and sauté for 2 minutes.
2. Add 2 tablespoons minced garlic. Stir and cook for a minute. Pour in the stock, stir and secure the lid. Select MANUAL and cook for 3 minutes on Low Pressure.
3. Do a quick pressure release and remove the lid. Throw in the chunks of brinjal, zucchini, and squash. Mix well. Distribute the diced tomatoes on top. Secure the lid.
4. Select MANUAL and cook for 3 minutes on Low Pressure. Do a quick pressure release. Remove the lid and check if the brinjal is cooked well. If not, cook for 1 minute using the similar procedure.
5. Transfer the content to a serving bowl. Drain out the excess liquid (if any). Mix in the remaining ingredients - garlic, basil, cilantro, balsamic vinegar, and ground coriander.
6. Season with salt and pepper. Serve warm.

Quick n Easy Zucchini

(Prep + Cook Time: 4 minutes | Servings: 2)

Ingredients:

- 1 tbsp olive oil
- 2 garlic cloves, minced
- 1 medium capsicum, diced
- 2 tbsp freshly chopped cilantro
- 2 tbsp freshly chopped basil
- 2 tbsp water/ veggie stock
- 2 cups zucchini, sliced
- Salt and pepper, to taste
- Toasted and chopped walnuts, to garnish

Directions:

1. Select SAUTE and preheat your Instant Pot. Add oil. Once hot, add the garlic and add the garlic and sauté for 20 seconds.
2. Add the diced capsicum and herbs and sauté for 15 seconds. Select Cancel. Pour in the water/ stock. Stir well while scrapping the bottom.
3. Throw in the sliced squash and secure the lid. Select MANUAL and cook for 30 seconds on LOW pressure.
4. When done, do a quick pressure release. Remove the lid, and transfer everything to a serving bowl.
5. Adjust the seasonings and garnish with toasted and chopped walnuts. Serve warm.

Couscous Burritos

(Prep + Cook Time: 25 minutes | Servings: 4)

Ingredients:

- 1 tsp olive oil
- 1 tbsp red onions, diced
- 1 green bell pepper, seeded and diced
- 1 tsp cumin powder
- 1 cup couscous, raw
- 1 cup salsa
- 1 cup vegan broth
- 1 can black beans, washed and drained
- Salt and pepper to taste

Toppings:
- 1 avocado, seeded and diced
- 1 sprig coriander, chopped finely
- 1 lime, cut into wedges
- 8 pcs. Romaine lettuce leaves

286

Directions:

1. Place the olive oil in the pot. Select the SAUTE button and cook the onion and bell pepper for a few minutes.
2. Once the onion turns translucent, add the cumin, salt, and pepper. Turn off the pot. Add the couscous, broth, salsa, and beans.
3. Cover and seal the lid. Select the RICE button and cook under low pressure for 10 minutes.
4. Leave the Instant Pot for another 5 minutes to naturally release the pressure. Uncover the lid.
5. Use a pair of forks to fluff the couscous. Transfer to a serving platter and serve with the toppings on a separate platter.
6. Use the romaine leaves as the burrito bread.

Vegan Mousaka
(Prep + Cook Time: 60 minutes | Servings: 4)

Ingredients:

For the lentils filling:
- 1 yellow onion, chopped
- 3 cups canned lentils, drained
- 14 oz canned tomatoes, chopped
- 2 celery stalks, chopped
- 4 carrots, chopped
- 2 bay leaves
- 1 yellow onion, chopped
- 1 garlic clove, minced
- 1 tsp thyme, dried
- 1 tsp oregano, dried

- Salt and black pepper to the taste
- 3 cups water

For the potato filling:
- 6 potatoes, sliced
- 2 yellow onion, finely chopped
- 2 tbsp extra virgin olive oil
- 2 garlic cloves, crushed
- Salt and black pepper to the taste
- A handful parsley, chopped

Directions:
1. Put 1 yellow onion, carrots, celery, 1 garlic clove, tomatoes, lentils, celery, oregano, thyme, bay leaves, salt, black pepper and water in your Instant Pot, cover and cook on HIGH for 6 minutes.
2. Release pressure, stir mix, transfer it to a bowl and leave aside.

3. Clean your Instant Pot, set on SAUTE mode, add 2 tablespoons oil, potatoes, 2 onions, salt, pepper and garlic, stir and cook for 4 minutes.
4. Add lentils mix on top, more salt and pepper if needed, cove pot and cook on LOW for 40 minutes.
5. Release pressure, divide the mousaka amongst plates and serve.

Vegan Chili
(Prep + Cook Time: 50 minutes | Servings: 6)

Ingredients:
- 1 pack veggie ground round (Yves is a good brand)
- 4 cups water
- 8 oz of pinto beans (soak before use)
- 8 oz red kidney beans (soak before use)
- 13 ounces chopped Roma tomatoes
- 2 chopped onions
- 3 minced garlic cloves
- 1 diced bell pepper
- 1 bay leaf
- 2 tbsp olive oil
- 1 tbsp chili powder
- 2 tsp cumin
- 1 ½ tsp oregano
- Salt to taste

Directions:
1. Heat olive oil in the Instant Pot. Sauté the garlic and onions.
2. Add veggie ground round and brown.
3. Add the bell pepper, chili powder, cumin, oregano, bay leaf, and salt. Mix. Put in the beans, tomatoes, and water. Stir.
4. Secure lid and maintain LOW pressure for 20 minutes.
5. Remove from heat and let the pressure drop naturally.
6. Pick out the bay leaf. Serve right away.

Assorted Mushrooms Chili (S&F)

(Prep + Cook Time: 20 minutes | Servings: 6)

Ingredients:

- 1 cup fresh button mushrooms, sliced
- 1 cup fresh Portobello mushrooms, chopped
- 1 cup oyster mushrooms, chopped
- 2 red onions, diced
- 8 cloves garlic, minced
- 2 cans crushed tomatoes, low-sodium
- 1 cup lima beans, soaked and peeled
- 1 cup red kidney beans, soaked and peeled
- 1 cup white beans, soaked and peeled
- 2 cup water
- 1 tsp mustard powder
- 1 tsp red pepper flakes
- ½ tsp dried thyme
- ½ tsp oregano powder
- ½ tsp paprika
- Salt and pepper to taste

Directions:

1. Put all ingredients in the Instant Pot. Cover and seal the lid.
2. Press the MANUAL button and cook on HIGH pressure for 8 minutes.
3. Release the pressure naturally. Remove the lid.
4. Serve in a bowl with a side of corn or vegan bread.

Vanilla Cake

(Prep + Cook Time: 35 minutes | Servings: 4)

Ingredients:

- ¾ cup whole wheat flour
- ¾ cup coconut sugar
- ½ cup unsweetened almond milk
- 3 tbsp canola oil
- ½ tsp baking soda
- 1 ½ tsp fresh lemon juice
- 1 tsp vanilla essence
- ¼ tsp salt

Directions:

1. Place a cup of water in the Instant Pot and place a circular wire stand over it. Set aside.
2. In a mixing bowl, combine the wet ingredients. In a separate mixing bowl, combine the dry ingredients.
3. Slowly add the wet ingredients to the dry ingredients. Mix with a spatula. Transfer the batter to a 6-inch tube pan.
4. Cover the pan with aluminum foil. Place the pan in the Instant Pot. 5. Manually cook over HIGH pressure for 15 minutes.
5. Let the pressure naturally release from the Instant Pot. Uncover the lid and remove the pan.
6. Leave the cake to cool before removing from the pan. Serve and enjoy.

Pineapple Crisps

(Prep + Cook Time: 30 minutes | Servings: 4)

Ingredients:

- 1 medium fresh pineapple, peeled and cut into 5 large chunks
- 2 tsp cinnamon powder
- ½ tsp nutmeg
- ½ cup water
- 1 tbsp organic maple syrup
- 4 tbsp olive oil
- ¾ cup steel cut oats
- ¼ cup whole wheat flour
- ¼ cup brown sugar Pinch of salt

Directions:

1. Place the pineapple chunks in the Instant Pot. Sprinkle with the spices and then pour in the water and maple syrup. Set aside.
2. In a mixing bowl, combine the oil, oats, flour, sugar, and salt. Pour this over each pineapple chunk. Cover and seal the lid.
3. Manually cook on HIGH pressure for 8 minutes. Leave the Instant Pot and wait for the pressure to release naturally.
4. Remove the lid. Transfer the pineapple chunks to individual serving bowls.
5. Add the thick sauce over each pineapple.
6. Serve with a side of vegan ice cream.

Apricot and Cranberry Cake
(Prep + Cook Time: 40 minutes | Servings: 4)

Ingredients:

- 2/3 cup whole wheat flour
- ½ tsp cardamom powder
- ½ tsp baking powder
- ½ tsp baking soda
- Pinch of salt
- ½ cup unsweetened almond milk
- ¼ cup organic maple syrup
- 2 tbsp flax seeds
- 2 tbsp applesauce
- 1 cup dried apricots, chopped
- ½ cup cranberries, chopped

Directions:

1. Brush a 6-inch tube pan with applesauce and set aside.
2. Using a mixing bowl, combine all dry ingredients together.
3. Using another mixing bowl, combine all wet ingredients.
4. Slowly add the wet ingredients to the dry ingredients. Fold the mix using a spatula.
5. Transfer the mixture to the tube pan and cover with aluminium foil.
6. Place the pan in the Instant Pot. Make sure to pour 1 ½ cups of water and place a circular wire stand before placing the tube pan. Cover and seal the lid.

7. Manually cook for 30 minutes over HIGH pressure. Leave the Instant Pot until the pressure naturally escapes the pot.
8. Open the lid and remove the tube pan.
9. Let the cake cool down before removing it from the tube pan.
10. Serve and enjoy.

Wintery Stew
(Prep + Cook Time: 20 minutes | Servings: 4)

Ingredients:
- 2 tbsp olive oil
- 3 cloves garlic, crushed and minced
- 1 cup yellow onion, diced
- 1 cup green bell pepper, chopped
- 2 cups carrots, chopped
- 2 cups parsnips, chopped
- 2 cups red potatoes, cubed
- 1 cup beets, cubed
- 2 cups tomatoes, chopped
- 1 tbsp fresh tarragon, chopped
- 1 tbsp fresh dill, chopped
- 1 tsp salt
- 1 tsp black pepper
- 1 tbsp molasses
- 4 cups vegetable stock

Directions:
1. Place the olive oil in a pressure cooker and turn on the SAUTE setting. 2. Add in the garlic and onion. Sauté for 2 minutes.
2. Add the green bell pepper, carrots, parsnips, red potatoes, beets and tomatoes.
3. Season with tarragon, dill, salt, black pepper and molasses. Mix well.
4. Add in the vegetable stock.
5. Cover and seal the pressure cooker. Set the pressure to HIGH and cook for 7 minutes.
6. Use the natural release method to release the steam before serving.

White Vegetable Stew

(Prep + Cook Time: 15 minutes | Servings: 4)

Ingredients:

- 1 ½ cups broth
- 3 cups diced celery root
- 2 bay leaves
- 1 cup diced carrot
- 1 cup sliced leek
- 1 cup diced parsnip
- 1 sprig rosemary
- 1 sprig thyme
- ½ cup green lentils
- ½ cup peas
- Squirt of lemon juice
- Salt and pepper to taste

Directions:

1. Put the leek in your Instant Pot, no oil, and cook for 1 minute on the SAUTE setting. Add garlic and cook for another minute.
2. Turn off the cooker and add carrot, parsnips, lentils, celery root, broth, and herbs.
3. Close the lid and select MANUAL, and then HIGH pressure for 6 minutes.
4. When time is up, hit CANCEL" and wait for the pressure to come down on its own.
5. When the pressure is gone, add the peas. Stir and close the lid for 2 minutes to heat everything.
6. Season with salt, pepper, and lemon juice before serving.

Homemade Pumpkin Purée

(Prep + Cook Time: 20 minutes | Servings: 12)

Ingredients:

- 4 pounds pie pumpkins, stem removed, cut in half, and seeds removed
- 1 ½ cups sugar
- 2 ½ cups water

Directions:

1. Place the steamer basket in your Instant Pot. Pour in the water.

2. Cut the pumpkin half into four pieces. Place the pumpkin in the steamer.
3. Close and lock the lid. Set the burner heat to HIGH. Set the timer to cook for 12 minutes.
4. Then open the cooker with the Quick pressure release method. Make sure not to overcook.
5. When it is cool enough to handle, scoop the flesh from the peel using a soup spoon.
6. Process the pumpkin along with sugar using an immersion blender for about 2 minutes.
7. Serve and enjoy.

Kidney Bean Salad
(Prep + Cook Time: 20 minutes | Servings: 4)

Ingredients:
- 1 ¼ cups dry kidney beans, soaked
- 4 ½ cups water
- 3/4 cup shallots, chopped
- 2 sprigs thyme
- 2 sprigs rosemary
- ½ cup green bell pepper, thinly sliced
- 1 cup red bell pepper, thinly sliced
- 2 ½ tbsp olive oil
- 2 tbsp apple cider vinegar
- 1 ½ tbsp sunflower seeds
- 1 tsp sea salt
- ½ tsp ground black pepper, or more to taste

Directions:
1. Add the water, soaked kidney beans, shallots, thyme, and rosemary to the inner pot of your cooker.
2. Cover and press the MANUAL button, set the cooking time to 20 minutes.
3. Then, open your Instant Pot by using natural pressure release.
4. Drain the cooked kidney beans and add the remaining ingredients.
5. Serve well chilled.

Farro and Cherry Salad

(Prep + Cook Time: 60 minutes | Servings: 6)

Ingredients:

- 1 cup raw whole-grain farro, raw
- 2 cups cherries, pitted and then cut in half
- ½ cup dried cherries, coarsely chopped
- 1 tbsp apple cider vinegar
- 1 tbsp olive oil
- 1 tsp lemon juice, freshly squeezed
- ¼ cup chives or green onions, finely minced
- ¼ tsp sea salt
- 8-10 mint leaves, minced
- 3 cups water

Directions:

1. Rinse the farro and put in the Instant Pot. Pour in 3 cups water. Cover and lock the lid. Turn the steam valve to SEALING. Cook on HIGH pressure for 40 minutes.
2. When the timer beeps, quick release the pressure. The grain should be plump and tender, but chewy.
3. Drain the farro and put into a bowl. Stir in the vinegar, oil, lemon juice, salt, chives, dried cherries, and mint.
4. Refrigerate until cold.
5. Just before serving, stir in the fresh cherries.

Hearty Mushroom-Bean Soup (S&F)

(Prep + Cook Time: 20 minutes | Servings: 4)

Ingredients:

- 4 ½ cups vegetable stock, preferably homemade
- 1 ¼ cups canned white beans
- ¼ tsp freshly ground black pepper
- ½ tsp sea salt
- 1 cup carrots, trimmed and thinly sliced
- ½ cup celery stalk, finely chopped
- ½ cup parsnip, chopped
- 1 tsp minced garlic
- 2 small-sized onions, chopped
- 1 ½ cups crushed fresh tomatoes
- 1 ½ pounds mushrooms, thinly sliced
- 1 tsp dried basil
- 1 tsp dried oregano

Directions:

1. Place all the ingredients into the Instant Pot; stir until everything is well combined.
2. Cover with the lid and secure it; choose MANUAL function and HIGH pressure for 22 minutes.
3. Serve hot.

Sweet Potato Soup with Peanut Butter

(Prep + Cook Time: 10 minutes | Servings: 6)

Ingredients:

- 4 sweet potatoes, cubed
- 12 oz canned coconut milk
- ½ tbsp lemon juice
- 2 ¼ cups vegetable stock
- 1 cup tomatoes, seeded and chopped
- 3 cloves garlic, finely chopped
- 1 ¼ cups scallions, chopped
- 1/3 cup peanut butter
- 2 tbsp grape seed oil
- ½ tsp black pepper, to taste
- ½ tsp sea salt
- A pinch of allspice

Directions:

1. Choose the SAUTE function. Then, heat the oil, and sauté the scallions and garlic, stirring frequently, until they are softened (about 5 minutes).
2. Press the CANCEL button. Stir in the other ingredients; stir until everything is combined well.
3. Close the lid and choose MANUAL. Let it cook for about 5 minutes.
4. Remove the lid according to the manufacturer's instructions.
5. Puree the soup to your desired consistency with an immersion blender.
6. Serve warm.

Warm Russet Potato

(Prep + Cook Time: 14 minutes | Servings: 6)

Ingredients:

- ¾ cup vegetable stock
- 1 tsp sea salt
- 1 tsp cayenne pepper
- ½ tsp ground black pepper, to your liking
- 1 tsp dried rosemary
- 2 pounds russet potatoes, cut into wedges
- ½ tsp cumin powder
- ½ tsp garlic powder
- ½ stick butter, softened

Directions:

1. Press the SAUTE button and add the butter; heat until it is warmed through.
2. Now, add the potatoes and cook for about 7 minutes.
3. Add the rest of the ingredients. Secure the lid according to manufacturer's directions; press the MANUAL button.
4. Cook for 9 minutes.
5. Transfer to a serving platter and serve.

Broccoli and Pineapple Salad

(Prep + Cook Time: 10 minutes | Servings: 6)

Ingredients:

For the Salad:
- ¾ cup water
- 2 ½ cups broccoli florets
- 1 large-sized carrot, thinly sliced
- ½ cup pineapple, peeled and sliced thinly

For the Vinaigrette:
- 3 tbsp extra-virgin olive oil
- ¾ orange, zested and squeezed
- 1 tsp fresh basil, roughly chopped
- ½ tsp white pepper, or more to taste
- 1 tsp kosher salt
- ¼ tsp cayenne pepper
- 1 ½ tbsp fresh cilantro, roughly chopped

Directions:

1. In your Instant Pot, place carrots, broccoli, and water.
2. Then, lock the cooker's lid. Choose MANUAL and 6-minute pressure cooking time.
3. To make the vinaigrette, thoroughly mix all the vinaigrette components.
4. Afterwards, open your cooker according to manufacturer's instructions.
5. Dress the salad and garnish with pineapple slices; serve chilled.

Broccoli and Garlic
(Prep + Cook Time: 35 minutes | Servings: 4)

Ingredients:
- 1 broccoli head, cut into 4 pieces
- ½ cup water
- 1 tbsp peanut oil
- 6 garlic cloves, minced
- 1 tbsp
- Chinese rice wine
- Salt, to taste

Directions:
1. Put the broccoli in the steamer basket of your Instant Pot, add ½ cup water to the pot, then cover and cook on Low for 12 minutes.
2. Release the pressure, transfer broccoli to a bowl filled with cold water, drain, and place it in another bowl.
3. Heat up a pan with the oil over medium high heat, add garlic, stir and cook for 3 minutes.
4. Add broccoli and rice wine, stir and cook for 1 minute more.
5. Add salt, stir and cook 30 seconds.
6. Transfer to plates and serve.

Squash and Pineapple Treat
(Prep + Cook Time: 20 minutes | Servings: 8)

Ingredients:
- 3 summer squashes, cut into bite-sized pieces
- 2 tsp brown sugar
- 2 tbsp arrowroot combined with
- 3 tbsp water
- 1 cup shallots, diced
- ¼ tsp freshly ground black pepper, or more to your liking
- ½ tsp sea salt
- 2 ½ tbsp soy sauce
- 1/3 cup pineapple juice
- 2 tbsp olive oil
- 10 ounces canned pineapple chunks

Directions:

1. Select the SAUTE function; warm the olive oil; now, sauté the shallot for about 5 minutes.
2. Add the squash, pineapple chunks, pineapple juice, and soy sauce; stir to combine well.
3. Next, lock the lid. Choose the MANUAL function and cook for 12 minutes.
4. Quick release the pressure. Combine the rest of the ingredients in a small-sized mixing bowl.
5. Add the mixture to the pot to thicken the liquid. Serve.

Maple Brussels Sprouts
(Prep + Cook Time: 10 minutes | Servings: 4)

Ingredients:
- 20 small-sized Brussels sprouts, cut in half
- 1 ½ tbsp maple syrup
- 1/3 cup water
- 2 medium-sized onions, diced
- 1 tbsp sesame oil
- ½ tsp freshly ground black pepper
- ½ tsp sea salt
- ½ tsp cayenne pepper

Directions:

1. Firstly, set your Instant Pot to SAUTE; now, warm the sesame oil; sauté the onions for 3 minutes.
2. In a mixing bowl, whisk the water and maple syrup; add your Brussels sprouts to the cooker.
3. Drizzle the maple mixture over them and sprinkle with cayenne pepper, salt, and black pepper.
4. Lock the lid and bring to HIGH pressure for 3 minutes.
5. Quick release the pressure.
6. Serve immediately.

Lemon-Garlic Corn on the Cob

(Prep + Cook Time: 10 minutes | Servings: 6)

Ingredients:
- 3 cloves garlic, minced
- ½ tsp ground black pepper
- 1 tsp salt
- 8 ears of corn, shucked
- 1 ½ tbsp lemon juice
- 2 ½ tbsp butter, room temperature
- 1 tbsp basil leaves, chopped

Directions:
1. Firstly, place the ears of corn on the metal rack in your cooker.
2. Make sure to add 1 cup of water and seal the lid. Select the MANUAL setting; adjust the cooking time to 5 minutes.
3. Carefully open the lid by following the manufacturer's instructions.
4. Meanwhile, heat up a pan over medium heat. Now, melt the butter and sauté the garlic along with the dried basil for 5 minutes or until they are fragrant.
5. Let it cool slightly; then, add the lemon juice, salt, and black pepper.
6. Transfer the prepared ears of corn to a serving.
7. Drizzle the pan sauce over ears of corn and serve.

Nutty Bulgur and Oat Porridge

(Prep + Cook Time: 30 minutes | Servings: 8)

Ingredients:
- 1/3 cup honey
- 1 cup steel-cut oats
- 1 cup bulgur
- ½ tsp ground cloves
- ½ tsp ground cinnamon
- ¼ tsp freshly grated nutmeg
- 1/3 cup walnuts, chopped
- 4 ½ cups water

Directions:
1. Mix everything in your Instant Pot. Lock the lid onto the Instant Pot.

2. Set the machine to cook at HIGH pressure. Cook for 27 minutes.
3. Use the quick-release method and remove the lid.
4. Set the cooker to its SAUTE function.
5. Bring to a simmer; cook for 3 more minutes.
6. Serve and enjoy.

Bean and Mint Salad

In this recipe, do not try to replace dry beans with canned beans.
(Prep + Cook Time: 10 minutes | Servings: 4)

Ingredients:

- 4 ¼ cups water
- ½ tsp black pepper, to taste
- 1 tsp sea salt
- 2 bay leaves
- 2 garlic cloves, smashed
- 1 ½ tbsp olive oil
- 1 ¼ cups dry beans, soaked
- 2 sprigs fresh mint

Directions:

1. Add the soaked beans (overnight), water, garlic clove, and bay leaf to the Instant Pot.
2. Close and lock the lid. Use the MANUAL mode and choose 9-minute cooking time.
3. Use natural pressure release to open the cooker.
4. Strain the beans and transfer to a salad bowl.
5. Toss with the remaining ingredients.
6. Serve chilled.

Yam Barley Congee (S&F)

(Prep + Cook Time: 50 minutes | Servings: 12)

Ingredients:

- 1 pound purple yam, cubed
- ½ pound barley
- ½ pound black eye beans
- ½ pound glutinous rice
- ½ pound brown rice
- ½ pound buckwheat
- 1 tsp salt
- ¼ tsp black pepper, or more to taste

Directions:
1. Add the ingredients to the inner pot. Pour in 7 cups of water. Close the lid.
2. Press the PORRIGE button and cook for 44 minutes.
3. Sweeten with honey if desired.
4. To serve, you can drizzle individual portions with truffle oil or soy sauce.

Butter Bean Casserole
(Prep + Cook Time: 25 minutes | Servings: 8)

Ingredients:
- 1 stick butter
- 1 ¼ cups sour cream
- 2 bay leaves
- 1 tsp sea salt
- 3 tbsp sugar
- ½ tsp mustard
- 1 ½ tsp granulated garlic
- 1 ½ pounds butter beans
- ½ cup fresh chopped chives, for garnish

Directions:
1. Firstly, soak the butter beans with 8 cups of water.
2. Then, add the salt and bay leaf, and press the MANUAL button. Cook for 5 minutes under HIGH pressure.
3. Press the KEEP WARM button and leave it for 9 minutes; next, quick release pressure.
4. Drain the butter beans; add them back to the Instant Pot.
5. Next, add the remaining ingredients, except for chives.
6. Cook for 11 minutes on MANUAL under HIGH pressure.
7. Serve garnished with fresh chives.

Butternut Squash Oatmeal

(Prep + Cook Time: 10 minutes | Servings: 2)

Ingredients:

- ½ cup Old fashioned oats
- 2 cup almond milk, unsweetened
- ½ tsp vanilla extract
- ½ cup butternut squash, peeled and cubed
- ½ tsp cinnamon powder
- Pinch of salt
- ½ cup pecans
- 2 tbsp coco sugar

Directions:

1. Place all ingredients except for the coco sugar and pecans in the Instant Pot. Cover and seal the lid.
2. Cook on HIGH pressure for 1 minute.
3. Let the pot sit and release the steam naturally.
4. Remove the lid. Stir the oats well.
5. Serve in a shallow bowl topped with pecans and coco sugar.

Spanish Paella

(Prep + Cook Time: 40 minutes | Servings: 8)

Ingredients:

- 2 cup raw brown rice
- 4 cup vegan broth
- 2 pinches saffron threads
- 1 red onion, diced
- 4 cloves garlic, minced
- 1 can crushed tomatoes
- 2 tsp tomato paste
- 2 tbsp Spanish paprika powder
- ½ cup frozen green peas
- 1 carrot, peeled and diced
- 1 red bell pepper, seeded and cut into thin strips
- ½ cup kidney beans
- 1 cup cauliflower florets, chopped

Directions:

1. Place all ingredients in the Instant Pot. Start with the rice, crushed tomatoes, tomato paste, and then the broth. Stir in all the spices, garlic, and onion using a wooden spoon.

2. Once the rice mix settle, carefully place the other ingredients on top of the rice – bell pepper, cauliflower, green peas, carrots and beans.
3. Arrange the vegetables nicely to create a beautiful finished product.
4. Cover and seal the lid. Select the RICE button and cook for 30 minutes.
5. Let the Instant Pot sit for 10 minutes to let off the pressure.
6. Serve and enjoy.

Mexican Chili Beans
(Prep + Cook Time: 50 minutes | Servings: 8)

Ingredients:
- 2 cup dried red kidney beans
- 4 cup water
- 3 tbsp olive oil
- 1 white onion, diced
- 6 cloves garlic, minced
- 2 tbsp jalapeno chili, sliced
- Salt and pepper to taste
- 2 tbsp green onions, chopped (for topping)

Directions:
1. Place beans, one tablespoon of olive oil, and water in the Instant Pot.
2. Cover and seal the lid. Select the MANUAL button and cook for 30 minutes.
3. Let the pressure naturally release after 30 minutes. Remove the lid.
4. Add the white onion, garlic, jalapeno, salt and pepper. Cover and seal the lid again. Select MANUAL and cook for another 10 minutes.
5. Mash the beans using a masher for better texture.
6. Serve in a bowl topped with green onions.

Mexican Rice Mix (S&F)

(Prep + Cook Time: 40 minutes | Servings: 8)

Ingredients:

- 2 cup raw California or Calrose rice
- 1 cup raw white beans
- 5 cup water
- 1 can tomato paste
- 4 cloves garlic, minced
- 1 red onion, diced
- 2 tsp chili powder
- Salt and pepper to taste

Directions:

1. Place all the ingredients into the Instant Pot. Stir before covering and sealing the lid.
2. Press the MANUAL option and cook for 25 minutes.
3. After 25 minutes, leave the Instant Pot for another 10 minutes to let off the pressure.
4. Fluff the rice using spatulas.
5. Serve and enjoy.

Assorted Mushrooms Chili (S&F)

(Prep + Cook Time: 15 minutes | Servings: 8)

Ingredients:

- 1 cup fresh button mushrooms, sliced
- 1 cup fresh Portobello mushrooms, chopped
- 1 cup oyster mushrooms, chopped
- 2 red onions, diced
- 8 cloves garlic, minced
- 2 cans crushed tomatoes, low-sodium
- 1 cup lima beans, soaked and peeled
- 1 cup red kidney beans, soaked and peeled
- 1 cup white beans, soaked and peeled
- 2 cup water
- 1 tsp mustard powder
- 1 tsp red pepper flakes
- ½ tsp dried thyme
- ½ tsp oregano powder
- ½ tsp paprika
- Salt and pepper to taste

Directions:

1. Put all ingredients in the Instant Pot. Cover and seal the lid.

2. Press the MANUAL button and cook for 8 minutes.
3. Release the pressure naturally. Remove the lid.
4. Serve in a bowl with a side of corn or vegan bread.

Asian Mushroom Dumpling
(Prep + Cook Time: 15 minutes | Servings: 2)

Ingredients:
- 1 tbsp olive oil
- 1 cup chopped mushroom
- 1-½ cups chopped cabbage
- ½ cup grated carrot
- 2 tbsp soy sauce
- 1 tsp ginger
- 1 tsp sesame oil
- 6 vegan dumpling wrappers

Directions:
1. Preheat a skillet over medium heat. Pour olive oil into the pot then stir in mushroom, chopped cabbage, grated carrots, ginger, sesame oil, and soy sauce then sauté until dry.
2. Remove from the heat. Place a wrapper on a flat surface then put a tablespoon of mushroom mixture on it. Press the wrapper then repeat with the remaining wrappers and filling.
3. Arrange the filled dumpling wrappers on the Instant Pot then select the STEAM menu and set time to 7 minutes.
4. Once it is done, naturally release the Instant Pot the open the lid.
5. Arrange the mushroom dumplings on a serving platter then enjoy.

Curry Tofu

(Prep + Cook Time: 25 minutes | Servings: 4)

Ingredients:

- 2 cup coconut milk
- 1 tbsp yellow curry powder
- 2 tbsp raw peanut, skin off
- 1 tbsp garam masala
- 2 large green bell peppers, cored and diced
- 1 cup tomato paste
- 1 white onion, diced
- 4 cloves garlic, minced
- 1 pack firm tofu, cubed
- Salt and pepper to taste

Directions:

1. On a non-stick pan, roast the peanuts on low heat. Keep moving the peanuts around to avoid burning them.
2. After 5 minutes, transfer the peanuts to a food processor and turn it into paste.
3. Before removing the peanut paste from the processor, add the other ingredients except for the tofu.
4. Blend these together to form a thick sauce.
5. Place the cubed tofu in the Instant Pot and then pour over the sauce. Cover and seal the lid. Press the MANUAL button and cook for 5 minutes.
6. After 5 minutes, let the Instant Pot release its pressure naturally. Uncover the lid.
7. Serve on a plate. Enjoy.

White Bean and Tofu Curry Bowl

(Prep + Cook Time: 20 minutes | Servings: 4)

Ingredients:

- 1 cup brown rice, raw
- 1 ½ c. vegan broth
- 1 pack firm tofu, cubed and dried
- 1 can white beans, washed and drained
- 1 cup coconut milk
- ½ cup diced tomatoes
- 1 tbsp garam masala
- 1 tbsp yellow curry powder
- 1 tsp red chili powder
- Salt and pepper to taste

Directions:

1. Place the tofu, white beans, coconut milk, diced tomatoes and spices in the Instant Pot. Cover and seal the lid. Press MANUAL and cook for 3 minutes.

2. Let the pressure release naturally from the pot. Uncover then and add the raw brown rice and the vegan broth.
3. Cover and seal the lid again. Press MANUAL and cook for 5 minutes. Let the pressure release naturally.
4. Serve in a bowl. Enjoy.

Japanese Udon in Pumpkin Soup

Udon is a type of thick wheat flour noodle of Japanese cuisine.
(Prep + Cook Time: 20 minutes | Servings: 2)

Ingredients:
- 1 cup vegan broth
- 2 cup organic pumpkin puree
- ¼ tsp light soy sauce
- 3 oz udon noodles
- ¼ cup soft tofu
- 4 stalk green onions, chopped
- ½ tsp toasted sesame seeds
- ½ tsp sesame oil
- 1 cup alfalfa sprouts
- Salt and pepper to taste

Directions:
1. Place the vegan broth and pumpkin puree in an Instant Pot. Season with soy sauce, salt and pepper and the stir well. Cover and seal the lid. Press MANUAL and cook for 3 minutes.
2. Quick release the pressure and uncover the lid. Add the soft tofu, udon noodles and sesame oil. Stir well. Seal the lid again, press MANUAL and cook for another 3 minutes. Let the Instant Pot release the pressure naturally.
3. Uncover the lid and then add the alfalfa sprouts and green onions.
4. Serve in a bowl with a sprinkle of toasted sesame seeds.

Corn bread
(Prep + Cook Time: 30 minutes | Servings: 8)

Ingredients:
- 17 ounce corn muffin mix
- 1 cup fat-free milk
- 2 eggs
- 8 fluid ounce water

Directions:
1. Place corn muffin mix in a medium sized bowl, add eggs, pour in milk and using electric mixture stir until blend and lumpy.
2. Take a Bundt pan, 7" diameter and 3 ¼" depth, brush the inner sides generously with oil and spoon corn bread mixture, use spatula to smooth the top.
3. Into pot of the Instant Pot, pour water, insert steamer basket and place pan. Close and lock with lid, switch on cooker, position valve, select HIGH pressure and enter 20 minutes cooking time on timer pad.
4. When time is up and timer buzz, switch off cooker and let pressure release naturally for 10 minutes and then quick release for remaining pressure.
5. Uncover cooker when pressure indicator has gone down and carefully remove the pan.
6. Insert wooden toothpick into dough, if toothpick comes out clean then bread is cook.
7. Then let pan cool slightly on cooling rack before turning out bread.
8. Slice to serve.

Greek-Style Eggplant Stew

(Prep + Cook Time: 40 minutes | Servings: 4)

Ingredients:
- 2 eggplants, cut into cubes
- 1 parsnip, chopped
- 1 carrot, chopped
- 1 (14 oz) can chickpeas, drained
- 2 cups water
- 4 cups vegetable broth
- 1 cup tomato paste
- 1 tsp celery seeds
- ½ tsp fennel seeds
- 1 tsp cumin
- ¼ tsp ground black pepper
- 1 tsp salt
- ¼ tsp cayenne pepper

Directions:
1. Add all of the above ingredients to your pressure cooker; lock the lid into place.
2. Bring to LOW pressure, maintaining the pressure for about 30 minutes.
3. Turn off the heat; allow pressure to release naturally.
4. Next, ladle the stew into individual serving dishes.
5. Serve warm topped with grated sharp cheese if desired.

Eggplant Pasta

(Prep + Cook Time: 25 minutes | Servings: 4)

Ingredients:
- 250 g. rigatoni pasta
- 1 large eggplant, washed and cubed
- 2 cup Portobello mushrooms, chopped
- 3 cloves garlic, minced
- 1 ½ cup pomodoro primavera sauce
- 2 tbsp. olive oil
- Salt and pepper to taste
- Fresh parsley, chopped (for topping)

Directions:
1. Press SAUTE button and sauté the garlic in olive oil in the Instant Pot.

2. Add the eggplant after a minute. Toss well and coat in garlic and oil. Season with salt and pepper. Finally, add the mushrooms. Cook for 3 minutes.
3. Add the rest of the ingredients, except for the parsley. Press MANUAL and cook for 10 minutes. Let the Instant Pot sit until the pressure is released. Uncover the lid.
4. Serve on a platter and top with chopped parsley.

Vegan Pasta
(Prep + Cook Time: 20 minutes | Servings: 4)

Ingredients:
- 9 oz. whole wheat vegan pasta
- 1 can chickpeas, washed and drained
- 2 cup vegan broth
- 1 cup marble tomatoes, quartered
- 3 cloves garlic, minced
- ½ white onion, sliced thinly
- 1 cup broccoli florets, chopped
- 1 green bell pepper, cored, seeded and sliced thinly
- 1 tbsp dried basil
- ½ tsp red pepper flakes (optional)
- 1 lemon, sliced into wedges
- Salt and pepper to taste

Directions:
1. Place all ingredients, except for the lemon wedges, in the Instant Pot. Cover and seal the lid.
2. Select the MANUAL option and cook for 10 minutes over medium pressure.
3. Leave the Instant Pot and let the pressure naturally release from it.
4. Transfer the pasta on a serving platter.
5. Serve with the lemon wedges. Enjoy.

Savoy Cabbage and Cream

(Prep + Cook Time: 30 minutes | Servings: 4)

Ingredients:

- 1 cup bacon, chopped
- 1 medium Savoy cabbage head, chopped
- 1 yellow onion, chopped
- 2 cups bone stock
- ¼ tsp nutmeg
- Salt and black pepper, to taste
- 1 bay leaf
- 1 cup coconut milk
- 2 tbsp parsley flakes

Directions:

1. Set your Instant Pot to SAUTE mode, then add bacon and onion. Stir and cook until bacon is crispy.
2. Add stock, cabbage, bay leaf, salt, pepper, and nutmeg. Stir, cover, and cook at HIGH pressure for 5 minutes.
3. Release the pressure, uncover pot, and set it on SAUTE mode again.
4. Add milk, more salt and pepper if needed, and parsley. Stir and cook for 4 minutes.
5. Divide among plates and serve.

Ratatouille

(Prep + Cook Time: 40 minutes | Servings: 4)

Ingredients:

- 1 big eggplant, peeled and thinly sliced
- 2 garlic cloves, minced
- 3 tbsp extra virgin olive oil
- Salt and black pepper, to taste
- 1 cup onion, chopped
- 1 green bell pepper, chopped
- 1 red bell pepper, chopped
- ½ cup water
- 1 tsp thyme
- 14 oz canned tomatoes, chopped
- A pinch of sugar
- 1 cup basil, chopped

Directions:

1. Set your Instant Pot to SAUTE mode, then add oil and heat it up.

2. Add green and red bell pepper, onion, and garlic. Stir and cook for 3 minutes.
3. Add eggplant, water, salt, pepper, thyme, sugar, and tomatoes. Cover the pot and cook at HIGH pressure for 4 minutes.
4. Release the pressure fast, uncover the pot, and add basil.
5. Stir gently, divide among plates and serve.

Couscous Burritos

(Prep + Cook Time: 25 minutes | Servings: 4)

Ingredients:

- 1 tsp olive oil
- 1 tbsp red onions, diced
- 1 green bell pepper, seeded and diced
- 1 tsp cumin powder
- 1 cup couscous, raw
- 1 cup salsa
- 1 cup vegan broth
- 1 can black beans, washed and drained
- Salt and pepper to taste

Toppings:
- 1 avocado, seeded and diced
- 1 sprig coriander, chopped finely
- 1 lime, cut into wedges
- 8 pcs Romaine lettuce leaves

Directions:

1. Place the olive oil in the pot. Select the SAUTE button and cook the onion and bell pepper for a few minutes.
2. Once the onion turns translucent, add the cumin, salt, and pepper. Turn off the pot.
3. Add the couscous, broth, salsa, and beans. Cover and seal the lid. Select the RICE button and cook under low pressure for 10 minutes.
4. Leave the Instant Pot for another 5 minutes to naturally release the pressure. Uncover the lid.
5. Use a pair of forks to fluff the couscous. Transfer to a serving platter and serve with the toppings on a separate platter.
6. Use the romaine leaves as the burrito bread.

Mexican "Baked" beans

(Prep + Cook Time: 45 minutes | Servings: 4)

Ingredients:

- 2 tbsp olive oil 1 cup red onion, diced
- 1 tbsp poblano pepper, diced
- 3 cloves garlic, crushed and minced
- 1 tsp Mexican oregano
- 1 tsp ground cumin
- 1 tsp chili powder
- ½ tsp salt
- 1 tsp black pepper
- 2 cups stewed tomatoes, chopped, with liquid
- 2 cups dry kidney beans, soaked overnight, rinsed and drained
- 5 cups vegetable stock
- 2 cups dry black beans, soaked overnight, rinsed and drained
- ¼ cup fresh cilantro, chopped

Directions:

1. Set the Instant Pot to the SAUTE setting and add the olive oil. Once the oil is hot, add the red onion, poblano pepper, and garlic.
2. Season the mixture with the Mexican oregano, cumin, chili powder, salt, and black pepper, and mix well.
3. Cook for 1-2 minutes. Next, add the stewed tomatoes with liquid, the kidney beans and the vegetable stock.
4. Set the machine to the HIGH pressure cooker setting. Cover and cook for 12 minutes.
5. Carefully release the steam using the quick release option and add the black beans. Cover and cook for an additional 25 minutes on HIGH pressure.
6. Use the natural release option to release the steam.
7. Stir in the fresh cilantro before serving.

Mung Beans Stew

(Prep + Cook Time: 10 minutes | Servings: 4)

Ingredients:

- 2 tbsp olive oil
- 1 red onion, diced
- 2 cloves garlic, minced
- 1 large carrots, peeled and diced
- ¼ tsp thyme
- 2 bay leaves
- 6 cups vegan broth
- 1 cup green mung beans, dried
- 1 cup yellow mung beans, dried
- 1 red potato, peeled and diced
- 3 handfuls spinach leaves
- Salt and pepper to taste

Directions:

1. SAUTE the garlic and onions in olive oil using the Instant Pot. After a few minutes, add the carrots.
2. Once the carrots start to soften, add the bay leaves, thyme, mung beans, potato, and vegan broth. Mix well. Cover and seal the lid.
3. Manually cook for 6 minutes over HIGH pressure.
4. Leave the Instant Pot until the pressure naturally releases. Uncover the lid.
5. Remove the bay leaf and then season with salt and pepper.
6. Finally, add the spinach leaves. Stir well.
7. Serve in a bowl.

Spaghetti Squash (S&F)

(Prep + Cook Time: 10 minutes | Servings: 4)

Ingredients:

- One 3-pound spaghetti squash
- 1 cup water

Directions:

1. Cut off the end of the squash with the stem and then cut in half.
2. Scoop out the seeds.

3. Pour water into your Instant Pot and lower in the steamer basket.
4. Put the cut squash in the basket and secure the lid.
5. Hit MANUAL and then cook for 8 minutes on HIGH pressure.
6. When the timer goes off, hit CANCEL and then quick-release.
7. When you can handle the squash without burning yourself, scrap the insides out with a fork.
8. Serve.

Vegan Feijoada

(Prep + Cook Time: 40 minutes | Servings: 6)

Ingredients:

- 2 ½ cups veggie broth
- 2 cups dried black beans (soaked overnight)
- 1 cup soy curls (softened in hot water for 15 minutes and drained)
- 2 peeled and cut carrots
- 2 sliced onions
- 4 minced garlic cloves
- 2 bay leaves
- 1 chopped red bell pepper
- 1 spicy chopped vegan sausage
- ⅓ cup dry red wine
- 1 tbsp cumin
- ½ tbsp smoked paprika
- ½ tbsp dried thyme
- ½ tbsp liquid smoke
- ½ tsp black pepper

Directions:

1. Turn on your Instant Pot to SAUTE and pour in a little water. Add onions, bell pepper, carrots, and garlic and stir for 5 minutes.
2. Add spices and cook for a few minutes.
3. Pour in the red wine, wait 2 minutes, and then add the sausage, broth, beans, soy curls, and bay leaves. Stir.
4. Lock the pressure cooker. Hit BEAN/CHILE and adjust time to 30 minutes.
5. When the timer goes off, hit CANCEL and wait for the pressure to come down.
6. Carefully open the lid and make sure the beans are soft.
7. Serve with herbs like parsley or cilantro!

Corn with Cilantro Butter

(Prep + Cook Time: 5 minutes | Servings: 4)

Ingredients:

- 1 ⅕ cups of water
- 4 ears of cleaned and shucked corn
- 6 tbsp butter, divided
- 2 tbsp minced cilantro
- ½ tsp chili powder
- ½ tsp salt
- ¼ tsp sugar

Directions:

1. In your Instant Pot, mix water, salt, sugar, and chili powder. Lower in corn niblets, along with 2 tablespoons of butter.
2. Close and seal the lid. Select MANUAL and cook on HIGH pressure for 3 minutes.
3. While that cooks, melt the remaining butter over the stovetop and add minced cilantro.
4. When the pressure cooker is done, hit CANCEL and quick-release.
5. Serve the corn with butter poured on top.

Spanish Zucchini Tortilla

(Prep + Cook Time: 15 minutes | Servings: 3)

Ingredients:

- 3 eggs
- 1 large zucchini
- 1 onion, chopped
- ½ tsp thyme, chopped
- ¼ tsp salt
- ¼ tsp white pepper
- 2 tbsp olive oil

Directions:

1. Cut the zucchini into thin strips and place aside. Crack the eggs in a medium bowl and whisk with a fork for 1 minute.
2. Add the zucchini strips, onion, thyme, salt, and pepper, mix well.
3. Add 3-4 cups of water into the Instant Pot and place a trivet or stand it in.

4. Now spray a medium sized baking dish with olive oil, transfer the eggs mixture into a pan and place into a trivet.
5. Cover the pot with a lid and let it cook on MANUAL mode for 10 minutes.
6. Serve hot and enjoy.

Vegan Rice and Veggies Dish
(Prep + Cook Time: 15 minutes | Servings: 3)

Ingredients:
- 2 cups long grain rice
- 1 red bell pepper, thinly sliced
- 1 tbsp extra virgin olive oil
- 1 yellow onion, finely chopped
- 1 carrot, grated
- Salt and black pepper to taste
- 4 cups water
- ½ cup peas

Directions:
1. Heat up a pan with the oil over medium high heat, add the onions, stir and cook for 4 minutes.
2. Transfer this mix to your Instant Pot, add rice, water, bell pepper, carrot, peas, salt and pepper, stir and cook on HIGH pressure for 10 minutes.
3. Release pressure naturally, divide rice mix amongst plates and serve.

Tasty Millet and Veggies

(Prep + Cook Time: 15 minutes | Servings: 3)

Ingredients:

- ½ cup oyster mushrooms, thinly sliced
- 1 cup millet, soaked and drained
- 1 cup leeks, finely chopped
- 2 garlic cloves, minced
- 1 tsp vegetable oil
- ½ cup green lentils, rinsed
- ½ cup bok choy, sliced
- 2 and ¼ cups veggie stock
- 1 cup asparagus, cut in medium pieces
- 1 cup snow peas, sliced
- ¼ cup mixed chives and parsley, finely chopped
- A drizzle of lemon juice
- Salt and black pepper to the taste

Directions:

1. Heat up a pan with the vegetable oil over medium high heat, add mushrooms, leeks and garlic, stir and cook for 2-3 minutes.
2. Add lentils and millet, stir, cook for 3-4 minutes and transfer to your Instant Pot.
3. Add bok choy, asparagus, snow peas and veggie stock, cover and cook on HIGH pressure for 10 minutes.
4. Release pressure naturally, add salt and pepper to the taste, stir and divide amongst serving bowls.
5. Drizzle lemon juice on top of each bowl, add chives and parsley and serve.

Wheat Berry Salad

(Prep + Cook Time: 60 minutes | Servings: 6)

Ingredients:

- 2 cups of Water
- ¼ cup of raspberry vinegar
- 1 cup of wheat berries
- 2 tsp of dijon mustard
- 1 tbsp of balsamic vinegar
- 3 tbsp of oil
- ¾ cup of dried blueberries
- ¾ cup of thinly sliced green onions
- ½ cup of slivered dried apricots
- ½ cup of chopped toasted almonds
- 2 tbsp of chopped fresh parsley
- ¾ tsp of salt
- ½ tsp of pepper

Directions:

1. Rinse your wheat berries well with cold water and place them in a bowl filled with cold water. Soak them over night. Rinse thoroughly and drain them.
2. Place your wheat berries in your Instant Pot with 2 cups of water and pressure cook for approximately 15 to 20 minutes, manually release the pressure when done. Rinse with cold water and drain.
3. Whisk together your raspberry vinegar, balsamic vinegar, mustard, salt, and pepper in your bowl. Gradually whisk in your oil until blended. Stir in your apricots, onions, almonds, blueberries, and parsley.
4. Allow it to stand for approximately 30 minutes. Stir in your wheat berries. Cover and refrigerate for 4 hours.
5. Garnish with your fresh parsley. Serve and enjoy.

Easy Soy Yogurt

(Prep + Cook Time: 14 hours | Servings: 2)

Ingredients:
- 1 ½ cups homemade soymilk
- 1 ½ tbsp soy yogurt

Directions:
1. Prepare 2 heatproof bowls without a lid. Divide and pour the soymilk into two containers then add half of the soy yogurt into each bowl.
2. Carefully place a trivet in the Instant Pot then put the bowls on the trivet then cover with the lid and seal tightly.
3. Select the YOGURT feature then set the time to 14 hours.
4. After 14 hours, open the Instant Pot lid, and you will see the yogurt that tends to separate.
5. Slowly stir the yogurt then take the bowl out of the Instant Pot. Let the yogurt cool then serve and enjoy.
6. The yogurt can be kept in the refrigerator up to 5 days.
7. It is better to start making yogurt in the evening, so it will be ready when the sun rises.

Gluten Free Quinoa Tabbouleh

(Prep + Cook Time: 10 minutes | Servings: 3)

Ingredients:
- 2 cups quinoa, rinsed and drained
- 1 ½ cup water
- 2 tbsp olive oil
- 1 medium tomato, thinly diced
- 1 small cucumber, thinly diced
- 3 garlic cloves, minced
- 2 tbsp mint, freshly chopped
- 2 tbsp parsley, freshly chopped
- 2 tbsp lemon juice
- Pinch of salt and black pepper powder, to taste

Directions:
1. Add 1 tablespoon oil, quinoa, salt and water into your Instant Pot. Secure the lid.

2. Hit the MANUAL and cook for 3 minutes on high pressure. Once cooked, let depressurize naturally for 5 minutes, then release the pressure manually.
3. Next, transfer the contents to a large mixing bowl. Keep aside for a minute to cool.
4. Once cooled, add in the diced tomatoes, cucumber, mint, parsley, 1 tablespoon oil and lemon juice.
5. Sprinkle salt (if needed) and pepper and mix everything up together.

Beet and Orange Salad
(Prep + Cook Time: 30 minutes | Servings: 4)

Ingredients:
- 1½ pounds beets
- 2 tsp orange zest, grated
- 3 strips orange peel
- 2 tbsp cider vinegar
- ½ cup orange juice
- 2 tbsp brown sugar
- 2 scallions, chopped
- 2 tsp mustard
- 2 cups arugula and mustard greens

Directions:
1. Scrub beets well, cut them in halves, and put them in a bowl.
2. In your Instant Pot, mix the orange peel strips with vinegar and orange juice, and stir.
3. Add beets, cover the pot, and cook at HIGH pressure for 7 minutes. Release the pressure naturally.
4. Uncover pot, and transfer beets to a bowl. Discard peel strips from the pot, then add mustard and sugar and stir well.
5. Add scallions and grated orange zest to the beets and toss them.
6. Add liquid from the pot over the beets, toss to coat, and serve on top of mixed salad greens. Serve.

Beets with Blue Cheese

(Prep + Cook Time: 30 minutes | Servings: 6)

Ingredients:
- 6 beets (about 1 ½ pounds)
- ¼ cup crumbled blue cheese
- ½ tsp kosher salt
- ½ tsp fresh ground black pepper
- 1 cup water, for the pot

Directions:
1. Trim the leaves from the beats, making sure not to cut the root off or into the beet. Rinse and remove any dirt.
2. Pour the water into the inner pot and set a rack. Put the beets on the rack. Close and lock the lid. Press PRESSURE, set the pressure to HIGH, and set the time for 20 minutes.
3. When the timer beeps at the end of the cooking cycle, turn the valve to VENTING for quick pressure release.
4. Carefully open the lid and transfer the beets onto a cutting board. Let them cool down for 1-2 minutes.
5. Using a paper towel, peel off the skin and then pull off the roots.
6. Trim the stems and then cut the beets into halves, then into quarters.
7. Sprinkle them with salt and pepper, then transfer into a serving bowl.
8. Top with the crumbled cheese and serve.

Babaganoush

(Prep + Cook Time: 25 minutes | Servings: 6)

Ingredients:
- 2 pounds eggplant, peeled and cut into medium chunks
- Salt and black pepper, to taste
- ¼ cup extra virgin olive oil
- ½ cup water
- 4 garlic cloves
- ¼ cup lemon juice
- 1 bunch thyme, chopped
- 1 tbsp tahini
- A drizzle of olive oil
- 3 olives, pitted and sliced

Directions:

1. Put the eggplant pieces in your Instant Pot, add ¼ cup oil, set the pot on SAUTE mode, and heat everything up.
2. Add garlic, water, salt and pepper, then stir. Cover and cook at HIGH pressure for 3 minutes.
3. Quick release the pressure and uncover pot, then transfer eggplant pieces and garlic to your blender.
4. Add lemon juice and tahini and pulse well.
5. Add thyme and blend again.
6. Transfer eggplant spread to a bowl, top with olive slices and a drizzle of oil and serve.

Corn on the Cob

(Prep + Cook Time: 5 minutes | Servings: 2)

Ingredients:

- Sweet Corn (3 ears, halved)
- 8 oz of water

Directions:

1. Pour the water into the bottom of your Instant Pot. Add the steamer basket.
2. Place the corn in the steamer basket. Depending on the size of your pressure cooker, you should be able to fit about 3 ears of corn in the basket.
3. For 3 ears of corn, you should use 8-ounces of water. For 5 or more ears of corn, you should use 12-ounces of water.
4. Close the lid on the pressure cooker. Allow the pressure to reach HIGH pressure. Set a timer for 2 minutes.
5. When the timer goes off, quick release the pressure.
6. Serve and enjoy.

Corn With Lime Sauce
(Prep + Cook Time: 20 minutes | Servings: 4)

Ingredients:
- 4 ears corn
- 1 ½ cups water
- 2 tbsp nutritional yeast
- 2 tbsp hemp hearts
- ½ cup almond milk
- 1 tbsp brown rice flour
- Salt and black pepper to the taste
- A pinch of cayenne pepper
- 1 garlic clove, crushed
- 1 tbsp lime juice
- Chopped cilantro for serving
- 1 jalapeno, chopped for serving

Directions:
1. Put a steaming basket in your Instant Pot, add corn, add the water, cover and cook on HIGH for 4 minutes.
2. Release pressure, take corn out and arrange it on plates. In your kitchen blender, mix almond milk with hemp, yeast, flour, garlic, salt and pepper and blend well.
3. Pour this into a small pan, heat up over medium high heat, add cayenne and lime juice, stir and cook 3-4 minutes.
4. Take sauce off heat, add cilantro and jalapeno, stir and drizzle over corn.
5. Serve.

Vegetarian Burritos (S&F)
(Prep + Cook Time: 20 minutes | Servings: 6)

Ingredients:
- 1 can crushed tomatoes
- 1 jalapeño minced
- 1 onion chopped
- flour tortillas
- 1 ½ cup vegan cheese
- 1 tsp chili seasoning
- ¼ cup vegetable stock
- 1 can vegan refried beans

Directions:
1. Add stock and tomatoes to pot.
2. Add onion.
3. Add jalapeño, chili seasoning.

4. Add beans.
5. Cook on HIGH pressure 15 minutes.
6. Serve.

Zucchini and Mushrooms
(Prep + Cook Time: 20 minutes | Servings: 6)

Ingredients:

- 8-12 oz mushrooms, sliced or separated depending on type of mushroom
- 4 medium zucchini, cut into
- ½-inch slices (about 8 cups)
- 1 can (15 oz) crushed or diced tomatoes with juice
- 1 large sprig fresh basil, sliced
- 1 tbsp extra-virgin olive oil
- ½ tsp black pepper, or to taste
- ½ tsp salt, or to taste
- 2 cloves garlic, minced
- 1 ½ cup onions, diced

Directions:

1. Press the SAUTE button of the Instant Pot. Add the olive oil and heat.
2. Add the garlic, onions, and mushrooms; cook, frequently stirring, until the onions are soft and the mushrooms lose their moisture.
3. Add the basil and sprinkle with the salt and pepper. Sauté for 5 minutes until the mushrooms are soft.
4. Add the zucchini, stir. Add the tomatoes with the juices over the zucchini; do not stir.
5. Close and lock the lid. Turn the steam valve to SEALING. Press the MANUAL button. Set the pressure to LOW and the timer to 1 minute.
6. When the timer beeps, turn the steam valve to VENTING to quick release the pressure. Carefully remove the cover.
7. If the zucchini are still a little undercooked, just cover the pot and let rest for 1 minutes to allow the zucchinis to soften.
8. Serve over pasta, rice, baked potatoes, or polenta. If desired, you can stir a can of white beans.

Fresh Berry Compote

(Prep + Cook Time: 36 minutes | Servings: 8)

Any kind of berries, fruit or cherries will work, so use whatever you love.

Ingredients:
- 1 pound Fresh Strawberries washed, trimmed and cut in half
- 1 pound Fresh Blueberries washed
- ¼ cup sugar
- 2 tsp Orange juice or 2 tsp Lemon juice

Directions:
1. Add fruit to Pressure Cooker cooking pot.
2. Sprinkle with sugar and let sit 20 minutes.
3. Add a little squeeze of orange juice.
4. Lock on lid and Close Pressure Valve.
5. Cook at HIGH Pressure for 1 minute.
6. When Beep sounds, allow a 15 minutes Natural Pressure Release.
7. Compote will thicken as it cools.

Peach Compote

(Prep + Cook Time: 30 minutes | Servings: 8)

Ingredients:
- 8 peaches, chopped
- 6 tbsp sugar
- 1 tsp cinnamon, ground
- 1 tsp vanilla extract
- 1 vanilla bean, scraped
- 2 tbsp grape nuts cereal

Directions:
1. Put peaches in your Instant Pot and mix with the sugar, cinnamon, vanilla bean, and vanilla extract.
2. Stir well, cover pot and cook at HIGH for 3 minutes. Release pressure for 10 minutes, then add grape nuts and stir well.
3. Transfer the compote to bowls and serve.

328

Fresh Currant Bread Pudding

(Prep + Cook Time: 15 minutes | Servings: 6)

This recipe calls for sweet bread in order to achieve a rich and delectable flavor.

Ingredients:

- 1/3 cup caster sugar
- 4 ½ cups sweet stale bread, cubed
- ½ tbsp candied lemon peel
- 1/3 cup dried currants
- 2 ½ tbsp butter
- ½ tsp vanilla essence
- A pinch of kosher salt
- ½ tsp cinnamon powder
- 2 ¼ cups milk
- 4 eggs, beaten
- 1 ½ cups heavy cream

Directions:

1. Prepare your cooker by adding 3 cups of water. Add the steam rack, too.
2. Take a casserole dish that will fit in the inner pot. Then, butter the casserole dish. Add bread cubes to the dish.
3. Combine the remaining ingredients in a mixing bowl; whisk vigorously until everything is well combined. Pour the mixture over the bread cubes.
4. Next, cover with two layers of foil.
5. Select the STEAM function and cook for 14 minutes or until the pudding is set.
6. Remove the casserole dish from the cooker.
7. Serve and enjoy!

Vegan Pumpkin Cake (VEG)

(Prep + Cook Time: 35 minutes | Servings: 10)

Here is a dairy-free and egg-free recipe that is actually lip-smacking good.

Ingredients:

- 1 ¼ cups pumpkin puree
- 1 cup applesauce
- 1 ¼ cups sugar
- A pinch of salt
- 2 cups flour
- 1 tsp ginger, grated
- ½ tsp vanilla extract
- 1 ½ tsp baking soda
- ½ tsp pumpkin pie spice

Directions:

1. In a mixing bowl, combine the flour, vanilla extract, baking soda, pumpkin pie spice, and the salt.
2. In a separate bowl, combine the applesauce and the sugar. Stir in the ginger and the pumpkins puree and mix well to combine.
3. Add the applesauce mixture to the dry flour mixture. Spoon batter into a cake pan oiled with cooking spray. Cover with a foil.
4. Pour 2 cups of water into the cooker. Lay a metal rack on the bottom of your cooker. Lay prepared cake pan on the metal rack. Cook for 24 minutes at HIGH pressure.
5. Transfer the pan to a wire rack before serving. Dust your cake with icing sugar or decorate with vegan frosting.
6. Enjoy!

Frozen Lime

(Prep + Cook Time: 32 minutes | Servings: 10)

In this gorgeous recipe, a good replacement for digestive biscuits would be ginger biscuits and even ginger nuts.

Ingredients:

- 1 tsp vanilla extract
- 3 tbsp flour
- 1 tsp anise seeds
- 1 tsp grated ginger
- 2 tbsp lemon zest, finely grated
- 2 tbsp lime zest
- 1 stick butter, at room temperature
- 3 whole eggs, room temperature
- ½ cup sour cream
- 1 ½ pounds full-fat cream cheese
- 1 ½ cups digestive biscuits, crumbled
- ½ cup caster sugar

Directions:

1. In a bowl, combine the crumbled biscuits and butter. Lightly grease the inside of a springform pan with a non-stick cooking spray. Now, press the biscuit mixture into the bottom of the spring-form pan.
2. Next, add 2½ cups of water to your Instant Pot. Now, lay a trivet at the bottom of the cooker.

3. In a food processor, mix the cream cheese together with caster sugar; process until creamy and smooth. Fold in the eggs, one at a time.
4. Add the rest of the ingredients. Pulse until everything is well blended.
5. Pour the batter into the springform pan. Cook at HIGH pressure; set the timer for 26 minutes.
6. Wrap your cheesecake in a foil and freeze overnight.
7. Serve and enjoy!

Festive Dessert with Prunes and Pecans
(Prep + Cook Time: 55 minutes | Servings: 8)

Pecans are a powerhouse of vitamin E, several important B-complex groups of vitamins, minerals, beta-carotene, and lutein.

Ingredients:
- 1 cup prunes, chopped
- ½ tsp ground ginger
- 1 ¼ cups sugar
- 2 tbsp orange liqueur
- 4 whole eggs
- 1 ½ sticks butter
- 2 tsp orange zest
- 1/8 tsp salt
- 1/3 cup pecans, chopped
- 1 tsp baking powder
- 1 ¼ cups self-rising flour
- ½ cup double cream, for garnish

Directions:
1. Firstly, beat together the butter and sugar in a dessert bowl. Add the sifted flour and baking powder. Now, whisk the eggs vigorously. Add the whisked eggs to the mixing bowl.
2. Stir in the ground ginger, salt, and orange zest. Next, add the prunes, pecans, and orange liqueur.
3. Add 3 cups of water to the Instant Pot's inner pot. Place a rack inside, and place the dessert bowl on top.
4. Select MANUAL function, HIGH pressure, and 55-minute cook time.
5. Meanwhile, whisk the double cream.
6. Press the CANCEL button; check for the doneness of your dessert.
7. Decorate the pudding with cream and serve.

Cheesecake with Cranberry Topping

(Prep + Cook Time: 45 minutes | Servings: 12)

This cheesecake has a mild flavor and flaky crust, so it pairs perfectly with fresh cranberries.

Ingredients:

For the Cake:
- 3 whole eggs
- ¾ tbsp flour
- 1 stick butter, melted
- 1 ¾ cups cream cheese, softened
- ½ tsp anise seed
- ¼ tsp cinnamon powder
- 1/3 cup sugar
- 1/3 cup sour cream
- 1 1/3 cups biscuits, roughly broken

For the Topping:
- 3/4 cup golden caster sugar
- 1 1/3 cups cranberries
- 2 tsp ground arrowroot
- Cold water

Directions:

1. In a bowl, combine the butter with biscuits. Spread the mixture around the bottom of a lightly springform pan.
2. Next, beat the sugar and cream cheese with an electric mixer. Add the sour cream, cinnamon, anise seed, and flour.
3. Fold in the eggs, one at a time; continue mixing until it is creamy. Pour the mixture onto the prepared crust.
4. Add 3 cups of water to the cooker. Lay the rack on the bottom. Then, lower the pan onto the rack.
5. Cover the cooker with the lid and choose the MANUAL mode. Set the timer for 35 minutes.
6. Refrigerate your dessert overnight.
7. Meanwhile, you can make the compote; place the cranberries, sugar, and 1 cup of water in a saucepan; then, bring to a simmer for 5 minutes, stirring periodically.
8. Then, mix the arrowroot with 2 tablespoons of cold water; add the mixture to the saucepan. Cook for 2 more minutes, stirring regularly. Allow the topping to cool completely.
9. Spread the topping over your cheesecake and serve chilled.

Banana-Vanilla Rice Pudding (S&F)

(Prep + Cook Time: 25 minutes | Servings: 6)

When you are in a hurry or you're just not in the mood to cook, it's good to have this recipe on hand.

Ingredients:

- 3 large-sized ripe bananas, divided
- 2 ½ cups vanilla rice milk
- 1 ½ cups basmati rice
- ½ tsp vanilla extract
- 1/8 tsp kosher salt
- ½ cup sugar
- 1 ½ cups water
- Ground cardamom, for garnish

Directions:

1. Add the rice, water, vanilla rice milk, sugar, and salt to your Instant Pot. Push the MANUAL button and cook for 11 minutes. Afterwards, remove the cooker's lid.
2. Let the pudding rest for 6 to 8 minutes before releasing pressure.
3. Add vanilla extract and 2 mashed bananas. Stir to combine. Cut the remaining banana into thin slices.
4. Divide the pudding among the serving bowls; serve topped with banana slices and ground cardamom.
5. Enjoy!

Orange Swirl Cheesecake

(Prep + Cook Time: 60 minutes | Servings: 8)

Ingredients:

- 1 cup of Crushed Oreo Cookie Crumbs (12 Oreos)
- 2 tbsp of Melted Butter

Filling:

- 16 oz of Cream Cheese (Room Temperature)
- 2 eggs
- 2 tbsp of Sour Cream
- ½ cup of Sugar
- 1 tsp of Vanilla Extract
- 1 tbsp of Orange Zest
- ½ cup of Melted & Cooled Orange Candy Melts

Directions:

1. Prepare a 7-inch springform pan by coating it with a non-stick spray.
2. In a small-sized bowl, combine your Oreo cookie crumbs and butter. Spread evenly in the bottom and 1-inch up the side of your pan. Place in your freezer for 10 minutes.
3. Place 8 ounces of cream cheese into your mixing bowl. Add ¼ cup of sugar and beat at a medium speed until smooth. Blend in your sour cream and vanilla. Mix in one egg until blended. Don't over mix.
4. In a second mixing bowl, place 8 ounces of your cream cheese and add ¼ cup of sugar and beat until smooth. Gradually beat in your melted candy melts. Mix in one egg until blended. Stir in your orange zest.
5. Scatter dollops of vanilla batter on top of your crust alternating with dollops of orange batter. Use a skewer to swirl the orange and vanilla batters together.
6. Pour 1 cup of water into your Instant Pot and place the trivet in the bottom. Carefully center the filled pan on a foil sling and lower it into your Instant Pot. Fold your foil sling down so that it doesn't interfere with closing your lid.
7. Lock your lid in place. Select HIGH pressure and set the timer for approximately 25 minutes. When the beep sounds, turn off your Instant Pot and use a Natural pressure release for 10 minutes, and then do a quick pressure release to release any of the remaining pressure.
8. When the valve drops carefully remove your lid. Remove your cheesecake and check the cheesecake to see if the middle is set but slightly jiggly like a set jello. If not, cook the cheesecake an additional 5 minutes. Use the corner of a paper towel to soak up any water on top of your cheesecake.
9. Remove the springform pan to a wire rack to cool. When your cheesecake is cooled, refrigerate covered with plastic wrap for at least 4 hours. Refrigerate until ready to serve.
10. Decorate with whipped cream, grated orange candy melts, and Oreo cookie crumbs.
11. Serve and enjoy!

Black Chocolate Cake (S&F)

(Prep + Cook Time: 15 minutes | Servings: 4)

Ingredients:
- 7 ounce Ghirardelli Chocolate 60% Cacao Bittersweet Chocolate Baking Chips
- 3 eggs
- 4 tbsp of Butter
- ¼ cup of Flour
- ½ cup of Sugar

Directions:
1. Melt your chocolate and butter together.
2. Add your sugar, flour, and eggs. Beat.
3. Put in your ramekin. Place on the trivet in your Instant Pot and add 250ml water in your pot.
4. Cook for 12 minutes on the MANUAL setting on HIGH pressure and then Quick release.
5. Serve and enjoy!

Applesauce (S&F)

(Prep + Cook Time: 15 minutes | Servings: 4)

Ingredients:
- 10 Large Jonagold Apples (Peeled, Cored, & Quartered)
- ¼ cup of Apple Juice
- ¼ cup of Sugar
- 1 tsp of Ground Cinnamon

Directions:
1. Place your apple pieces, apple juice, cinnamon, and sugar in your Instant Pot and stir well to combine. Select HIGH pressure and set cook time for 4 minutes.
2. After the timer beeps, turn off your Instant Pot. Wait 5 minutes and then use a Quick pressure release. Carefully remove your lid.
3. Stir in your apples, breaking up large chunks, until you've achieved your desired consistency.
4. Serve and enjoy!

Star Anise Chocolate Cake

(Prep + Cook Time: 15 minutes | Servings: 10)

Inspired by black chocolate, you can come up with this dessert idea that's so easy and literally scrumptious.

Ingredients:

- 3 eggs
- ¼ cup flour
- ½ tsp grated nutmeg
- ½ tsp grated ginger
- 1 tsp anise seeds
- 1 cup sugar
- 1 stick butter
- 1 ½ cups black chocolate chips Icing sugar, for garnish

Directions:

1. Microwave the chocolate chips and butter until they are completely melted or about 1 minute. Add sugar, anise seeds, ginger, nutmeg, flour and eggs.
2. Beat for 5 minutes, until everything is well mixed or until there are no lumps.
3. Pour the batter into a buttered cake pan. Insert the trivet into your Instant Pot. Pour in 3 cups of water. Place the cake pan on the trivet.
4. Cook for 7 minutes on MANUAL mode.
5. Afterwards, perform the quick release. Let it cool completely. After that, invert the cake onto a serving platter and dust it with icing sugar.
6. Serve and enjoy!

Tropical Tapioca Pudding (S&F)

(Prep + Cook Time: 10 minutes | Servings: 4)

Tapioca is high in iron and carbohydrates but low in fat.

Ingredients:

- 1 ¼ cups pineapple, diced
- 3/4 cup nectarine, diced
- 2 ¼ cups whole milk
- ½ tsp vanilla paste
- ½ tsp cardamom
- ½ tsp lemon zest, grated
- 1/3 cup sugar
- ½ cup small pearl tapioca, soaked

Directions:

1. Prepare your Instant Pot by adding 1½ cups of water; then, insert the rack and set aside.
2. Rinse tapioca and add it to a heat-proof bowl. Add the milk, sugar, lemon zest, cardamom, and vanilla paste. Add the bowl to the cooker.
3. Cover and choose MANUAL setting; cook for 9 minutes under HIGH pressure.
4. While your tapioca pudding is still warm, add the fruits.
5. Gently stir to combine and serve at room temperature.

Pumpkin Chocolate Bundt Cake
(Prep + Cook Time: 15 minutes | Servings: 10)

Add a festive look to your dessert table every day with this appetizing cake.

Ingredients:

- 1 ¼ cups pumpkin puree
- 1 tsp ginger, grated
- 1 ½ sticks butter, room temperature
- ¼ tsp grated nutmeg
- ½ tsp ground cinnamon
- ½ tsp ground cloves
- 1 tsp baking soda
- ½ tsp baking powder
- 2 cups all-purpose flour
- ¼ tsp salt
- 3 large eggs
- 1 ¼ cups sugar
- 1 cup chocolate chips

Directions:

1. In a bowl, mix the flour, baking soda, baking powder, nutmeg, cloves, cinnamon, and salt. Now, set it aside.
2. Then, cream the butter together with sugar using an electric mixer. Then, fold in the eggs (one at a time). Stir in the ginger and pumpkin; mix until everything is well blended.
3. Combine the reserved dry mixture with the butter mixture. Lastly, add the chocolate chips and stir to combine.
4. Spoon batter into a half-sized Bundt pan greased with non-stick cooking spray. Cover with an aluminum foil.
5. Next, prepare your Instant Pot by adding 1 ½ cups of water. Then, place the rack on the bottom. Lay the Bundt pan on the rack. Cook at HIGH pressure for 25 minutes.

6. Place your cake on a wire rack to cool before slicing and serving.
7. Enjoy!

Vegan Key Lime Cheesecake (VEG)
(Prep + Cook Time: 25 minutes | Servings: 8)

Ingredients:
for the Crust:
- 1 cup instant oats
- ½ cup almonds
- ½ cup raisins, low sugar
- ¼ cup water

Ingredients for filling:
- 1 cup cashews, soaked in water

- ½ cup almond flour
- ¼ cup coconut sugar
- ½ cup almond milk
- Zest of one lime
- 2 tbsp lime juice
- 1 tsp vanilla essence
- 1 tbsp arrowroot powder
- ½ cup fresh fruit in season (topping)

Directions:
1. Place the ingredients for the crust in a food processor to turn it into a coarse paste. Place the dough in a spring form pan that will fit in the Instant Pot.
2. Place about a cup of water in the Instant Pot and place a circular wire stand over it.
3. Place the cashews in a food processor and blend until smooth. Add in a little of water to create a smooth paste. Slowly add the almond flour, sugar, almond milk, lime zest, lime juice, and vanilla essence to the processor. Pulse again. Add the arrowroot and pulse one last time.
4. Place the prepared filling over the crust. Cover the spring form pan with aluminium foil. Place the pan in the Instant Pot. Cover and seal the lid. Manually cook for 20 minutes over HIGH pressure.
5. Quick release the pressure and carefully uncover the lid. Remove the pan using tongs and remove the foil. Let the cake cool for an hour and then place in the refrigerator overnight.
6. Place the fresh fruits as toppings before serving.

Apricot and Cranberry Cake

(Prep + Cook Time: 30 minutes | Servings: 12)

Ingredients:

- 2/3 cup whole wheat flour
- ½ tsp cardamom powder
- ½ tsp baking powder
- ½ tsp baking soda
- Pinch of salt
- ½ cup unsweetened almond milk
- ¼ cup organic maple syrup
- 2 tbsp flax seeds
- 2 tbsp applesauce
- 1 cup dried apricots, chopped
- ½ cup cranberries, chopped

Directions:

1. Brush a 6-inch tube pan with applesauce and set aside. Using a mixing bowl, combine all dry ingredients together.
2. Using another mixing bowl, combine all wet ingredients.
3. Slowly add the wet ingredients to the dry ingredients.
4. Fold the mix using a spatula. Transfer the mixture to the tube pan and cover with aluminium foil. Place the pan in the Instant Pot.
5. Make sure to pour 1 ½ cups of water and place a circular wire stand before placing the tube pan. Cover and seal the lid.
6. MANUALy cook for 30 minutes over high pressure. Leave the Instant Pot until the pressure naturally release the pot.
7. Open the lid and remove the tube pan.
8. Let the cake cool down before removing it from the tube pan.
9. Serve and enjoy.

Sweet Coconut Rice with Walnuts

(Prep + Cook Time: 15 minutes | Servings: 4)

Ingredients:

- 2 cup unsweetened almond milk
- 1 cup low fat coconut milk
- 1 cup Japanese rice
- ½ cup coconut sugar
- 1 tsp vanilla essence
- ¼ cup desiccated coconut
- ¼ cup crushed walnuts

Directions:

1. Place the almond milk and coconut milk in the Instant Pot. Press the SAUTE button and wait for the mixture to boil.

2. Make sure to stir the mix continuously. Once it boils, add the Japanese rice and stir. Cover and seal the lid. Manually cook the mix for 5 minutes.
3. Let the pressure naturally escape the pot for 5 minutes.
4. Carefully uncover the lid. Add the vanilla essence and sugar. Stir well.
5. Transfer in a serving bowl. Sprinkle over the desiccated coconut and walnuts.
6. Serve and enjoy.

Rice Pudding
(Prep + Cook Time: 30 minutes | Servings: 6)

Ingredients:
- 1 cup basmati rice
- ¾ cup heavy cream OR coconut cream
- 2 cups milk, your choice (soaked nut milk OR raw milk)
- 1/8 tsp sea salt
- ¼ cup maple syrup
- 1 vanilla bean scrapings OR 1 tsp vanilla extract
- 1 ¼ cups water

Directions:
1. Put the rice in a fine mesh colander. Rinse well with several changes of water. Transfer into the Instant Pot. Add the milk, water, sea salt, and maple syrup in the pot. Briefly stir.
2. Cover and lock the lid. Press the PORRIDGE key and let cook on preset time of 20 minutes.
3. When the Instant Pot timer beeps, press the CANCEL key and unplug the Instant Pot. Let the pressure release naturally for 10-15 minutes or until the valve drops.
4. Using an oven mitt or a long handled spoon, turn the steam valve to VENTING to release remaining pressure. Unlock and carefully open the lid.
5. Add the cream and the vanilla. Stir well until mixed.
6. Serve with optional toppings.

Vegan Vanilla Cake (VEG)

(Prep + Cook Time: 25 minutes | Servings: 12)

Ingredients:

- ¾ cup whole wheat flour
- ¾ cup coconut sugar
- ½ cup unsweetened almond milk
- 3 tbsp canola oil
- ½ tsp baking soda
- 1 ½ tsp fresh lemon juice
- 1 tsp vanilla essence
- ¼ tsp salt

Directions:

1. Place a cup of water in the Instant Pot and place a circular wire stand over it. Set aside.
2. In a mixing bowl, combine the wet ingredients. In a separate mixing bowl, combine the dry ingredients.
3. Slowly add the wet ingredients to the dry ingredients. Mix with a spatula. Transfer the batter to a 6-inch tube pan. Cover the pan with aluminium foil. Place the pan in the Instant Pot.
4. Set MANUAL setting and cook over HIGH pressure for 15 minutes. Let the pressure naturally release from the Instant Pot. Uncover the lid and remove the pan.
5. Leave the cake to cool before removing from the pan.
6. Serve and enjoy.

Butter Cake

(Prep + Cook Time: 45 minutes | Servings: 8)

Ingredients:

- 2 egg whites
- 10 tbsp butter
- 2 cups flour
- ½ cup milk
- ½ cup caster sugar
- 1 cup sugar
- 1 tsp vanilla extract
- 1 tsp baking soda
- 1 tbsp lemon juice
- ½ tsp ground cardamom

Directions:

1. Melt the butter and combine it with the milk, flour, sugar, vanilla extract, baking soda, lemon juice and ground cardamom.
2. Knead the smooth dough and place it in the Instant Pot form.

3. Pour water in the Instant Pot and add the trivet with the butter dough form.
4. Close the lid and cook the dish at the MANUAL mode for 25 minutes.
5. Then open the Instant Pot lid and check if it is done with the help of the wooden stick.
6. Transfer the cooked butter cake in the plate and chill it. Meanwhile, whisk the egg whites carefully till you get strong white peaks.
7. Then add caster sugar and continue to whisk the mixture for 1 minute more – the icing is cooked.
8. Then sprinkle the butter cake with the icing and chill it. Enjoy the cake!

Carrot Pecan Bread (VEG)
(Prep + Cook Time: 70 minutes | Servings: 12)

Ingredients:
- 1 ½ cup sugar
- 1 ½ cup water
- 1 cup raisins, chopped
- 2 large carrots, peeled and grated
- 1 tsp cinnamon powder
- ¼ tsp nutmeg powder
- ¼ tsp salt
- 2 tbsp coconut oil
- 1 cup pecan, crushed
- 2 cups whole wheat flour
- 2 tsp soda water

Directions:
1. Place the water, sugar, raisins, nutmeg, cinnamon, oil, and carrots in a saucepan.
2. Over low heat, cook while constantly stirring until the mixture comes to a boil. Turn off the heat. Let the mixture cool down for about 10 minutes.
3. Add the pecans, flour, salt, and soda water to the mix. Stir well.
4. Transfer the mixture to a greased 6-inch circular cake pan.
5. Pour a cup or two of water in the Instant Pot. Place a circular wire stand over it and place the cake pan on it. Cover and seal the lid.
6. Cook on MANUAL setting on HIGH pressure for an hour.

7. Wait for the pressure the naturally release from the Instant Pot before uncovering the lid.
8. Remove the cake pan and let the bread cool down on a wire rack.
9. Slice the carrot bread and serve with a side of fresh fruits.

Carrot Cake
(Prep + Cook Time: 45 minutes | Servings: 8)

Ingredients:
- 1 cup flour
- 1 tsp baking soda
- 1 tsp lemon juice
- 1 carrot
- 1 tsp apple juice
- ½ cup yogurt
- ½ cup milk
- 1 tsp pumpkin pie spices
- 2 eggs
- 1 cup sugar
- 1 tbsp semolina

Directions:
1. Peel the carrot and grate it. Combine the eggs with the grated carrot and whisk the mixture.
2. Then add yogurt and milk. Sprinkle the mixture with the apple juice, lemon juice, baking soda, pumpkin pie spices, semolina, and flour.
3. Knead the smooth dough. Pour the carrot dough in the Instant Pot form.
4. Pour water in the Instant Pot and place the trivet.
5. Put the Instant Pot form in the trivet and close the lid.
6. Cook the carrot pie at the MANUAL mode for 35 minutes.
7. When the carrot pie is cooked wait for the pressure to naturally release and remove it from the Instant Pot and chill well.
8. Cut the pie into the slices. Enjoy!

Mango Cake
(Prep + Cook Time: 45 minutes | Servings: 8)

Ingredients:
- 1 ¼ cups flour
- ¾ cup milk
- ½ cup sugar
- ¼ cup coconut oil
- 1 tbsp lemon juice
- 1 tsp mango syrup
- 1 tsp baking powder
- ¼ tsp baking soda
- ⅛ tsp salt

Directions:
1. Grease a baking pan that will fit in your Instant Pot.
2. Mix the sugar, oil, and milk in a bowl until the sugar has melted.
3. Pour in mango syrup and mix again. Pour all the dry ingredients through a sieve into the wet. Add lemon juice and mix well.
4. Pour into the baking pan. Pour 1 cup of water into the Instant Pot and lower in a trivet.
5. Lower the baking pan into the cooker and close the lid.
6. Select MANUAL, and cook on HIGH pressure for 35 minutes.
7. When time is up, hit CANCEL and wait for the pressure to come down naturally.
8. Check the cake for doneness before cooling for 10 minutes. Serve.

Sweet Tapioca Pudding (VEG)
(Prep + Cook Time: 70 minutes | Servings: 12)

Ingredients:
- ½ cup tapioca pearls, washed and drained
- 1 ½ cup unsweetened almond milk
- ½ cup water
- ½ cup granulated sugar
- 1 tsp lime zest
- ½ tsp vanilla essence

Directions:
1. Place a cup of water in the Instant Pot and place the steamer basket over.
2. In an oven-safe mixing bowl, combine the tapioca pearls, almond milk, water, lime zest, vanilla essence, and sugar.

344

3. Mix using a spatula until the sugar has fully dissolved. Place the mixing bowl on the Instant Pot's steamer basket. Cover and seal the lid.
4. Set STEAM setting for 8 minutes.
5. Wait for the pressure to naturally release from the Instant Pot before removing the lid.
6. Carefully remove the mixing bowl and set it on counter. Use a spatula to stir the pudding before transferring it to individual serving bowls.
7. Cover each bowl with plastic cling-wrap and place in the refrigerator for at least 4 hours before serving.

Pineapple Crisps (VEG)
(Prep + Cook Time: 20 minutes | Servings: 5)

Ingredients:
- 1 medium fresh pineapple, peeled and cut into
- 5 large chunks
- 2 tsp cinnamon powder
- ½ tsp nutmeg
- ½ cup water

- 1 tbsp organic maple syrup
- 4 tbsp olive oil
- ¾ cup steel cut oats
- ¼ cup whole wheat flour
- ¼ cup brown sugar
- Pinch of salt

Directions:
1. Place the pineapple chunks in the Instant Pot. Sprinkle over the spices and then pour in the water and maple syrup. Set aside.
2. In a mixing bowl, combine the oil, oats, flour, sugar, and salt. Pour this over each pineapple chunk. Cover and seal the lid.
3. Manually cook on HIGH pressure for 8 minutes. Leave the Instant Pot and wait for the pressure to release naturally. Remove the lid.
4. Transfer the pineapple chunks to individual serving bowls.
5. Add the thick sauce over each pineapple.
6. Serve with a side of vegan ice cream.

Greek Yogurt Cheesecake

(Prep + Cook Time: 45 minutes | Servings: 6)

Ingredients:

- 1 ½ cups graham-cracker finely-ground crumbs
- 1 ½ cups whole-milk Greek yogurt
- 4-ounces softened, regular cream cheese
- 4 tbsp melted butter
- 2 big eggs
- ¼ cup sugar
- 1 tsp vanilla

Directions:

1. Mix the cracker crumbs with melted butter.
2. Press down into the bottom of a 7-inch springform pan, so the bottom is covered and the crust is halfway up the pan.
3. Mix the cream cheese, sugar, yogurt, and vanilla until very smooth.
4. Add the eggs one at a time and mix. Be careful not to overmix.
5. Pour into the pan, covering the crust completely up the sides.
6. Lower a trivet into the pressure cooker, along with 1 cup of water.
7. Put the pan on the trivet and lock the lid.
8. Select MANUAL and cook 30 minutes on HIGH pressure.
9. When time is up, hit CANCEL and wait for the pressure to come down on its own.
10. Carefully open the lid. With a paper towel, blot any excess moisture from the cake.
11. Take out the cake and let it cool on the counter for 1-2 hours.
12. Chill in the fridge for at least 4 hours before serving.

Mini Pumpkin Puddings

(Prep + Cook Time: 35 minutes | Servings: 4)

Ingredients:

- 1 cup water
- 1 cup pumpkin puree
- ¼ cup sugar
- ¼ cup half-and-half
- 1 egg yolk
- 1 beaten egg
- 1 tbsp butter
- ½ tsp ground cinnamon
- ½ tsp pure vanilla extract
- ¼ tsp ground ginger
- ¼ tsp salt
- Pinch ground cloves

Directions:

1. Pour the water into the Instant Pot and lower in the steam rack.
2. Grease four heat-safe mugs.
3. In a bowl, whisk the sugar, pumpkin, and spices together.
4. Add the egg, egg yolk, vanilla, and half-and half, and whisk until thoroughly blended.
5. Pour into the containers.
6. Place on the steam rack in the Instant Pot.
7. Lock the lid.
8. Press MANUAL and select 15 minutes on HIGH pressure.
9. When the timer goes off, hit CANCEL and wait for the pressure to go down on its own.
10. Open the lid. Wait till the steam dissipates before taking out the puddings.
11. Cool for 1 ½ hours on the counter.

Orange-Chocolate Bread Pudding

(Prep + Cook Time: 40 minutes | Servings: 4)

Ingredients:

- 2 cups water
- 3 ½ cups stale French bread, cut into ¾-inch pieces
- 3 big eggs
- 3 oz chopped dark chocolate
- ¾ cups heavy cream
- ½ cup whole milk
- ⅓ cup sugar + 1 tbsp
- Zest and juice of one orange
- 1 tsp butter
- 1 tsp almond extract
- Pinch of salt

Directions:
1. Pour water into the Instant Pot and insert the steamer rack.
2. Grease a 6-7 inch round baking dish.
3. In a bowl, mix the eggs and ⅓ cup of sugar.
4. Pour in the milk, cream, almond extract, orange juice, orange zest, and salt. Mix.
5. Toss the bread pieces in the mixture. Let it soak for 5 minutes.
6. Add the chopped chocolate and stir.
7. Pour in the baking dish and make sure all the bread is submerged.
8. Sprinkle on 1 tablespoon of sugar.
9. Put on the steamer rack (do not wrap in foil) and close the lid. Hit MANUAL and cook for 15 minutes on HIGH pressure.
10. When time is up, hit CANCEL and wait for the pressure to come down by itself.
11. When depressurized, open the lid and take out the pudding.
12. Serve.

Red-Wine Baked Apples
(Prep + Cook Time: 40 minutes | Servings: 6)

Ingredients:
- 6 cored apples
- 1 cup red wine
- ½ cup sugar
- ¼ cup raisins
- 1 tsp cinnamon

Directions:
1. Set the apples inside the Instant Pot.
2. Pour in wine and add the sugar, cinnamon, and raisins.
3. Secure the lid.
4. Select MANUAL and cook for 10 minutes on HIGH pressure.
5. When the timer beeps, hit CANCEL and wait 20-30 minutes for the pressure to come down.
6. Serve the apples in a bowl with the cooking liquid spooned over.

Brownie Cakes

(Prep + Cook Time: 30 minutes | Servings: 4)

Ingredients:

- 2 eggs
- ⅔ cup sugar
- ½ cup flour
- 4 tbsp cocoa powder
- 4 tbsp unsalted butter
- 2 tbsp chocolate chips
- 2 tbsp powdered sugar
- ¼ tsp vanilla extract

Directions:

1. Melt the butter and chocolate chips together in a heatproof bowl.
2. Add the sugar and beat until mixed.
3. Add in the eggs and vanilla and beat again.
4. Sift in the flour and cocoa into the wet ingredients and blend.
5. Pour 1 cup of water into the Instant Pot and insert the steamer rack.
6. Pour the brownie batter into 4 ramekins and cover the top with foil.
7. Lower into the Instant Pot on top of the rack.
8. Select MANUAL and choose HIGH pressure for 18 minutes.
9. When time is up, quick-release the pressure.
10. Remove the ramekins and cool for a few minutes.
11. Dust on some powdered sugar and serve!

Cherry Jam

(Prep + Cook Time: 30 minutes | Servings: 7)

Ingredients:

- 2 cup brown sugar
- 2 cups cherry, pitted
- 1 tbsp fructose syrup
- 1 tsp lemon zest
- ½ tsp ground cardamom

Directions:

1. Chop the cherries and sprinkle them with the brown sugar.
2. Stir the mixture and transfer it to the Instant Pot.
3. Sauté the mixture for 5 minutes. Stir it frequently with the help of the wooden spoon.

4. Then sprinkle the cherry mixture with the fructose syrup, ground cardamom, and lemon zest.
5. Stir it carefully and sauté the mixture for 15 minutes more till it is reduced in 2 times.
6. Then transfer the cooked cherry jam in the big bowl.
7. Chill it well. Serve.

Raspberry Jam
(Prep + Cook Time: 25 minutes | Servings: 2)

Ingredients:
- 2 pounds fresh raspberries
- 1 ½ pounds light honey

Directions:
1. Pour raspberries and honey into your Instant Pot.
2. Turn the cooker to the KEEP WARM setting and stir for 3 minutes until the honey has become liquid.
3. Turn to SAUTE and stir until the pot begins to boil. Close and seal the lid immediately. Adjust time to 2 minutes after pressing MANUAL.
4. When the timer beeps, hit CANCEL and wait for the pressure to release on its own.
5. Take the lid off and on sauté, bring the jam to a boil again until it reaches 220-degrees F.
6. Pour jam into clean half-pint jars and screw on the lids.
7. Jam will keep in the fridge for 4-6 weeks.

Blueberry Jam

(Prep + Cook Time: 25 minutes | Servings: 8)

Ingredients:

- 2 pounds blueberries, frozen or fresh
- 1 pound honey, preferably local

Directions:

1. Put the blueberries in the Instant Pot. Pour in the honey. Press the KEEP WARM function to melt the honey, occasionally stirring. If you are using frozen berries, this may take a while, but this step is worth it.
2. When the honey is melted, press the SAUTE key and let the honey boil – there will be white-pink bubbles around the blueberries.
3. When the honey is boiling, quickly press the CANCEL key to stop the sauté function. Cover and lock the lid. Press the MANUAL key, set the pressure to HIGH, and set the timer for 2 minutes.
4. When the Instant Pot timer beeps, press the CANCEL key and unplug the Instant Pot. Let the pressure release naturally for 10-15 minutes or until the valve drops.
5. Using an oven mitt or a long handled spoon, turn the steam valve to VENTING to release remaining pressure.
6. Unlock and carefully open the lid. Press the SAUTÉ key and let boil until some of the water has evaporated off and the jam is nicely gelled when dripped off with a spoon.
7. Make sure to scrape the bottom of the pot frequently with a wooden spoon to ensure even gelling.
8. Pour the jam into clean half-pint jars. Store the jars in the fridge.

Pineapple whisked cake
(Prep + Cook Time: 45 minutes | Servings: 8)

Ingredients:
- 9 oz. pineapple, canned
- 4 eggs
- 1 cup flour
- 1 cup sour cream
- 1 tsp baking soda
- 1 tbsp lemon juice
- 1 tsp cinnamon
- 1 cup sugar
- 2 tbsp butter

Directions:
1. Beat the eggs in the mixing bowl and whisk them with the help of the whisker.
2. After this, add sour cream and continue to whisk the mixture for 1 minute more.
3. Then add baking soda and lemon juice. Stir the mixture gently. Then add sugar, cinnamon, butter, and flour. Mix the mixture up with the help of the hand mixer for 5 minutes.
4. Then chop the canned pineapples and add them to the dough. Mix up the dough with the help of the spoon.
5. Then pour the dough in the Instant Pot and close the lid. Cook the dish at the MANUAL mode for 30 minutes.
6. When the time is over – open the Instant Pot and check if the cake is cooked.
7. Remove the cake from the Instant Pot and chill it well.
8. Slice the cake and serve.

Mocha Cheesecake
(Prep + Cook Time: 40 minutes | Servings: 6)

Ingredients:
- 11 tbsp chocolate graham cracker crumbs
- 2 pkgs softened cream cheese
- 11 tbsp sugar
- 16 tbsp semi-sweet chocolate chips
- 3 tbsp melted butter
- 3 tbsp espresso
- 4 tbsp whipping cream
- 2 eggs
- 1 tsp vanilla
- 3 tbsp Kahlua

Directions:

1. Pregrease a soufflé dish and line with foil that has been greased. Mix crumbs and butter with ¼ of the sugar.
2. Press this into the bottom of the pan and chill it in the freezer. In a separate bowl, use a mixer to beat the rest of the sugar and cream cheese mix until smooth.
3. Add one egg and beat in, then add the other egg. Blend in the vanilla and whipping cream.
4. Cook over low heat while stirring in the coffee, chocolate chips, and Kahlua until melted. Pour the mix over the cheese mixture and blend well. Ladle this over the prepared crust.
5. Make a foil strip sling to make it easier to lower into the pot. Pour 1 ½ c water into the pot. Set the trivet in the bottom so that the cheesecake is above the water.
6. Place the cheesecake in the center of the foil and lower it in the trivet. Lock the lid down and bring it to HIGH pressure. Reduce the heat and maintain pressure.
7. Cook for fifteen minutes. Turn the heat off and let the pressure out on its own. Take off the lid. Lift out the pan and cool the cake on a rack.
8. Cover and chill for four hours or overnight.

New York Cheescake
(Prep + Cook Time: 55 minutes | Servings: 12)

Ingredients:

- 16 oz cream cheese
- 15 Oreo cookies
- 1 tbsp vanilla
- 1 cup sugar

- 2 eggs
- 2 tbsp butter, melted

Equipment:
7-inch spring-form pan

Directions:

1. Put the Oreo cookies into a food processor and process until crumbled. Stir in the melted butter. Transfer the Oreo cookie mix into the spring-form pan and press into an even layer.
2. In a medium-sized to large-sized bowl, put the eggs, cream cheese, vanilla, and sugar; mix until creamy and smooth. Transfer in the spring-form pan and spread into an even layer.

3. Put a trivet in the Instant Pot and pour in 1 cup water. Take a long piece of foil and fold it lengthwise to create a strip long enough to allow you to lower the cheesecake onto the trivet and retrieve it later when the cooking time is done.
4. Using the foil sling, lower the pan onto the trivet. Cover and lock the lid. Press the MANUAL key, set the pressure to HIGH, and set the timer for 40 minutes.
5. When the Instant Pot timer beeps, press the CANCEL key and unplug the Instant Pot.
6. Using an oven mitt or a long handled spoon, turn the steam valve to VENTING to quick release the pressure.
7. Unlock and carefully open the lid. Using the foil sling, carefully remove the cheesecake from the pot.
8. Chill for about 1 hour. Top with your favorite topping or fruits.

Chocolate Cheesecake
(Prep + Cook Time: 25 minutes | Servings: 8)

Ingredients:
- 16 oz cream cheese
- 2 eggs
- 2 tbsp powdered peanut butter
- 1 tbsp cocoa
- 1 tsp vanilla extract
- ½ cup Swerve sugar substitute

Directions:
1. Make sure all ingredients are at room temperature. Add cream cheese and eggs into your blender and blend until smooth.
2. Then add additional ingredients, blending to incorporate together.
3. Once blended, add to 4 or 8 ounce mason jars and cover with foil or the mason jar lid.
4. Add 1 cup of water to your Instant Pot and insert trivet.
5. Place jars inside Instant Pot and cook in 2 batches.
6. Cook on HIGH pressure for 15-18 minutes. Let it naturally release and chill for a few hours up to overnight.
7. Top with whipped heavy cream and a drizzle of peanut butter or a few chopped peanuts for some texture. Serve.

Strawberry Cheesecake

(Prep + Cook Time: 35 minutes | Servings: 6)

Ingredients:
- 1 cup strawberries
- 1 cup cream
- 2 eggs
- 1 cup sugar
- 7 oz. crackers
- 5 tbsp butter
- 1 tsp vanilla sugar
- ¼ tsp nutmeg
- 3 tbsp caramel

Directions:
1. Crush the crackers well and combine them with the butter. Mix up the mixture carefully till you get smooth mass.
2. Then beat the eggs in the mixing bowl and whisk them well.
3. Add sugar, vanilla sugar, nutmeg, and cream. Whisk the mixture very well with the help of the mixer.
4. Wash the strawberries and slice them. Then put the cracker mixture in the Instant Pot and flatten it well to make the crust.
5. Then pour the cream mixture over the crust and flatten it with the help of the fork.
6. Then dip the sliced strawberries in the cream mixture and close the Instant Pot lid.
7. Cook the dish at the PRESSURE mode for 24 minutes.
8. When the time is over – remove the cheesecake from the Instant Pot carefully and chill it.
9. Then sprinkle the chilled cheesecake with the caramel. Serve.

Strawberry and Mango Crunch

(Prep + Cook Time: 35 minutes | Servings: 4)

Ingredients:
- 2 cups strawberries, sliced
- 2 cups mango, chunks
- 1 cup mango juice
- 1 package biscuits, crumbled
- ½ cup all-purpose flour
- 1 cup milk
- 1 egg, whisked
- ¼ cup caster sugar
- 4 tbsp butter, melted

Directions:
1. In a bowl add all-purpose flour, biscuits, egg, sugar, mango juice, and milk, mix well.

2. Spread into a greased baking dish and press with a spoon a little bit.
3. Now drizzle butter, place the mango chunks and strawberry chunks on top.
4. Place a trivet into the Instant Pot and add 3-4 cups of water in it.
5. Put a baking dish on a trivet and cover the pot with a lid.
6. Cook on MANUAL mode for 30 minutes.
7. Serve and enjoy.

Applesauce
(Prep + Cook Time: 30 minutes | Servings: 6)

Ingredients:
- 1-pound apples
- 2 cup water
- 1 tsp cinnamon
- 1 tsp sugar

Directions:
1. Wash the apples carefully and peel them.
2. Chop the peeled apples and place them in the Instant Pot.
3. Add water and mix up the mixture gently.
4. Then close the lid and cook the apples under the PRESSURE for 16 minutes.
5. Then release the remaining pressure and open the Instant Pot lid.
6. Transfer the cooked apples to the blender and blend them well.
7. Add cinnamon and sugar and continue to blend the apple mixture for 1 minute more.
8. When you get smooth applesauce – remove it from the blender and chill it.
9. Serve the applesauce.

Apple Sweet Oatmeal
(Prep + Cook Time: 20 minutes | Servings: 2)

Ingredients:
- 2 red apples
- 1 cup oatmeal
- 1 cup coconut milk
- 1 tsp coconut
- 1 tsp vanilla extract
- ½ cup brown sugar
- ½ tsp ground ginger
- 1 cup cream
- ¼ tsp ground anise

Directions:
1. Wash the apples and peel them.
2. Then grate the apples and combine them with the brown sugar, coconut, vanilla extract, ground ginger, and ground anise.
3. Mix up the mixture. Place the apple mixture in the Instant Pot.
4. Add oatmeal. Then sprinkle the mixture with the coconut milk and cream.
5. Combine all the ingredients well with the help of the spoon.
6. Close the lid and cook the dish at the PORRIGE mode for 10 minutes.
7. When the time is over -- transfer the cooked dish in the serving bowls.

Apple Crisp
(Prep + Cook Time: 35 minutes | Servings: 6)

Ingredients:
- 5-6 apples, medium-sized (I used Fuji – or any variety)
- 1 cup oats, gluten free
- 2 tsp ground cinnamon
- ½ cup water
- ½ cup flour blend (I used Bob's Red Mill 1: 1 Gluten Free)
- ½ cup butter, melted
- ½ cup brown sugar, organic

Directions:
1. Peel the apples, remove the seeds, and then slice into thin pieces. Put the apple slices into the bottom of the Instant Pot. Add the water and cinnamon and stir to combine.

2. In a bowl, stir the remaining ingredients until combined. Spread on top of the apple mix in the pot. Cover and lock the lid. Press the MANUAL key, set the pressure to HIGH, and set the timer for 8 minutes.
3. When the Instant Pot timer beeps, press the CANCEL key and unplug the Instant Pot. Let the pressure release naturally for 10-15 minutes or until the valve drops.
4. Using an oven mitt or a long handled spoon, turn the steam valve to VENTING to release remaining pressure.
5. Unlock and carefully open the lid. Let cool for a couple of minutes. Enjoy!

Notes: If you like more crumble topping, double the oats, butter, and brown sugar.

Apple Tacos
(Prep + Cook Time: 20 minutes | Servings: 6)

Ingredients:
- 4 red apples
- 2 tbsp honey
- 1 tsp cinnamon
- ½ tsp ginger
- 6 oz corn tortillas
- 1 tbsp caster sugar

Directions:
1. Peel the red apples and chop them. Sprinkle the chopped apples with the cinnamon, ginger, and caster sugar.
2. Mix up it carefully and leave the apples for 5 minutes or till they give the juice.
3. Then place the apples in the Instant Pot and cook them at the MANUAL mode for 4 minutes.
4. Then spread the corn tortillas with the honey. Remove the cooked apples from the Instant Pot and chill it till the mixture is warm.
5. Then place the apple mixture in the tortillas and wrap them.
6. Serve the dish immediately.

Baked Apples

(Prep + Cook Time: 30 minutes | Servings: 6)

Ingredients:
- 6 apples, fresh picked fruits, cored
- ¼ cup raisins
- ½ cup raw Demerara sugar
- 1 tsp cinnamon powder
- 1 cup red wine

Directions:
1. Put the apples in the Instant Pot. Pour the wine in the pot and then sprinkle with the cinnamon powder, sugar, and raisins.
2. Cover and lock the lid. Press the MANUAL key, set the pressure to HIGH, and set the timer for 10 minutes.
3. When the Instant Pot timer beeps, press the CANCEL key and unplug the Instant Pot. Let the pressure release naturally for 10-15 minutes or until the valve drops.
4. Using an oven mitt or a long handled spoon, turn the steam valve to VENTING to release remaining pressure.
5. Unlock and carefully open the lid.
6. Scoop out the apples into small-sized serving bowls with lots of the cooking liquid.

Cream Cheese Coffee Cake

(Prep + Cook Time: 45 minutes | Servings: 8)

Ingredients:
- 6 tbsp of butter (room temperature)
- 3 egg yolks (room temperature)
- 2 whole eggs (room temperature)
- 1 ½ cups of cake flour butter and flour for dusting pan
- ¾ cup of sugar
- 1 ¾ tsp of baking powder
- 8 oz of cream cheese (room temperature)
- 3 cups of powdered sugar (add some more for dusting)
- 1 tsp of vanilla
- ¼ tsp of salt
- 1 ½ cups of water

Directions:
1. Grease a spring-form pan with butter and dust it with flour. In a bowl, cream the sugar and butter.

2. Add 3 egg yolks and continue mixing. Stir in the vanilla, salt, baking powder and flour. Pour the mixture to the prepared pan and press to make an even layer.
3. Mix the cream cheese and 2 eggs in another bowl. Gradually add the powdered sugar.
4. Once well-combined, pour the mixture on top of the crust. Cover the pan with a dry paper towel and aluminum foil.
5. Pour 1 ½ cups of water into the pot. Place a trivet inside and put the pan on top. Lock the lid and set the cooker on a HIGH. Cook for 25 minutes. Perform a 10-minute natural pressure release once done.
6. Take off the lid and place the pan on a wire rack to cool.
7. Remove the cover of the pan. Sprinkle the top of the cake with powdered sugar while it is still warm.
8. Wait around 3 hours for the cake to cool completely at room temperature.
9. To speed up the process, you can refrigerate it after 30 minutes.
10. Slice and enjoy the treat.

Vanilla Cake
(Prep + Cook Time: 55 minutes | Servings: 6)

Ingredients:
- 5 eggs
- 1 tsp vanilla extract
- 1 tbsp vanilla sugar
- ½ cup flour
- ½ cup sugar
- 3 cups milk
- 6 oz butter

Directions:
1. Melt butter and combine it with the vanilla sugar, vanilla extract, sugar, milk, flour, and eggs.
2. Whisk the mixture well with the help of the hand whisker.
3. Pour ½ cup of water in the Instant Pot. Then pour the butter mixture into the glass form.
4. Place the trivet in the Instant Pot. Then transfer the glass form in the trivet and close the Instant Pot lid. Cook the dish at the MANUALmode for 45 minutes.

5. When the dish is cooked – open the Instant Pot lid and chill the cake.
6. Transfer the cake to the serving plate carefully and sprinkle it with the caster sugar if desired.

Carrot Cake (VEG)

(Prep + Cook Time: 40 minutes | Servings: 6)

Ingredients:

- 5 oz coconut flour
- A pinch of salt
- ¾ tsp baking powder
- ½ tsp baking soda
- ½ tsp cinnamon powder
- ¼ tsp nutmeg, ground
- ½ tsp allspice
- 1 tbsp flaxseed mixed well with
- 2 tbsp water
- 3 tbsp coconut yogurt
- ½ cup palm sugar
- ¼ cup pineapple juice
- 4 tbsp coconut oil, melted
- 1/3 cup carrots, grated
- 1/3 cup pecans, toasted and chopped
- 1/3 cup coconut flakes
- Cooking spray
- 2 cups water

Directions:

1. In a bowl, mix flour with baking soda and powder, salt, allspice, cinnamon and nutmeg and stir.
2. In another bowl, mix flaxseed with coconut yogurt, palm sugar, pineapple juice, oil, carrots, pecans and coconut flakes and stir well.
3. Combine the two mixtures and stir very well everything.
4. Pour this into a sprayed spring form, add 2 cups water in your Instant Pot and place the form into the steamer basket.
5. Cover the Instant Pot and cook on HIGH pressure for 32 minutes.
6. Release pressure for 10 minutes, remove cake from the pot, leave it to cool down.
7. Then cut and serve it.

Mini Lava Cakes

(Prep + Cook Time: 25 minutes | Servings: 6)

Ingredients:
- ¼ tsp orange zest
- Pinch of salt
- 4 tbsp flour
- 4 tbsp sugar
- 1 medium egg
- 2 tbsp evoo
- 4 tbsp milk
- 1 tbsp bitter cocoa powder

Directions:
1. Put one cup of water in the pressure cooker. Prepare by putting olive oil on the inside of the pot.
2. Add flour, sugar, salt, cocoa, orange zest and baking powders. Mix this with a fork.
3. Add milk, egg, and olive oil. Mix until you have a cake batter. Pour into a mug.
4. Place the uncovered cup into the cooker. Close and lock the lid. Turn to HIGH pressure.
5. Turn down the heat when it reaches pressure and cook for 15 minutes. Quick release the pressure. Open and remove.
6. Serve in a saucer.

Sweet Spaghetti Casserole

(Prep + Cook Time: 30 minutes | Servings: 6)

Ingredients:
- 8 oz. spaghetti, cooked
- 1 cup cottage cheese
- 6 eggs
- ¼ cup cream
- 1 tbsp olive oil
- 1 tsp salt
- 1 cup sugar
- 1 tsp vanilla sugar
- 1 tsp nutmeg

Directions:
1. Combine the cottage cheese, cream, eggs, and sugar together in the blender.
2. Blend the mixture well till it is smooth.

3. Then transfer the cottage cheese mixture in the bowl and add cooked spaghetti, nutmeg, and vanilla sugar. Mix up the mixture.
4. Pour the olive oil in the Instant Pot and transfer the cottage cheese mixture. Close the lid and cook the dish at the RICE mode for 20 minutes.
5. When the dish is cooked – chill it well and remove from the Instant Pot.
6. Cut it into pieces and serve.

Strawberry Delight Bundt Cake
(Prep + Cook Time: 35 minutes | Servings: 12)

Ingredients:
- 1½ cups all-purpose flour
- 1½ tsp baking mixture (mixture of baking powder and baking soda)
- ½ cup frozen strawberries
- ½ cup Greek yogurt
- ¾ cup sugar

Directions:
1. Blend the wet and dry ingredients separately and then mix them together to make the cake batter.
2. Pour the batter in a greased bundt pan and cover the pan with a foil.
3. Put the steamer rack inside the Instant Pot and pour a cup of water.
4. Place the bundt pan on the rack and close the lid. Cook on MANUAL setting for 35 minutes and let the pressure release naturally.
5. Cool down the cake and then place in the fridge for chilling.
6. Serve chilled.

Banana Balls

(Prep + Cook Time: 20 minutes | Servings: 8)

Ingredients:
- 4 bananas
- 1 cup flour
- 1 tbsp cream
- 1 tsp butter
- 1/3 cup olive oil
- ½ cup caster sugar
- 1 tsp vanilla extract
- 1 tsp baking soda

Directions:
1. Peel the bananas and mash them Combine the mashed bananas with the flour, cream, and butter.
2. Add vanilla extract and baking soda. Knead the non-sticky dough.
3. Make the small balls from the dough.
4. Pour the olive oil in the Instant Pot and preheat it.
5. When the olive oil starts to boil – toss the banana balls in the Instant Pot and cook them for 5 minutes at the SAUTE mode.
6. Stir the balls frequently. Put the caster sugar in the bowl.
7. When the banana balls are cooked – dip them in the caster sugar and coat well.
8. Serve the banana balls immediately.

Cream Mousse With the Strawberries

(Prep + Cook Time: 25 minutes | Servings: 6)

Ingredients:
- 1 cup cream cheese
- 1 cup whipped cream
- 3 egg yolks
- 1 cup sugar
- 1 tbsp cocoa powder
- 1 tbsp butter

Directions:
1. Whisk the egg yolks with the sugar and combine the mixture with the cream cheese.
2. Transfer the mixture to the Instant Pot and cook it at the SAUTE mode for 7 minutes.
3. Stir the cream cheese mixture constantly.

4. Then transfer the cooked cream cheese mixture into the mixing bowl.
5. Add whipped cream and cocoa powder.
6. Add butter and mix it up carefully with the help of the hand blender.
7. Transfer the mousse in the serving glasses. Enjoy!

Blueberry Muffins
(Prep + Cook Time: 25 minutes | Servings: 6)

Ingredients:
- 1 cup frozen blueberries
- 1 ½ cup flour
- 1 tsp baking powder
- 1 tbsp apple cider vinegar
- 1 tbsp coconut
- ½ cup milk
- 2 eggs
- 1 tsp vanilla extract
- 1 tsp olive oil

Directions:
1. Place the flour, baking soda, apple cider vinegar, coconut, milk, eggs, and vanilla extract in the food processor. Blend the mixture well.
2. Then add the frozen blueberries and blend the mixture for 30 seconds more.
3. Take the muffin molds and pour the ½ of every mold with the dough.
4. Place the muffins on the trivet and transfer it to the Instant Pot. Close the lid and set the HIGH pressure mode. Cook the muffins for 10 minutes.
5. When the muffins are cooked – remove them from the Instant Pot.
6. Chill them well. Serve.

Lemon Loaf

(Prep + Cook Time: 40 minutes | Servings: 8)

Ingredients:
- 1 cup lemon juice
- 3 tbsp lemon zest
- 3 cups flour
- ½ cup cream
- 1 egg
- 1 tsp baking soda
- ½ tsp baking powder
- ½ cup caster sugar
- 1 tsp turmeric

Directions:
1. Combine the flour, baking powder, baking soda, turmeric, and caster sugar together. Stir the mixture and add lemon juice and cream
2. After this, add egg and lemon zest. Knead the soft dough from the mixture.
3. Place the lemon dough in the loaf form. Pour water in the Instant Pot and put the trivet.
4. Transfer the loaf form with the dough in the Instant Pot and close the Instant Pot lid. Cook the dish at the MANUAL mode for 30 minutes.
5. Then open the Instant Pot lid and remove the form from the machine.
6. Chill it well and after this, discard the lemon loaf.
7. Slice it and serve.

Cream Cheese Mousse

(Prep + Cook Time: 20 minutes | Servings: 6)

Ingredients:
- 2 cups cream cheese
- ¼ cup chocolate
- 1 tsp vanilla extract
- ½ cup cream
- ½ cup sugar
- 1 tsp cocoa powder

Directions:
1. Combine the chocolate, vanilla extract, sugar, cocoa powder, and cream together.
2. Mix up it carefully with the help of the hand mixer.

3. Then place the cream mixture in the Instant Pot and SAUTE it for 4 minutes.
4. Then chill the mixture little and add the cream cheese.
5. Whisk the mixture till it is smooth.
6. Transfer the cooked mousse in the freezer and chill it for 10 minutes.
7. Serve it immediately.

Caramel Bites
(Prep + Cook Time: 20 minutes | Servings: 6)

Ingredients:
- 7 oz. puff pastry
- 1 tbsp butter
- 1 tsp cinnamon
- 1 egg yolk
- 1 tsp olive oil
- 4 tbsp caramel

Directions:
1. Roll the puff pastry with the help of the rolling pin. Then make the circles from the dough with the help of the cutter.
2. Whisk the egg yolk and sprinkle every dough circle with it. Put the butter and caramel in the center of the puff pastry circle and make the small puffs.
3. Then spray the Instant Pot with the olive oil inside.
4. Add the puff pastry bites and cook them at the SAUTE mode for 3 minutes from the each side or till all the sides are light brown.
5. Make the cooked caramel bites dry with the help of the paper towel.
6. Serve the dish warm.

Walnuts Bars
(Prep + Cook Time: 25 minutes | Servings: 8)

Ingredients:
- 1 cup walnuts
- 1/3 cup cream
- 1 tbsp starch
- 1/3 cup sugar
- 5 tbsp butter
- 1 cup flour
- 1 tsp baking soda
- 1 tsp lemon juice
- 1 egg
- ¼ tsp salt
- 1 tsp turmeric

Directions:

1. Place the butter, baking soda, lemon juice, egg, and flour in the food processor. Blend the mixture well till it is smooth.
2. Then place the smooth dough mixture in the silicon form and flatten it well. Place the form in the Instant Pot and close the lid.
3. Cook the dish at the MANUAL pressure for 10 minutes. Meanwhile, combine the starch, cream, sugar, and turmeric together.
4. Mix up the mixture with the help of the hand mixer till it is increased in two times.
5. Crush the walnuts and add them to the cream mixture. Stir it.
6. When the time is over – release the remaining pressure and chill the crust.
7. Spread it with the cream mixture and transfer it to the Instant Pot again.
8. Cook the dish for 5 minutes more at the MANUAL mode.
9. Then chill the dish well and cut it into the bars. Serve it.

Cottage Cheese Prune Soufflé

(Prep + Cook Time: 20 minutes | Servings: 5)

Ingredients:

- 6 oz. prunes
- 1 cup cottage cheese
- ½ cup sour cream
- 5 eggs
- ½ cup sugar
- 1 tbsp honey
- 1 tsp ground ginger
- 3 egg yolks

Directions:

1. Beat the eggs in the bowl and add egg yolks. Then sprinkle the eggs with the sugar and mix up the mixture with the help of the hand mixer.
2. Add the cottage cheese and sour cream. Combine the mix up the mixture for 3 minutes more.
3. Then add honey and ground ginger. Mix up the mixture for 10 seconds. Remove the hand mixer from the egg mixture.

4. Chop the prunes and add them to the egg mixture. Then transfer the cottage cheese mixture in the ramekins and place the ramekins in the Instant Pot trivet.
5. Pour water in the Instant Pot and transfer the trivet with the soufflé.
6. After this, close the Instant Pot lid and cook the soufflé at the MANUAL mode for 10 minutes.
7. When the soufflé is cooked – chill it well.

Pears Stewed in Red Wine
(Prep + Cook Time: 15 minutes | Servings: 6)

Ingredients:
- 6 pears, firm ripe, peeled
- 4 cloves (the spice)
- 2 cups sugar, optional
- 1 stick cinnamon OR 1 teaspoon cinnamon
- 1 piece fresh ginger OR 1 teaspoon ginger
- 1 bunch herbs, for decoration - mint, sage, basil, or oregano
- 1 bottle red wine (something dry, tarty, and tannic, like Barbaresco or Sangiovese)
- 1 bay laurel leaf

Directions:
1. Peel the pears – leave the stem attached. Pour the bottle of wine into the Instant Pot. Add the sugar, ginger, cinnamon, cloves, and bay. Mix well until the sugar is dissolved.
2. Add the pears into the pot. Cover and lock the lid. Turn the steam valve to SEALING. Press the MANUAL key, set the pressure to HIGH, and set the timer for 5-7 minutes.
3. When the Instant Pot timer beeps, press the CANCEL key.
4. Let the pressure release naturally for 10 minutes.
5. Using an oven mitt or a long handled spoon, turn the steam valve to VENTING to release remaining pressure. Unlock and carefully open the lid.
6. Using 2 spoons or tongs, carefully pull out the pears from the pot.

7. Transfer them onto a plate and set aside. Press the SAUTE key. Cook the cooking liquid until reduced to a third of its original amount.
8. Drizzle the syrup over the pears, decorate with some herbs, and serve at room temperature or chilled.

Coconut Rice Pudding
(Prep + Cook Time: 35 minutes | Servings: 8)

Ingredients:
- 1 cup arborio rice
- 1 cup water
- 1 whole vanilla bean
- ½ tsp cloves, freshly ground
- 2 cans sweetened condensed milk
- 2 cups almond milk, unsweetened
- 3 cinnamon sticks
- 3 cups coconut milk, unsweetened
- 3 strips orange zest strip

Directions:
1. Except for the condensed milk, pour all of the liquid ingredients into the Instant Pot. Press the START key to turn the heating element on.
2. Add the spices into mixture, leaving the orange zest strips and cinnamon sticks whole. Grind the cloves into fine powder and add into the pot. With a knife, gently slice a long slit down the middle of the vanilla pod. Scrape all the vanilla bean out and into the pot. Add the vanilla pod in the pot and stir to mix.
3. Press the SAUTE key and bring the mix to a light simmer. Press the CANCEL key to stop the sauté function. Add the rice and stir briefly to mix.
4. Cover and lock the lid. Turn the steam valve to SEALING. Press the MANUAL key, set the pressure to HIGH, and set the timer for 15 minutes.
5. When the Instant Pot timer beeps, press the CANCEL key and unplug the Instant Pot. Let the pressure release naturally for 10-15 minutes or until the valve drops. Using an oven mitt or a long handled spoon, turn the steam valve to VENTING to release remaining pressure. Unlock and carefully open the lid.

6. Remove the orange zest strip, cinnamon sticks, and vanilla pod; discard.
7. Open 2 cans of sweetened condensed milk and add it all into the rice pudding. Stir until mixed thoroughly. Let the pudding slightly cool, cover, and put in the fridge to completely cool.
8. Serve in pretty dishes.
9. Garnish each serving with honey and sliced blueberries and strawberries.

Polenta with Honey and Pine Nuts
(Prep + Cook Time: 20 minutes | Servings: 6)

Ingredients:
- 5 cups water
- 1 cup polenta
- ½ cup heavy cream
- ½ cup honey
- ¼ cup pine nuts
- Salt to taste

Directions:
1. Mix pine nuts and honey with water in your Instant Pot. Turn on the SAUTE function and bring to a boil while stirring. Mix in polenta.
2. Close and seal lid. Select MANUAL and adjust time to 12 minutes.
3. When time is up, hit CANCEL and quick-release the pressure.
4. Mix in cream and wait 1 minute before serving with a sprinkle of salt.
5. Serve.

Pea And Pineapple Curry

(Prep + Cook Time: 1 hour 20 minutes | Servings: 4)

Ingredients:

- 1 cup black eyed peas, dry and soaked
- 1 cup brown lentils
- 3 tbsp extra virgin olive oil
- 1 yellow onion, chopped
- 3 cups water
- ½ cup cashew butter mixed with
- 1 tbsp water
- ½ tsp turmeric
- Salt and black pepper to the taste
- ½ tsp cumin
- ¼ tsp cinnamon
- 2/3 cup pineapple chunks

Directions:

1. Put the lentils in your Instant Pot, add ¼ cup water, cook on HIGH pressure for 30 minutes, release pressure naturally, transfer to a bowl and leave them aside for now.
2. Put the peas in your Instant Pot, add 2 cups water, cook on HIGH pressure for 30 minutes, release pressure naturally, transfer them to another bowl and leave them aside for now.
3. Heat up a big pan with the oil over medium high heat, add onion, stir and cook for 2-3 minutes.
4. Add turmeric, salt, pepper, cumin, cinnamon, peas and lentils, stir well and cook for 3 minutes more.
5. Add cashew butter, the rest of the water and the pineapple, stir and cook for 4-5 minutes more.
6. Divide amongst plates and serve right away.

Pina Collada Pudding

(Prep + Cook Time: 30 minutes | Servings: 8)

Ingredients:

- 1 tbsp coconut oil
- A pinch of salt
- 1½ cups water
- 1 cup Arborio rice
- 14 oz canned coconut milk
- 2 eggs
- ½ cup milk
- ½ cup sugar
- ½ tsp vanilla extract
- 8 oz canned pineapple tidbits, drained and halved

Directions:

1. In your Instant Pot, mix the oil, water, rice, and salt. Stir, cover, and cook on HIGH Pressure for 3 minutes.
2. Release the pressure for 10 minutes, then uncover pot, add sugar and coconut milk, and stir well.
3. In a bowl, mix the eggs with the milk and vanilla. Pour this over the rice.
4. Combine well, set the pot to Sauté mode, and bring to a boil.
5. Add pineapple tidbits, stir, then divide into dessert bowls and serve.

Lemon Marmalade
(Prep + Cook Time: 40 minutes | Servings: 8)

Ingredients:

- 2 pounds lemons, washed, sliced and cut into quarters
- 4 pounds sugar
- 2 cups water

Directions:

1. Put lemon pieces in your Instant Pot, add 2 cups water, then cover and cook on HIGH pressure for 10 minutes.
2. Release the pressure naturally, then uncover pot, add sugar and stir.
3. Set pot to Simmer mode and cook for 6 minutes, stirring all the time.
4. Divide in jars and serve when needed.

Creme Brulee

(Prep + Cook Time: 30 minutes | Servings: 6)

Ingredients:

- 8 egg yolks
- 1/3 cup granulated sugar
- Pinch of salt
- 2 cups heavy cream
- 1 ½ tsp vanilla
- 6 tbsp superfine sugar

Directions:

1. Add 1 1/2 cups of water to the pressure cooking pot and place the trivet in the bottom.
2. In a large mixing bowl, whisk eggs yolks, 1/3 cup granulated sugar and a pinch of salt.
3. Add cream and vanilla and whisk until blended. Strain into a large measuring bowl with pour spout or a pitcher.
4. Pour mixture in to six custard cups, cover with foil, and place on trivet in pressure cooking pot. Stack the cups in a second layer.
5. Lock the lid in place. Select HIGH pressure and set the timer for 6 minutes.
6. When beep sounds, turn off pressure cooker and use a natural pressure release for 10 minutes and then do a quick pressure release to release any remaining pressure.
7. When valve drops carefully remove lid. Carefully remove the cups to a wire rack to cool uncovered.
8. When cool, refrigerate covered with plastic wrap for at least 2 hours or up to 2 days.
9. When ready to serve, sprinkle about a tablespoon of sugar to cover the entire surface of each custard.
10. Working with one at a time, move the flame of the torch 2 inches above the surface of each custard in a circular motion to melt the sugar and form a crispy, caramelized topped.

Grated pie

(Prep + Cook Time: 55 minutes | Servings: 6)

Ingredients:

- 1 cup strawberry jam
- 7 oz margarine
- 2 cups butter
- 1 tsp salt
- 1 tsp vanilla extract
- 1 tbsp lemon zest
- 1 tbsp turmeric
- 1 tsp nutmeg
- ½ tsp ground ginger

Directions:

1. Grate the margarine in the mixing bowl. Sprinkle it with the salt, vanilla extract, lemon zest, turmeric, nutmeg, and ground ginger.
2. After this, sift the flour in the bowl and knead the smooth and non-sticky dough with the help of the hands.
3. Then place the dough in the freezer for 15 minutes. Remove the dough from the freezer and cut it into 2 parts.
4. Grate the one part of the dough in the Instant Pot.
5. Then sprinkle the grated dough with the strawberry jam. Flatten it well to make the layer.
6. After this, grate the second part of the dough in the Instant Pot.
7. Close the lid and cook the dish at the HIGH pressure mode for 25 minutes.
8. When the time is over – transfer the cooked pie on the serving plate.

Paleo Diet Recipes

Baked Eggs
(Prep + Cook Time: 10 minutes | Servings: 4)

Ingredients:
- 8 eggs
- ¾ cup almond milk
- 5 pieces diced bacon
- 2 cups sweet potatoes, shredded
- 1 diced onion
- ½ tsp salt

Directions:
1. First, add the bacon to the Instant Pot. Brown it on SAUTE mode for two minutes.
2. Add the onion and sauté for an additional two minutes.
3. Next, add the sweet potatoes over the bacon.
4. To the side, beat together the eggs, almond milk, and salt, and pour the mixture over the sweet potato and bacon.
5. Place the lid on the Instant Pot at this time. Close the valve, and set the timer on MANUAL. Cook for 7 minutes.
6. When time is up, quick-release the pressure.
7. Serve the egg bake with additional salt and pepper, to taste.

Nutritional Information Per Serving: 451 calories, 22 grams net carbohydrates, 21 grams protein, 29 grams fat, 948 mg sodium.

Beef + Broccoli Soup
(Prep + Cook Time: 30 minutes | Servings: 6)

Ingredients:
- 4 ¾ cups beef stock
- 2 pounds tri-tip beef
- 2 pounds frozen broccoli florets
- 4 garlic cloves
- 1 small chopped onion
- 1 cup cheddar cheese
- 2 tbsp salt
- Black pepper to taste

Directions:
1. Turn on your Instant Pot and when it reads "HOT," add a little bit of olive oil, just to coat the bottom.
2. Season the beef with salt and pepper. Lay in the Pot and brown on both sides for 5 minutes.

3. Remove meat and plate for now. Add onion and garlic, and cook until softened.
4. Return beef and pour in broth. Seal the lid and cook for 20 minutes on HIGH pressure.
5. When time is up, hit CANCEL and quick-release the pressure.
6. Add broccoli florets, and stir.
7. Close lid and select MANUAL, and cook on high pressure again for just 4 minutes.
8. Quick-release again when time is up.
9. If you're adding cheese, stir into the Pot before serving.
10. Season to taste.

Nutritional Info (⅙ recipe) Total calories: 270 Protein: 37 Fat: 7.5 Carbs: 13 Fiber: 3

Southern Glory Beef Chili
(Prep + Cook Time: 45 minutes | Servings: 4)

Ingredients:
- 1 pound grass-fed organic ground beef
- 5 chopped carrots
- 1 diced green pepper
- 1 diced onion
- ½ tsp pepper
- 1 tsp onion powder

- 1 tbsp Worcestershire sauce
- 1 tsp onion powder
- 1 tsp paprika
- 3 tsp chili powder
- 1 tsp garlic powder
- ½ tsp cumin

Directions:
1. First, press the button SAUTE on the Instant Pot. Add the ground beef to the pot, and cook until no longer pink.
2. Next, add the rest of the ingredients, stirring them well.
3. Place the lid and lock it. Press the button KEEP WARM/CANCEL and then press the MEAT/STEW button.
4. This will set the chili to cook for 35 minutes.
5. Know that the steam valve should be closed at this time.
6. Next, allow the pressure in the Instant Pot to release naturally.
7. Remove the lid, and serve the chili warm.

Nutritional Information Per Serving: 381 calories, 38 grams net carbohydrates, 2 grams protein, 24 grams fat, 6 mg sodium.

Apple, Cabbage, and Beet Stew (S&F)

(Prep + Cook Time: 25 minutes | Servings: 4)

Ingredients:

- 2 chopped beets
- 1 ½ diced apples
- 3/4 head of a cabbage, chopped into bite-sized pieces
- 4 cups vegetable broth
- 1 diced onion
- 1 tbsp grated ginger
- 3 carrots, chopped
- 2 tbsp chopped parsley, fresh
- 1 tsp salt

Directions:

1. First, prepare the ingredients.
2. Add the listed ingredients to the Instant Pot. Place the lid on the Instant Pot, and cook on HIGH pressure for 22 minutes.
3. Afterwards, release the pressure immediately, releasing it away from your face to avoid burning yourself.
4. Serve the stew warm, and enjoy.

Nutritional Information Per Serving: 172 calories, 24 grams net carbohydrates, 8 grams protein, 1 gram fat, 1442 mg sodium.

Chicken Veggie Lemon Soup

(Prep + Cook Time: 20 minutes | Servings: 4)

Ingredients:

- 1 pound chicken breast, diced
- 1 tbsp. coconut oil
- 2 carrots, diced
- 4 minced garlic cloves
- 1 diced tomato
- 1 diced zucchini
- 4 sprigs of thyme
- 1 diced summer squash
- 1/3 pound asparagus, chopped
- 1 lemon, juiced
- 2 ½ cups spinach, fresh
- 2 ½ cups water
- 5 cups bone broth
- 1 tsp salt

Directions:

1. First, add the coconut oil to the bottom of the Instant Pot. Melt it on SAUTE.
2. Afterwards, add the garlic, cooking until fragrant, about 2 minutes.

3. Next, add the chicken and cook for about 8 minutes, until it's golden brown on all sides.
4. As the chicken cooks, prepare the vegetables.
5. Afterwards, remove the chicken from the Instant Pot. Set it to the side.
6. Next, add one cup of the bone broth to the Instant Pot. Scrape at the bottom of the Instant Pot with a wooden spoon, deglazing it.
7. Add the vegetables and thyme at this time. Season with salt.
8. Add the chicken back to the soup, and stir well.
9. Add the water, the remainder of the bone broth, and the lemon juice at this time.
10. Press the SOUP button on the Instant Pot, place the lid and then cook for a full 5 minutes.
11. Afterwards, remove the lid, releasing the pressure immediately.
12. Add the spinach, and stir well.
13. Serve the soup warm, and enjoy.

Nutritional Information Per Serving: 192 calories, 4 grams net carbohydrates, 28 grams protein, 5 grams fat, 560 mg sodium.

Chicken "Pho"
(Prep + Cook Time: 45 minutes | Servings: 8)

Ingredients:
- 2 pounds chicken, diced
- 2 diced onions
- 1 tbsp coriander seeds
- 1-inch piece of ginger, chopped
- 1 cinnamon stick
- 3 cloves
- 1 tsp cardamom pods, green
- ¼ cup fish sauce
- 1 chopped head of bok choy
- 1 spiralized daikon
- 1 stalk of lemon grass
- 1 tsp salt

Directions:
1. First, add the coriander seeds to a skillet, without oil. Toast them over medium-low on the stovetop, until they're fragrant. This should take about 6 minutes.

2. Next, rinse off the chicken. Add the chicken to the Instant Pot, along with the spices, cardamom pods, onion, lemon grass, and the fish sauce.
3. Add cold water to the Instant Pot, completely covering the ingredients. Place the lid on the Instant Pot, and lock. Select SOUP option and cook for 30 minutes.
4. Next, release the pressure immediately, and add salt.
5. Bring the mixture to a simmer on the warm setting, and add the spiralized daikon and the bok choy.
6. Stir well, and cook for about 7 minutes.
7. Next, divide up the soup, and serve warm with coriander seeds.

Nutritional Information Per Serving: 186 calories, 3 grams net carbohydrates, 33 grams protein, 4 grams fat, 1058 mg sodium.

Chicken Pina Colada
(Prep + Cook Time: 30 minutes | Servings: 4)

Ingredients:
- 1 cup pineapple chunks, frozen or fresh
- 2 pounds chicken thighs, organic, cut into 1-inch chunks
- 1/8 tsp salt
- ½ cup green onion, chopped, for garnish
- ½ cup coconut cream, full fat
- 1 tsp cinnamon
- 2 tbsp coconut aminos

Directions:
1. Except for the green onions, put all of the ingredients in the Instant Pot. Cover and lock the lid. Press the POULTRY key and cook on preset HIGH pressure and 15 minutes cooking time.
2. When the Instant Pot timer beeps, press the CANCEL key and turn off the Instant Pot. Let the pressure release naturally for 10-15 minutes or until the valve drops.

3. Using an oven mitt or a long handled spoon, turn the steam valve to VENTING to release remaining pressure. Unlock and carefully open the lid.
4. Stir to mix. If you want a thick sauce, stir in 1 teaspoon arrowroot starch with 1 tablespoon water.
5. Press the SAUTE key of the Instant Pot. Add the arrowroot starch mixture into the pot and cook until thick to preferred thickness.
6. Turn the Instant Pot off. Serve garnished with green onions.

Nutrition Information per serving: 531 Cal, 24.1 g total fat (11 g sat. fat), 202 chol., 778 mg sodium, 731 mg potassium, 9 g total carbs, 2 g fiber, 5.5 g sugar, 67.7 g protein, 5% vitamin A, 38% vitamin C, 6% calcium, and 21% iron.

Caribbean Chicken
(Prep + Cook Time: 30 minutes | Servings: 4)

Ingredients:
- 2 pounds chicken, sliced into bite-sized pieces
- 1 cup pineapple, fresh or frozen
- 1 tsp salt
- 1 tsp cinnamon
- ½ cup coconut cream, full-fat
- 2 tbsp coconut aminos
- ¼ cup chopped green onions

Directions:
1. First, add the chicken, pineapple, salt, cinnamon, coconut aminos, and the coconut cream into the Instant Pot.
2. Close the lid, lock the seal, and press the button that says POULTRY. The Instant Pot will then cook your chicken for 15 minutes at HIGH pressure.
3. After the 15 minutes have passed, turn off the Instant Pot, and allow the pressure to release naturally for 10 minutes.
4. Remove the lid. Stir well, and serve the chicken warm sprinkled with green onions.

Nutritional Information Per Serving: 435 calories, 7 grams net carbohydrates, 66 grams protein, 14 grams fat, 568 mg sodium.

Sweet 'n Sour Mango Chicken

(Prep + Cook Time: 50 minutes | Servings: 4)

Ingredients:

- 8 boneless chicken thighs
- 4 chopped garlic cloves
- 1 chopped mango
- ½ chopped red onion
- ½ cup chicken broth
- ¼ cup chopped cilantro
- ¼ cup + 1 tbsp coconut aminos
- 1-inch piece of chopped ginger
- 2 tbsp lime juice
- 2 tbsp apple cider vinegar
- 2 tbsp honey
- 1 tbsp olive oil
- 1 tsp fish sauce
- Salt to taste

Directions:

1. Heat the olive in your Instant Pot turned to the SAUTE setting.
2. Put the chicken thighs in with the skin down, and brown for three minutes. Flip and brown on that side for two minutes. Plate the thighs.
3. Put the mango, garlic, and onion in your cooker. When the onion is translucent and mango is beginning to brown, turn off the Pot.
4. Add the chicken back in, along with the lime juice, ¼ cup coconut aminos, cilantro, honey, broth, ginger, fish sauce, and 1 tablespoon of apple cider vinegar.
5. Seal the lid. Cook on HIGH pressure for 15 minutes.
6. When time is up, turn off the cooker and quick-release.
7. Plate the thighs. Pour in 1 tablespoon of coconut aminos, 1 tablespoon apple cider vinegar, and salt into your cooker.
8. Hit SAUTE again and reduce for 10-15 minutes, or until you get a nice thick sauce.
9. Serve chicken with sauce on top.

Nutritional Info (¼ recipe) Total calories: 379 Protein: 38 Fat: 13 Carbs: 26 Fiber: 4

Butternut Squash Paleo Soup

(Prep + Cook Time: 35 minutes | Servings: 8)

Ingredients:

- 6 cups butternut squash, peeled and cubed
- 2 cups diced celery
- 3 cups diced carrots
- 5 garlic cloves, peeled
- 2 tbsp chopped thyme leaves
- 6 cups vegetable stock
- 1 tsp cayenne pepper
- 1 tbsp dried oregano
- 1/3 cup parsley leaves, chopped
- ½ tbsp pepper
- 1 tbsp salt
- 2 cups full-fat coconut milk

Directions:

1. First, slice the butternut squash in half and then peel both halves.
2. Afterwards, trim off the ends and remove the seeds.
3. Dice the butternut squash, and then prep the rest of the vegetables.
4. Add the vegetables into the Instant Pot, along with the parsley, garlic, thyme, oregano, salt, and cayenne pepper. Add the vegetable stock over the soup.
5. Next, close the lid on the Instant Pot. Press the SOUP function, and cook for thirty minutes. Afterwards, release the pressure manually, making sure that the steam doesn't burst on your skin.
6. Use your immersion blender to blend the soup, mixing it to your desired consistency.
7. Next, add the coconut milk, and stir well to combine.
8. Season to taste and serve warm.

Nutritional Information Per Serving: 215 calories, 17 grams net carbohydrates, 3 grams protein, 14 grams fat, 936 mg sodium.

Pork Egg Roll Soup

(Prep + Cook Time: 30 minutes | Servings: 4)

Ingredients:

- 1 pound pork, ground
- 1 tbsp coconut oil
- ½ chopped head of cabbage
- 1 diced onion
- 4 cups chicken broth
- 2 cups shredded carrot
- 1 tsp onion powder
- 1 tsp garlic powder
- 1 tsp ground ginger
- ½ tsp salt
- ½ cup coconut aminos

Directions:

1. First, add the coconut oil to the bottom of the Instant Pot.
2. Press the SAUTE button, and then add the diced onion and the pork. Cook until the pork browns.
3. Next, add the rest of the ingredients, giving them a good stir.
4. Place the lid on the Instant Pot, locking it into place.
5. Cook the mixture for 25 minutes on HIGH pressure.
6. Afterwards, release the pressure manually, making sure to release the pressure away from your face.
7. Stir well, and serve warm.

Nutritional Information Per Serving: 292 calories, 11 grams net carbohydrates, 36 grams protein, 8 grams fat, 1174 mg sodium.

Pork Ribs

(Prep + Cook Time: 40 minutes | Servings: 8)

Ingredients:

- 1 cup water
- 2 ½ pounds pork ribs

Dry Rub

- 1 tsp black pepper
- 1 tsp paprika
- 1 tsp onion powder

- ½ tsp garlic powder
- ½ tsp dry mustard
- ½ tsp chili powder

BBQ Sauce Ingredients:

- 2 slices of chopped bacon
- 3 minced garlic cloves
- ½ diced onion
- 1/3 cup coconut aminos
- 1/3 cup apple cider vinegar
- ½ tsp. paprika, smoked

- 6 ounces tomato paste
- 1 cup tomato sauce
- ½ cup apple juice, natural
- ½ tsp salt
- ½ tsp pepper
- 1 tbsp olive oil

Directions:

1. First, make the dry rub for the pork shoulder, stirring together the listed spices.
2. Slice the pork ribs into individual pieces or slabs, knowing that you can stack them in the Instant Pot.
3. Coat the ribs with the dry rub at this time. Next, add the water to the Instant Pot, and add the ribs, stacking them.
4. Place the lid on the Instant Pot, and cook on HIGH pressure for 15 minutes.
5. To the side, make the BBQ sauce.
6. Heat the olive oil in a skillet over medium heat. Add the bacon, and cook the bacon until it's crispy.
7. Next, add the onion and the garlic and sauté them for six minutes.
8. Add the rest of the listed ingredients for the BBQ sauce at this time, and stir well. Next, bring the mixture to a boil.
9. Once it begins to boil, reduce the heat and allow the mixture to simmer for 10 minutes.
10. After the ribs have completed their cooking, release the pressure manually.

11. Place the ribs on a plate to the side. Remove the liquid from the Instant Pot at this time.
12. Next, add some of the BBQ sauce to the Instant Pot, coating it, and then add a single layer of ribs.
13. Then, add more sauce, and then another layer of ribs, until you've used all the sauce and all the ribs.
14. Next, place the lid back on the Instant Pot, and cook on HIGH pressure, pressing the manual button, for 10 minutes. After 10 minutes, release the pressure manually, and remove the ribs from the Instant Pot.
15. Serve warm, and enjoy.

Nutritional Information Per Serving: 446 calories, 8 grams net carbohydrates, 39 grams protein, 27 grams fat, 415 mg sodium.

Pork Loin with a Cherry Apple Glaze
(Prep + Cook Time: 45 minutes | Servings: 6)

Ingredients:
- 1 cup diced apple
- 1 cup pitted cherries
- ½ cup chicken broth
- 1/3 cup water
- 1 1/3 pound pork loin
- ½ cup diced onion
- ½ cup diced celery
- ½ tsp black pepper
- ½ tsp sea salt

Directions:
1. First, place the pork, water, broth, salt, and pepper in the Instant Pot. Place the lid on the Instant Pot, and close the valve.
2. Press the button that says MEAT/POULTRY and adjust the time for 30 minutes.
3. Afterwards, allow the pressure to release naturally for five minutes. Then, release the pressure manually.
4. Add the rest of the ingredients, including the onion, apple, cherries, celery, and more salt and pepper.
5. Place the lid back on the Instant Pot, and lock it.
6. Press the button that says MANUAL and adjust the timer for 3 minutes.
7. After three minutes, release the pressure manually.
8. Serve the pork warm, and enjoy.

Nutritional Information Per Serving: 331 calories, 19 grams net carbohydrates, 28 grams protein, 14 grams fat, 299 mg sodium.

Pork Carnitas

(Prep + Cook Time: 40 minutes | Servings: 8)

Ingredients:
- 2 pounds pork
- 4 minced garlic cloves
- 2 cups chicken stock
- 1 tsp sea salt
- ½ cup onion, chopped
- ½ tsp black pepper

Directions:
1. First, add the pork to the Instant Pot. Pour the chicken stock into the Instant Pot, along with the onions and the garlic.
2. Season the very top of the pork with pepper and salt.
3. Next, place the lid on the Instant Pot, and cook on HIGH pressure for 25 minutes.
4. Afterwards, shred the pork using two forks, and serve the pork in lettuce wraps.

Nutritional Information Per Serving: 170 calories, 1 gram net carbohydrate, 30 grams protein, 4 grams fat, 490 mg sodium.

Southern Belle's Pulled Pork

(Prep + Cook Time: 75 minutes | Servings: 8)

Ingredients:
- 2 pounds pork shoulder
- 1 diced onion
- 1 tsp onion powder
- 1 tsp garlic powder
- 1 tsp dried mustard
- 1 tsp cinnamon
- 1 tsp cayenne pepper
- 1 tsp sea salt
- ½ tsp black pepper
- 1 cup apple cider vinegar
- 4 minced garlic cloves
- ½ cup coconut aminos
- 1 tbsp molasses

Directions:
1. First, add the onions to the Instant Pot. To the side, stir together the spices, including the garlic, and coat the pork with the spice rub.
2. Place the pork in the Instant Pot at this time. To the side, stir together the apple cider vinegar, molasses, and coconut aminos. Pour the sauce over the pork.

3. Place the lid on the Instant Pot, and lock the lid. Press the MANUAL button, and set the timer to 50 minutes, on HIGH pressure.
4. After it's done cooking, allow the pressure to release naturally. Afterwards, remove the lid carefully.
5. Remove the pork, and shred it with two forks.
6. Press the SAUTE button to reduce the sauce at the bottom for about ten minutes.
7. Pour the sauce over the pork, and serve warm.

Nutritional Information Per Serving: 358 calories, 5 grams net carbohydrates, 24 grams fat, 26 grams protein, 315 mg sodium.

Lime and Chili Salmon
(Prep + Cook Time: 10 minutes | Servings: 2)

Ingredients:
- 2 five-ounce salmon fillets
- 1 cup water

Sauce Ingredients:
- 1 tbsp honey Juice from
- 1 lime 1 diced jalapeno
- 1 tbsp olive oil

- ½ tsp pepper
- ½ tsp salt

- 1 tbsp chopped parsley
- ½ tsp cumin
- ½ tsp paprika

Directions:
1. First, stir together the listed sauce ingredients in a medium-sized bowl. Set the mixture to the side.
2. Next, add the cup of water to the Instant Pot. Place the steam rack in the Instant Pot, and then place the salmon fillets on the steam rack.
3. Season the salmon with salt and pepper, and then place the lid on the Instant Pot.
4. Lock the lid, and press the STEAM button.
5. Adjust the cooking time to five minutes. After 5 minutes, release the pressure manually, and unplug the Instant Pot.
6. Open the lid, and move the salmon from the Instant Pot to a side plate.
7. Add the sauce over the salmon, and serve warm.

Nutritional Information Per Serving: 333 calories, 9 grams net carbohydrates, 34 grams protein, 18 grams fat, 666 mg sodium.

Beef & Plantain Curry

(Prep + Cook Time: 1 hour 40 minutes | Servings: 5)

Ingredients:

- 2 pounds cubed bottom blade pot roast
- 2 peeled and sliced onions
- 1 cup coconut milk
- 1 stick cinnamon

- 1 black (very ripe) sliced and chopped plantain
- 1 tbsp chopped coriander leaves
- 3 tsp coconut oil
- Sea salt to taste

Marinade:

- 2 tsp coconut oil
- 1 tsp ground turmeric
- 1 tsp ground garlic

- 1 tsp ground ginger
- 1 tsp sea salt

Directions:

1. Mix the marinade ingredients. Store in a plastic baggie with the beef for at least a half hour.
2. Turn your cooker to SAUTE and add three teaspoons coconut oil. Cook onion until they become clear. Plate.
3. Brown the meat all over and plate for now. Pour coconut milk into the cooker, deglazing and scraping up any bits of onion and meat.
4. Add meat and onions back into the pot, along with the cinnamon stick. Seal the lid and hit MANUAL.Adjust time to 35 minutes.
5. When time is up, hit CANCEL and wait for a natural pressure release. When safe, open the lid and turn the cooker back to SAUTE.
6. Add plantain and salt. Stir until the fruit is cooked and the sauce has thickened.
7. Pick out the cinnamon stick. Serve with chopped coriander.

Nutritional Information Per Serving: 360 calories, 41 protein, 14 carbs, 15 fat, 1.6 fiber

French Beef with Red Wine Sauce

(Prep + Cook Time: 55 minutes | Servings: 8)

Ingredients:
- 1 pound steak
- ½ pound bacon tips
- 3 minced garlic cloves
- 4 diced carrots
- 2 tsp sea salt
- 2 large diced onion
- 2 tbsp chopped parsley, fresh
- 2 tbsp chopped thyme, fresh
- 2 tsp black pepper
- 1 cup red wine
- 2 large sweet potatoes, sliced and cubed
- 1 tbsp olive oil
- ½ cup beef stock
- 1 tbsp maple syrup

Directions:
1. First, press the SAUTE button on the Instant Pot, and add the olive oil.
2. Next, season the beef with salt and pepper, and sauté the beef in batches, making sure to brown it.
3. Set the beef to the side, and then add the bacon, browning it with the onions.
4. Next, add the beef back to the Instant Pot, along with the remaining ingredients. Press the MANUAL button, which will force the Instant Pot into high pressure, and set the Instant Pot to 30 minutes.
5. After 30 minutes, allow the pressure to release naturally for 15 minutes.
6. Then, release the pressure manually and serve the beef warm.

Nutritional Information Per Serving: 412 calories, 22 grams net carbohydrates, 32 grams protein, 15 grams fat, 1228 mg sodium.

Olive and Lemon Chicken

(Prep + Cook Time: 25 minutes | Servings: 4)

Ingredients:
- 4 chicken breasts, boneless and skinless
- ½ tsp sea salt
- ½ tsp cumin
- ½ cup ghee
- ½ tsp pepper
- 1 cup green olives, pitted juice from
- 1 lemon
- 1 cup bone broth
- ½ cup sliced onions

Directions:

1. First, salt, pepper, and rub cumin over the chicken breasts. Press the SAUTE button on the Instant Pot, and add the ghee.
2. After the ghee has melted, place the chicken breasts inside, and brown on both sides for about five minutes each side.
3. Add the remaining ingredients listed above, and allow the mixture to simmer.
4. Once it begins to simmer, cover the Instant Pot with a lid.
5. Cook under pressure for a full 10 minutes, and then release the pressure manually, allowing the steam to escape.
6. Serve the chicken warm, and enjoy.

Nutritional Information Per Serving: 443 calories, 1 gram net carbohydrates, 40 grams protein, 29 grams fat, 324 mg sodium.

Paleo Butter Chicken
(Prep + Cook Time: 35 minutes | Servings: 6)

Ingredients:

- 1 ½ pounds chicken, skinless and boneless, sliced into bite-sized pieces
- 1 diced onion
- 4 minced garlic cloves
- 2 tbsp ghee
- 1-inch minced piece of ginger
- 1 tsp garam masala
- 1 tsp coriander
- 1 tsp paprika
- ½ tsp cayenne
- ½ tsp cumin
- ½ tsp turmeric
- 1 diced green pepper
- ½ tsp black pepper
- 15 oz tomato sauce
- 1 cup coconut cream

Directions:

1. First, press the button that says SAUTE on the Instant Pot, and then add the ghee and the onions.
2. Stir well, and then allow the onions to cook for 10 minutes, or until they begin to brown.
3. Next, add the ginger and the garlic cloves, and stir-fry them for about 45 seconds.
4. Then, add the rest of the spices, along with the chicken, and stir well until the chicken is coated in the spices.

5. Stir occasionally for the next five minutes, until the chicken is seared.
6. Next, add the green pepper and the tomato sauce, and cover the Instant Pot.
7. Lock the lid, and press the button that says KEEP WARM/CANCEL.
8. Next, press the POULTRY button to cook the chicken. This will set the Instant Pot to 15 minutes.
9. After the chicken is done cooking, the Instant Pot will switch over to the KEEP WARM functionality.
10. Allow the pressure in the Instant Pot to release naturally, and then unlock the lid.
11. Add the coconut cream, and stir slowly. Serve the butter chicken warm, with the sauce, and enjoy.

Nutritional Information Per Serving: 335 calories, 6 grams net carbohydrates, 17 grams fat, 35 grams protein, 452 mg sodium.

Caribbean Chicken (S&F)
(Prep + Cook Time: 30 minutes | Servings: 4)

Ingredients:
- 2 pounds chicken, sliced into bite-sized pieces
- 1 cup pineapple, fresh or frozen
- 1 tsp salt
- 1 tsp cinnamon
- ½ cup coconut cream, full-fat
- 2 tbsp coconut aminos
- ¼ cup chopped green onions

Directions:
1. First, add the chicken, pineapple, salt, cinnamon, coconut aminos, and the coconut cream into the Instant Pot. Close the lid, lock the seal, and press the button that says POULTRY.
2. The Instant Pot will then cook your chicken for 15 minutes at HIGH pressure.
3. After the 15 minutes have passed, turn off the Instant Pot, and allow the pressure to release naturally for 10 minutes.
4. Afterwards, release the pressure and remove the lid.

5. Stir well, and serve the chicken warm sprinkled with green onions.

Nutritional Information Per Serving: 435 Cal, 7 grams net carbohydrates, 66 grams protein, 14 grams fat, 568 mg sodium.

Quick Garlick Spanish Chicken (S&F)
(Prep + Cook Time: 20 minutes | Servings: 6)

Ingredients:
- 1 pound chicken breasts
- 1 ½ cups homemade tomato salsa
- ½ tsp sea salt
- ¼ tsp black pepper
- ½ tsp garlic powder

Directions:
1. Place all the ingredients in the pressure cooker and stir well.
2. Seal the lid and press the POULTRY button.
3. This will let it cook for 15 minutes at HIGH pressure.
4. When done, use the quick release method and open the lid.
5. Serve immediately.

Enchilada Soup
(Prep + Cook Time: 30 minutes | Servings: 6)

Ingredients:
- 1 ½ pounds chicken thighs, boneless, skinless
- 1 bell pepper, thinly sliced
- 1 can (14.5 ounces) fire-roasted crushed tomatoes
- 1 onion, thinly sliced
- 1 tbsp chili powder
- 1 tbsp cumin
- 1 tsp oregano
- ½ cup water
- ½ tsp ground pepper
- ½ tsp sea salt
- ½ tsp smoked paprika
- 2 cups bone broth
- 3 cloves garlic, minced

For garnish: Fresh cilantro 1 avocado

Directions:
1. Except for the garnish ingredients, put all of the ingredients in the pot in the following order: chicken, tomatoes, bell pepper, onion, garlic, broth, water, cumin, chili powder, oregano, paprika, sea salt, pepper.
2. Cover and lock the lid. Turn the steam valve to SEALING. Press the MANUAL key, set the pressure to HIGH, and set the timer for 20minutes.
3. When the Instant Pot timer beeps, press the CANCEL key and unplug the Instant Pot.
4. Using an oven mitt or a long handled spoon, turn the steam valve to VENTING to quick release the pressure.
5. Unlock and carefully open the lid.
6. Using 2 forks, shred the chicken right in the Instant Pot.
7. Ladle into servings bowls and top each serving with fresh cilantro and avocado.

Nutrition Information per serving: 347 Cal, 16 g total fat (3.9 g sat. fat), 101 chol., 637 mg sodium, 630 mg potassium, 13.4 g total carbs, 4.7 g fiber, 5.3 g sugar, 36 g protein, 35% vitamin A, 89% vitamin C, 5% calcium, and 18% iron.

Curry in a Hurry

(Prep + Cook Time: 20 minutes | Servings: 6)

Ingredients:

- 2 pounds chicken breast or thighs
- 2 tbsp curry powder
- 3 tbsp honey
- 6 ounces can tomato paste
- 2 cloves garlic, minced
- 16 oz canned tomato sauce
- 16 oz canned coconut milk
- 1 tsp salt
- 1 cup onion, chopped OR
- ¼ cup dry minced onion

Directions:

1. Except for the chicken, put all of the ingredients into the Instant Pot. Stir to combine and then add the chicken. Cover and lock the lid.
2. Turn the steam valve to SEALING. Press the MANUAL key, set the pressure to HIGH, and set the timer for 15 minutes.
3. When the Instant Pot timer beeps, press the CANCEL key and unplug the Instant Pot.
4. Let the pressure release naturally for 10-15 minutes or until the valve drops.
5. Using an oven mitt or a long handled spoon, turn the steam valve to VENTING to release remaining pressure.
6. Unlock and carefully open the lid. Serve with rice and/ or peas.

Nutrition Information per serving: 319 Cal, 20.8 g total fat (16.7 g sat. fat), 25 chol., 850 mg sodium, 891 mg potassium, 25.6 g total carbs, 5.1 g fiber, 18.7 g sugar, 12.9 g protein, 14% vitamin A, 26% vitamin C, 10% calcium, and 20% iron.

Leftvofer Turkey Paleo Stew

(Prep + Cook Time: 50 minutes | Servings: 6)

Ingredients:
- 3 cups turkey, cooked, diced
- 2 cups sweet potatoes, potatoes, or parsnips, peeled and diced
- 2 carrots, large-sized, peeled and then diced
- 1 tsp dried minced garlic OR 2-3 fresh garlic cloves
- 1 tbsp cranberry sauce, you can leftover
- 1 tbsp avocado oil, or your choice of cooking oil
- 1 onion, small-sized, diced
- 1 can (4.5-ounce) diced tomatoes with juice
- 3 stalks celery, diced
- 5 cups turkey broth
- Salt and pepper, to taste

Directions:
1. Press the SAUTE key of the Instant Pot. Put the oil in the pot and wait until hot.
2. Add the onion, celery, and carrot. Stir-fry for about 3-5 minutes or until the onion is translucent.
3. Add the diced tomatoes, potatoes, and pour in the turkey broth. Stir to mix. Add the cranberry sauce, minced garlic, and thyme.
4. Press the CANCEL key to stop the sauté function. Cover and lock the lid.
5. Turn the steam valve to SEALING. Press the SOUP key and let cook preset time of 30 minutes.
6. When the Instant Pot timer beeps, press the CANCEL key and unplug the Instant Pot.
7. Using an oven mitt or a long handled spoon, turn the steam valve to VENTING to quick release the pressure.
8. Unlock and carefully open the lid. Remove the thyme and then discard. Adjust the salt and pepper as needed.

Nutrition Information per serving: 278 Cal, 6 g total fat (1.9 g sat. fat), 0 chol., 1352 mg sodium, 823 mg potassium, 20.7 g total carbs, 5.4 g fiber, 8.1 g sugar, 35.1 g protein, 108% vitamin A, 34% vitamin C, 5% calcium, and 65% iron.

Crab Legs
(Prep + Cook Time: 30 minutes | Servings: 4)

Ingredients:
- 2 pound of crab legs
- 1 cup of water
- 1 cup of white wine
- Lemon wedges
- Melted butter

Directions:
1. Pour the water and wine into the inner pot.
2. Put in the crab legs Set the pot at high pressure and let it cook for 7 minutes.
3. Once done, simply wait for 10 minutes and let the pressure release naturally.
4. Open and top it up with some melted butter and dashes of sherry.

Paleo Chili
(Prep + Cook Time: 25 minutes | Servings: 8)

Ingredients:
- 2 ½ lb Ground beef
- ½ large Onion (chopped)
- 8 cloves Garlic (minced)
- 2 15-oz can Diced tomatoes (with liquid)
- 1 6-oz can Tomato paste
- 1 4-oz can Green chiles (with liquid)
- 2 tbsp Worcestershire sauce
- ¼ cup Chili powder
- 2 tbsp Cumin
- 1 tbsp Dried oregano
- 2 tsp Sea salt
- 1 tsp Black pepper
- 1 medium Bay leaf (optional)

Directions:
1. Select the SAUTE setting on the Instant Pot (this part is done without the lid).
2. Add the chopped onion and cook for 5-7 minutes, until translucent (or increase the time to about 20 minutes if you like them caramelized).
3. Add the garlic and cook for a minute or less, until fragrant.
4. Add the ground beef. Cook for 8-10 minutes, breaking apart with a spatula, until browned.

5. Add remaining ingredients, except bay leaf, to the Instant Pot and stir until combined. Place the bay leaf into the middle, if using.
6. Close the lid. Press KEEP WARM/CANCEL to stop the saute cycle. Select the MEAT/STEW setting (35 minutes) to start pressure cooking.
7. Wait for the natural release if you can, or turn the valve to "vent" for quick release if you're short on time. If you used a bay leaf, remove it before serving.

Paleo Sausage Stew
(Prep + Cook Time: 30 minutes | Servings: 6)

Ingredients:
- 1 pound boneless, skinless chicken thighs
- 1 pound andouille pork sausage
- 1 tbsp coconut oil
- 1 medium white onion, sliced
- 2 stalks celery, chopped
- 3 bell peppers, diced
- 2 large carrots, chopped
- 2 cloves garlic, minced
- cups chopped tomatoes
- 2 cups bone broth
- ¼ cup parsley, minced
- 1 tsp salt
- 1 tsp thyme

Directions:
1. Set the pressure cooker to SAUTE, heat the oil and toss in the chicken and sausage. Cook until browned on all sides.
2. Transfer the meat from the pressure cooker and set aside.
3. Toss the onion, celery, peppers and carrots into the pressure cooker and sauté for a few minutes.
4. Add the garlic and sauté for another minute.
5. Pour in the bone broth and add the chopped tomatoes.
6. Bring everything to a simmer. In the meantime, cut the meat into bite-size pieces.
7. Transfer them back to the pressure cooker, along with minced parsley, salt, thyme, red chili flakes, pepper and bay leaf.
8. Press the SOUP button and let it cook for 5 to 10 minutes.
9. When done, release the pressure naturally. Serve warm.

Chocolate Cake

(Prep + Cook Time: 25 minutes | Servings: 4)

Ingredients:
- ¼ cup avocado, mashed
- ½ tsp apple cider vinegar
- ½ ripe banana
- 1 green plantain
- 1 cup water
- 1/8 tsp cream of tartar
- 2 tbsp coconut oil, melted PLUS more for greasing the pans
- 2 tbsp honey
- 3/4 tsp baking soda
- 5 tbsp carob powder (or, if you have reintroduced cocoa, use cocoa powder)

Optional garnishes (any): Coconut flakes Coconut cream Fruit

Directions:
1. Put the banana, plantain, avocado, honey, coconut oil, carob, baking soda, vinegar, and cream of tartar into a food processor and blend until the mixture is smooth.
2. Grease 3 pieces of mini ramekins and fluted pan with extra coconut oil. Divide the batter between the ramekins/ pans until each is ¾ full.
3. Pour the water in the pot and set a steaming rack. Put the ramekins/ pans into the steaming rack. Cover and lock the lid.
4. Turn the steam valve to SEALING. Press the MANUAL key, set the pressure to HIGH, and set the timer for 18 minutes.
5. When the Instant Pot timer beeps, press the CANCEL key and unplug the Instant Pot.
6. Using an oven mitt or a long handled spoon, turn the steam valve to VENTING to quick release the pressure.
7. Unlock and carefully open the lid.
8. Garnish each with the coconut flakes, coconut cream, or fruit.
9. Serve warm.

Nutrition Information per serving: 256 Cal, 12.9 g total fat (9.2 g sat. fat), 0 chol., 323 mg sodium, 683 mg potassium, 41.1 g total carbs, 5.4 g fiber, 23.1 g sugar, 2.9 g protein, 14% vitamin A, 23% vitamin C, 2% calcium, and 11% iron.

51489695R00236

Made in the USA
Middletown, DE
11 November 2017